In Memory of
My Brother, Richard
(1942-1965)

BETWEEN HEAVEN AND EARTH

A Journey With My Grandfather

Robert Nurden

About the author

Robert Nurden is a writer and journalist who has worked for the *Guardian, Independent on Sunday* and *Daily Telegraph*, as well as many other national newspapers and magazines. He has reported on worker exploitation in the international garment trade, reindeer herding in the Arctic, racial stereotyping by the Western media and cider-making in Herefordshire. He lives in East London, not far from where his grandfather was minister.

First published in the UK in November 2020
Text copyright © 2020 Robert Nurden

Edited by Jennifer Barclay
Book design by Adam Hay Studio
Back cover photograph: Glenbow Museum, Calgary

ISBN: 9798666160022
Printed in the UK

PRAISE FOR
BETWEEN HEAVEN AND EARTH

'*This beautifully written and somewhat unconventional biography of an unorthodox character has plenty of twists and turns to keep the reader riveted, while providing an illustration of a fascinating era. A cracking read.*'
Jennifer Barclay, author of *Wild Abandon*

'*Stanley James is the ideal subject for a biographer: a complex, restless and ultimately elusive man who lived large and held in his past a dark secret. In this diligently researched and well-written book, Robert Nurden does his wide-ranging and enigmatic grandfather full justice.*'
Ian Robert Smith

'*A remarkable life which intrigues, informs, amuses, astonishes - and shocks.*'
Jane Sutton

'*Robert Nurden sits you down, makes you comfortable and spins an enthralling tale. Cowboy, hobo and preacher, Stanley shines in the light of his grandson's level gaze.*'
Richard C. McNeff, author of *With Barry Flanagan: Travels through Time and Spain*

'*In this excellent, immensely readable, and meticulously researched portrait of his extraordinary and complex grandfather, Robert Nurden has disinterred a trove of precious things past, and shed invaluable light on the tough, turbulent and violent lives of our latter-day forebears.*'
Eamonn Shanahan

'*Cowboy, preacher. Soldier, pacifist. Husband, adulterer. This is a biography with whopping great contradictions at its heart. And it's written by the subject's grandson who has shrugged off any embarrassment his findings might have induced and come up with a stonking story.*'
Susana Sutherland

ACKNOWLEDGEMENTS

I am greatly indebted to the many people who took up the challenge of reading and editing the text and offered invaluable advice. They are Jennifer Barclay, Simon Ely, Carmen Frowd, Tim Frowd, Susan Rowlands, Kevin Scanlan, Eamonn Shanahan and Ian Smith. Others who provided guidance are Tracey Beresford, Professor Clyde Binfield, Richard Clark, Rosemary Ely, Mark Gorman, Hugh Greener, Mark Hapgood, Pushpinder Khaneka, Richard McNeff, Adam Newey, Nigel Pollitt, Tony Prouse, Susana Sutherland, Jane Sutton, Peter Williams and William Wood.

I would like to thank my wonderful designer Adam Hay, for whom nothing was too much trouble, and Tony Morrison who talked me through JPEGs and TIFs with admirable patience. The family scoured their brains and cupboards to come up with memories and photographs. Thank you Rosemary Ely, Tim Frowd and Sue Morgan in particular.

I am grateful to Trinity Church, Walthamstow, for letting me rummage through their attic. I would like to pay special tribute to Tierl Thompson, whose book *Dear Girl* provided me with vital material and utterly changed the nature of this biography.

So many kind Canadians aided my Alberta research, but in particular Bev Copithorne who rounded up every Jumping Pound rancher there was, plus Kathleen Rogers and Sandy Pedlar of the Southern Alberta Pioneers and their Descendants, and a long-lost cousin, Professor Gregory Ball, for his reminiscences. Then, of course, there were innumerable archivists – especially those at the Women's Library of the London School of Economics – who bent over backwards to solve the mysteries of the past, in which they succeeded over and over again. Without everyone's generosity, this book would not have been possible.

CONTENTS

INTRODUCTION

The flint-fronted Chiltern house looked much as it did in those faded photographs from the late 1940s, my family squinting awkwardly against the glare of the summer sun.

I told the taxi driver not to wait. I really didn't know how long this would take. I walked slowly towards Long Dene Cottage, then stood for a moment and listened to the rooks busying themselves in the copse behind the house. I raised the knocker and let it fall once, then twice, against the sturdy front door.

A woman stood in the doorway, smiling. 'Hello. Can I help you?' She seemed relaxed, almost as if she had been expecting me, so unfazed was she by the stranger arriving unannounced.

'I'm sorry to disturb you. My grandfather and his family lived in this house years ago and I'm writing a book about him. I was wondering if I could possibly look round.' It all came out wrong – too abrupt – as it had done every time I tried to explain my project: researching the life of my mother's father, Stanley Bloomfield James, a man who had nine books to his name and was sufficiently well known to have received an obituary in *The Times*.

'Well, I don't see why not. John, there's someone here who…'

Her husband appeared and leaned forward to shake my hand. 'When were they here? Do you know?' he asked.

'Well, he died in 1951. They lived here for about ten years before that.'

They invited me in. As I walked inside, my mother's words came back to me. 'When we showed you to him the first time, he took you, held you in his arms and blessed you.' I was three months old and he had only a short while to live, here in this house. My hosts ushered me into the garden where we drank tea from mugs. I'd brought his obituary, just in case they needed proof of my story. I handed over the photocopy in which Stanley's quizzical features stared out across the decades.

'He wasn't *that* famous then, was he?' said the man after skimming through it. An enigmatic smirk played at the corners of his mouth. 'He wasn't a game changer by any stretch of the imagination, was he?'

I bridled. Who did he think he was, dismissing my grandfather in such an offhand manner? This was my grand opus, something I'd been thinking about for years. 'Yes, second division, I reckon,' I replied caustically. 'But I always think that people with slightly lower profiles are more interesting than full-on celebrities, don't you?'

The man changed tack. 'Actually, I think we heard about him from our vendors. They said he used to write in the garden shed. Bit of an eccentric, by all accounts. We had the hut removed about ten years ago.' He pointed out the rectangular patch of raised ground and irregular grass growth, the only sign that the hut had once been there.

I wandered down the garden and looked back at the cottage with its tiny, diamond-shaped panes of glass. There was so much more I wanted to know about him. And now all his children – my mother and her brothers and sisters – had died and there was no one left to ask. Why hadn't I pressed them for information while they were still alive? I took a photo of the cottage and rejoined my hosts.

'I'm afraid there's nothing much more we can tell you,' said the woman. 'But it's always nice to make a connection with the past, so thank you for coming.'

I walked down Bunkers Lane, where the green shoots of spring were appearing in the hedgerows. The Chilterns undulated on the horizon. It must have been an idyllic spot for Stanley to see out his final days. His grave was just a few miles away in the next village and I decided to do the journey on foot. I headed for St Lawrence Church, Abbots Langley.

Plot E49, I'd been told by the church secretary. There it was – a plain granite cross and headstone, tilted at an awkward angle. The grass was growing over it and the stonework was splattered with bird droppings. Probably no one had been there for years. I never remembered my mother or anyone from the family visiting the grave. I only found out the name of the village where he was buried from the last line of his obituary. Then I'd had to phone round the different churches to find the record of his burial.

I leant forward and tried to decipher the inscription. At the intersection of the cross the letters IHS were carved, denoting Jesus Christ. The wording on the headstone said:

'Stanley Bloomfield James. Author. Born Dec 9th 1869. Died All Saints Day 1951. Strong and content I travel the open road'.

The quotation was from 'Song of the Open Road' by one of his favourite poets, Walt Whitman. There was a space underneath the words, left blank I presume, so that when Jess, my grandmother, was buried with him, her name could be added. But she died in Winchester twelve years later, and had her own grave. On his headstone there was no reference to her or to his children. It struck me as odd. The Whitman line made it almost pagan. Yet for fifty years he had supposedly been a committed Christian – first an inspirational Congregational minister, then a Catholic writer, one of the best known in the English-speaking world.

The complex image we had grown up with was of a man who had rebelled against his father's Nonconformist religion, travelled to Canada and become, in turn, cowboy, shepherd, navvy, hobo, journalist and soldier – a kind of 1890s hippy. Someone who in his mature years married and had seven children but who had ruffled conventional feathers by embracing pacifism, socialism and feminism and then converting to Catholicism; who had worked alongside Bertrand Russell and numbered G. K. Chesterton among his friends; who had published nine books, including two autobiographies, and over a thousand articles. And, to cap it all, someone who was intelligent, sensitive, kind and compassionate.

All of which was true. But my research into his life had thrown up a different side to his character. I had unearthed hitherto unseen private letters and diaries which turned that image upside down. The respectful little book I'd had in mind was gathering metaphorical dust. Now I was sitting down to write a very different kind of story.

THE WORLD ACCORDING TO DANIEL

~ 1 ~

FARMERS, MINISTERS – AND THE CROOK

The village of Nevern nestles so close to Cardigan Bay you can smell the salt on the air, and the squat trees on the surrounding hills bend sharply away from the prevailing wind. It was here, in this green, fecund valley, that generations of James farmers – my grandfather's ancestors – lived and worked. My research visit in the watery May sunshine to this wild corner of Pembrokeshire in west Wales was as impressionistic as it was factual, but none the less satisfying for that.

The River Nevern divides the village in two. With a current population of 865, it boasts a castle, the fine church of St Brynach's, and a cluster of houses. I walked into the churchyard looking for headstones carved with the name James and, despite some of the inscriptions being hard to decipher, I identified about forty. Although the family members had worshipped in the nearby Nonconformist chapel, many of them had been buried in the parish churchyard. I headed for the old chapel – now the village hall – and looked through the plain windows at the place where generations of Jameses had spent their Sunday mornings.

At least three of the Jameses had lived at 'Coledge, Bayvil' according to their headstones. It turned out that Bayvil was the parish and the 'college' in question was in nearby Felindre, a handsome building on the edge of the village. At the village's only pub, the Salutation Inn, the friendly bar staff commented on my English accent. I told them I was trying to trace my Welsh ancestors. 'What's the name?' asked the barmaid.

'James,' I said.

'Really? That's my maiden name. There are lots of us around here. We're probably the biggest family group in the area. She's a James, too.' She pointed out a woman sitting with a man at a table in the otherwise empty public bar. 'Winnie, he's looking for his relatives. Jameses, like us.'

Winnie waved me over. She introduced the man at her table. 'This is my lover. Who are you?' I explained what I was up to. She went on: 'I'm from Cardigan but the Jameses cross the county boundary into Pembrokeshire. My relatives would have known yours without a doubt.' She beamed me a friendly smile.

I bought her and her companion another drink so that I had an excuse for extending the conversation. But I quickly realised there was little more to say. The passage of time had swallowed up our linked, but separate, pasts. I downed my pint and bid them farewell. I sat for a moment in the car, taking in the walls and country lanes, the thin mist and the soggy fields where the Jameses had once worked.

* * *

Stanley's branch of the James family migrated from the Nevern district to Llangybi in Monmouthshire about the middle of the eighteenth century. One of the first to make the journey was Daniel James, a farmer, who was born in 1720. He is listed as an elder at the Congregational chapel at New Inn, a hamlet near Llangybi, in 1775. It seems he was ordained in order to assist the presiding minister at New Inn. When the minister died in 1783, the by now Reverend Daniel James became responsible for the chapel, running the ministry from his farm and travelling the ten miles on horseback to take services. He is thought to have died a bachelor late in 1796, but he was a pioneer in the family's movement east.

There was a second Daniel James, the son of a Thomas James, who was baptised near Nevern in 1775. He spent years there as a farm labourer; then in 1817 he, too, appeared in Llangybi, at Cwmbwrwch Farm. This was Stanley's grandfather (and my great-great-grandfather).

The facts are that on 31 December 1831, at the age of fifty-six, this second Daniel married Mary Powell of Llangybi, who was just twenty-three. The thirty-three-year age difference probably meant this was his second marriage. The wedding took place at St Philip and St Jacob Anglican Church, Bristol, and on the register they were described as residents of the city, but they were soon back at Cwmbwrwch where they spent the rest of their lives as tenant farmers. They had three children – Miriam, born 1834; Lemuel, born 1838; and Daniel (the third Daniel in this story), born 1841, who was Stanley's father and my great-grandfather.

This third Daniel James is the only one to play an important part in this story. But in official documents and records he always referred to himself as 'Bloomfield James', and according to his son, Stanley, he wanted the family name to change to Bloomfield. His family knew him as plain Daniel, and that's how I'll refer to him. But the name Bloomfield was clearly important to him as it appears on all personal papers and documents. He later gave it to his four children; some of their children inherited it and it is still alive today. Yet none of my family ever knew where it came from.

Having almost given up finding out its provenance, I stumbled across a possible answer in the words of one long-gone and almost forgotten poet from Suffolk called Robert Bloomfield (1766-1823). In his day he was highly regarded, being admired by fellow poets William Wordsworth and John Clare. He was a cobbler and received acclaim for his poem 'The Farmer's Boy'. In 1811 he published 'The Banks of Wye', following a long walking tour in the region. Bloomfield's poem includes affectionate references to the 'tumbling Usk', a river, and to Caerleon, a Monmouth village, both of which Daniel senior would have known intimately. Did Daniel admire the poet and could 'The Banks of Wye' have been a favourite of his? And did he want to preserve the poet's memory through his own children? It's possible, though it's just speculation.

For me, this was more than an amble down the highways and byways of family history. I was trying to connect first with my great-grandfather Daniel, who died fifty-one years before I was born, and with his son Stanley, with whom I overlapped by a mere seven months. There was the familiar sense of adventure, of almost illicit pleasure, in chasing something alluring yet ultimately unattainable.

One thing that was far from clear was the whereabouts of Cwmbwrwch Farm. I knew it was set in a deep, enclosed valley, north of Caerleon, according to a description of my grandfather's. He didn't waste the opportunity to wax lyrical about Caerleon's romantic associations with King Arthur, Lancelot and Guinevere. I looked up the meaning of Cwmbwrwch and found it meant 'the Hollow of the Badger'. I instantly loved the name. I reread the relevant passage in his book and learned how the settle in the kitchen had doubled up as a pulpit for itinerant preachers. I read of Celtic warmth, of the poetic spirit that had created the stories of the Grail, and of silk gowns with Geneva bands.

Finding what I reckoned was the right area, I encountered Llandegfedd Reservoir, which I had seen on the Ordnance Survey map. On the west side of this large stretch of water was a small area of trees marked Cwmbwrwch Wood. The water lapped a few feet away. Was the elusive farmhouse one of a number of properties submerged beneath the reservoir when it was created in the early 1960s to supply water to Cardiff? I would have to make the trip to Gwent Archives in Ebbw Vale to find out.

The next day, Frances Younson showed me some old maps that clinched it. There was Cwmbwrwch on a pre-1961 map, a farm perched above the banks of Sor Brook, its hedged fields rising up on the eastern side to a point above the shoreline of today's reservoir. A photograph that later came my way showed Cwmbwrwch's white façade in the distance. Ms Younson showed me photographs of the dam being constructed, of pick-up trucks, caterpillar bulldozers and earth removers but, disappointingly, the scarred landscape was all that was left by that point in time. An engineer told me that in such situations, buildings are usually demolished rather than merely submerged.

Cwmbwrwch, top right, where generations of the James family lived and worked as tenant farmers, before the property was demolished to make way for Llandegfedd reservoir, seen here under construction. Credit: Nic Henderson

I drove back to Llandegfedd Reservoir which the previous day had kept its secret from me. This time when I parked I realised I was where my ancestors' cows, sheep and chickens had once grazed and pecked. There was an overgrown copse behind the car park which my maps showed had previously contained outhouses. The staff in the visitor centre had time on their hands to chat. 'Yes,' said one, 'the foundations are very near the shoreline. When the water's low, we can see the site of the old well and the feeding troughs. Even now, if the house was still there, the water would only come up to the bedroom windows. Come back in the summer if it's been very hot and you may see some remains.'

Having located the farm, I now needed to locate the chapel where the first Daniel James had been a Nonconformist minister and countless Jameses had worshipped. New Inn was about two miles away, just over the hill on the road to Pontypool. I was helped by what Stanley had written: 'I saw the ruins of the whitewashed chapel where, in my boyhood days, the descendants of those who had worshipped in the farm kitchen met. Underneath it had been a stable, a necessary adjunct for worshippers who came from a distance and spent the whole Sunday in religious exercises.'

A brown, tall, frankly unattractive chapel, built towards the end of the nineteenth century, matched the leaden, rain-filled sky. Although the whitewashed chapel and stables were no more, it was confirmed for me that they had until recently been there. The next day was Sunday so I phoned the minister, the Reverend Gordon Cooke, and asked if I could attend the morning service, explaining that an ancestor of mine had been minister there in the eighteenth century. I was warmly welcomed and, in his sermon, Mr Cooke remarked that, as a result of my visit, the congregation had the chance to connect with worshippers – my ancestors – from the chapel's past.

* * *

While at Gwent Archives, I'd been told of another enquiry they had received relating to the James family of Cwmbwrwch Farm. 'Would you like to be put in touch?' they asked. 'We think he may be a relative of yours.'

I contacted the man and arranged a visit. Hugh Greener, a distant cousin, lived in Pontyclun and was in his eighties. He was descended from Lemuel James, who was my great-grandfather's brother and Stanley's uncle.

Hugh, a tall, kindly man with a winning smile and thick south Wales accent, told me that from a young age Lemuel had helped his mother Mary farm Cwmbwrwch; his father Daniel was no longer present, presumably dead. By 1861 Lemuel was a farmer in his own right. In the early 1860s he married Worcestershire girl Martha Bradley and it was around this time that he was 'an ardent follower of the hounds and the assistant overseer' for Llangybi, an official responsible for looking after the poor of the district. Kelly's Directory of 1871 also records that Lemuel farmed at Cwmbwrwch.

So far, so conventional. But over the next two hours, surrounded by photos and documents he'd spent years collecting, Hugh gave me a picture of a very different side to Stanley's uncle. 'Lemuel was a crook,' he announced with a wide grin on his face, munching a digestive biscuit. It was as if he'd been impatiently waiting for the necessary formalities to be over before revealing this family secret.

I beamed back. 'Really?' I swigged my tea and settled down to hear the tale.

'In 1876 at the age of thirty-seven he was charged with forging two cheques – one for £60 (£5,500 in 2020) and another for £30 – in the name of his wife's stepfather. He was also declared a bankrupt.'

Hugh showed me the documents he'd photocopied for me. He seemed distinctly proud of his ancestor's act of criminality and there was certainly a frisson of illicit pleasure for me, too, as if a relative had satisfied a secret desire of mine to act outside the law.

Hugh had used a genealogist in Cardiff to help him unearth the facts. She had found reports of the case in no less than five local newspapers of the time – the *Western Mail*, the *South Wales Daily News*, the *County Observer and Monmouthshire Central Advertiser*, the *Pontypool Free Press and Herald of the Hills* and the *Monmouthshire Merlin*. At the petty sessions – the preliminary hearing – in Usk on 6 May 1876 Lemuel was charged with having forged and presented two bills of exchange with intent to defraud.

He had gone into the Usk branch of the London and Provincial Bank and presented the bills of exchange which had seemingly been signed by Isaac Hobbis, his wife's stepfather, also a farmer. The bank, knowing Lemuel, cashed them but Hobbis later said the signatures were not his, adding that he knew James's 'affairs were in a bad state'. The chairman of the magistrates, Colonel G. Relph, in indicting Lemuel for trial, said that 'it was the most unpleasant duty he had had for some time'. Lemuel was summoned to appear at the next assizes and bailed for the sum of £220 (£20,000 in 2020).

Lemuel James, who was sentenced to a year's hard labour for forgery

At the assizes, Lemuel's defence lawyer, a Mr Lawrence, tried to discredit Hobbis's version of events by making out he was frequently drunk. In answer to Lawrence's cross-questioning, Hobbis denied it and said he had not fallen out of a trap while drunk – it was someone else who had run into his trap.

Lawrence: Do you get drunk?
Hobbis: Sometimes. [Laughter.] No more than he does.
Lawrence: Do you mean me? [Renewed laughter.]
His Lordship: Do you get drunk oftener than your neighbours?
Hobbis: No, nor so often.

The line of inquiry tailed away and the attempt by Lemuel's lawyer to deflect the blame from his client and to discredit Hobbis's good character came to nothing and the jury found Lemuel guilty of forgery. In passing sentence, the judge said that Lemuel was guilty of 'a most serious offence' but that the bank 'had acted with a great want of caution' and he had never heard of a more 'indiscreet act than appeared to characterise their transactions'.

He sentenced Lemuel to twelve months' imprisonment with hard labour. Hugh told me that this involved breaking up rocks, day after day.

What made this seemingly respectable figure in the community break the law? By 1876 he and Martha had seven children. Was he under financial pressure with so many mouths to feed? Did he have debts? Probably both. Once he was out of jail, Martha took Lemuel back and he continued to work on the land, with the last child Daisy being born in 1878. The 1881 census shows that he was no longer at Cwmbwrwch but merely living in the district. It now describes him as an 'agricultural labourer'. Out of disgrace he must have lost the right to farm the land and had to move out of the farmhouse. The 1881 census – taken in April – shows him living with Martha and the family, but by the end of the year he had married again – this time to an Elizabeth Williams. One assumes Martha had died. Ten years later, Lemuel regained the status of 'farmer' and was living at Great House Farm, a few miles to the east in Llanthewy Vach. He was still there in 1901 with Elizabeth, but by 1911 he was living with his grocer son in Griffithstown, where he died two years later. The notice of his death in a local newspaper states that Lemuel was 'an old and respected inhabitant of the district'.

The story finished, Hugh and I sat silent in his living room, letting the sounds of the town drift through the net-curtained windows and pull us back to the present day. I wondered how Daniel and Lemuel had got on – and how well Stanley had known his criminal uncle.

* * *

Any hope that Stanley might inherit from his mother a counterbalancing secular strain to the overwhelming Nonconformist influence of the Jameses would prove misplaced. Not only were Clara Pulsford and her ancestors from Newton Abbot in Devon Nonconformists, they were Congregationalists, too. Indeed, that common thread between the families may well have been what brought Daniel and Clara together, but I have no evidence of that. Clara was the oldest of six children, and had a grandfather who had been a notable religious revivalist in the county. And two of her uncles made their mark in Congregational churches, largely in Scotland.

Her oldest uncle, Dr John Pulsford (1815-1897), published books and sermons and preached in Edinburgh and London for many years, drawing large congregations. Congregationalists dubbed him the 'the last of the mystics' for his visionary approach to faith. Certainly, *Infoldings and Unfoldings of the Divine Genius in Nature and Man*, despite its rather off-putting title and intense prose style, has something of Wordsworthian pantheism about it. Another volume considers the writings of Nietzsche. Along with ten or so of his books available on the Internet is one of his pulpit addresses: 'Fear Not: A Sermon Preached in Offord Road Chapel, London'.

In 1868 John, who at one point was chairman of the Congregational Union, took over the pastorate of Albany Street Chapel, Edinburgh, where his younger brother William had been in charge four years previously. By all accounts he was an impressive preacher. Edwin Paxton Hood describes his speaking:

like the writing of Richter, it reminds us of all soft, soothing, lulling tones in Nature. The voices of flutes over the still mountain lakes at evening, or beneath the moonlight night – bells wafted on a calm Sabbath-day to a listener on the mountain height – an

organ from some lake-girt and taper-illumined minster at midnight
– such are the images which rise to our mind; or, say in a word,
it is the music of crystals shooting into shape, and beauty, and
cohesion – aerial, soft, but clear.

John's obituary in The *Illustrated London News* of 1897 says he 'lived a very active life, both with voice and pen... Most of Dr Pulsford's religious writings are characterised by a fine spiritual insight which gives them a place of their own in Nonconformist literature.' A gushing Victorian portrait if ever there was one, typical of the time.

Dr John Pulsford, the 'last of the mystics', well known
for his sermons with a pantheistic theme

John's younger brother, Dr William Pulsford (1822-1886), also took the route north to work as a Congregational minister. His first charge as pastor of Albany Street Church, Edinburgh, was a nine-year tenure that lasted until 1864. William then moved to Trinity Congregational Church, Glasgow. His time there seems to have been a successful one, if an 1880 article in the series Men You Know, published in *The Bailie*, a popular Scottish magazine of the day, is to be believed. It states rather grandly: 'There are stars which... are so far remote that their greatness remains unknown beyond their particular spheres. Something of this is the case with the Rev. Dr William Pulsford.

[He] has been one of the most potent ministerial influences in our midst – a great educative power.'

After studying in Germany, William returned speaking the language fluently and translated many important texts, an achievement recognised when Glasgow University conferred the degree of Doctor of Divinity on him. A volume of his sermons, the article claims, contained 'probably as exquisite productions of the pulpit as any [of] recent date'.

Dr William Pulsford, a Biblical scholar who translated German texts

Although Clara's father, Thomas, born in 1825, earned his living as a linen draper in Devon, he too was a Congregationalist like his brothers. It was impossible for Stanley to escape these religious influences, firstly from his father Daniel and his forebears, and secondly from the Pulsfords, that is from Clara his mother, her father and uncles, and their ancestors. Further back, both the Jameses and Pulsfords had been farmers and these men and women of the soil – and possibly Lemuel the crook, too – would play a huge part in shaping Stanley's thinking.

~ 2 ~
IN THE SHADOWS

In 1869 a mysterious piece of graffiti was scrawled across the walls of a busy Nonconformist church in Bristol. The hastily chalked word read 'Ichabod'. Quite what the motivation was for broadcasting this strange message for all the world to see is lost in the pages of history. And at the time only those well versed in ancient scripture would have known that this perfunctory quotation came from the First Book of Samuel in the Old Testament and referred to an obscure, tragic figure whose name translates as 'the glory has departed from Israel'. There would be no great significance in this were it not for the fact that this writing on the wall greeted Daniel James, my great-grandfather, when he arrived to take up his first Congregational ministry at the city's Castle Green Church. Did the scribbler know something unsavoury about his new pastor and want to make his feelings known?

If there was a hidden meaning, Daniel, newly married to Clara Pulsford and eager to make his mark at his first church, chose to ignore it. The couple had almost certainly met when Daniel, newly qualified as a Congregational minister from Western College, Bristol, was visiting various churches around the southwest of England as an itinerant preacher, among them Newton Abbot in Devon, where Clara lived. They fell in love but shortly afterwards

– we're not sure why – Clara moved to London, to 175 Sloane Street to be exact. But it was only a temporary separation and on New Year's Eve 1868 they were married at Westminster Chapel. Daniel was twenty-nine, Clara twenty. Shortly afterwards he took up the Bristol post.

ABOVE LEFT: The Reverend Daniel Bloomfield James was said to have 'one of the most wonderful voices ever given to man' **ABOVE RIGHT:** Clara Pulsford came from a long line of Congregational ministers

The couple moved into Shargar Villa on the Cheltenham Road, which, as with so many locations in this story, I managed to obsessively track down by overlaying ancient and modern maps supplied by Bristol Archives. Standing in the road, the house was hard to spot because a pub, the Bishops Tavern, had been built on to the front of the once-elegant Victorian frontage. Daniel's church was a good distance away, the network of streets comprising Castle Green having long since disappeared after being flattened in devastating bombing raids during the Second World War.

Towards the end of 1869 Daniel was preoccupied with writing and publishing a pamphlet entitled 'A Manual for the Use of the Church & Congregation Assembling in Castle Green'. He writes: 'Although like a true Brother he must point out some of your faults, yet, on the whole, thanks be to God, there is much reason for congratulation in reference to the past and hopefulness in regard to the future.'

He talks about the good work that was being done in the Sunday school and Bible classes and underlines the importance of engaging with young people. Then his gentleness and compassion emerge from the pages: 'We are none of us perfect, but so far as I know, you are ready to pass by the little infirmities of human nature, and to love each other in spite of faults and differences.' He appears to have been criticised for not giving enough 'spiritual food', but he replies that unless people approach him there's nothing he can do for them. Almost in passing, he makes reference to the fact that the church had added a hundred members since he arrived. In summing up he says:

I have spoken very freely to you, but as a brother. I am conscious of my own imperfections, and it is only the knowledge that God is with you that keeps up my strength. When I am tired and weak I lean upon him... my preaching may not profit all my hearers, but rest assured I think of you all in my sermon preparations and prayers, and try to enter into all your circumstances and feelings... Be thoughtful, prudent, modest in all your walks and conversation... I am always Your friend and affectionate pastor, D. Bloomfield James.

But a far more significant event had occurred even as Daniel was writing this rather defensive missive to his congregation. On 9 December in Shargar Villa Clara gave birth to my grandfather. It wasn't until March of the following year that Stanley was baptised – Stanley Bloomfeld James – not by his own father but, surprisingly, by one Urijah Thomas, pastor of the neighbouring Congregational church. Why didn't Daniel himself perform the baptism? Did he feel that such a meaningful act would have appeared too familiar if done to one of his own? If so, Stanley at a young age was on the receiving end of his father's awkward reserve. It appears that Clara's warmth, kindness and steadying influence were needed to counteract her husband's diffident manner from the very start of their married life.

Perhaps, reading between the lines of Daniel's end-of-year note, it is possible to detect a feeling of disquiet. Whether that was the case or not, within two years he had resigned and moved to the first of his four London churches. He took up his second post, the pastorate of East Hill Congregational Church, Wandsworth, in 1871. Stanley was in his second year when they moved into 26 Oberstein Road, a four-storey house a stone's throw from Clapham Junction station. The move was prestigious for Daniel because East Hill was one of the largest Congregational churches in the country and was known in some quarters as the 'Cathedral to Congregationalism'. During Daniel's day, East Hill church was enlarged to seat nearly a thousand people and given a new entrance in a road off the High Street. Even today, after some restoration, it looks much as it did then, with the original marble pulpit, arches, galleries and wood-panelling. A plaque at the entrance marks the placing of the memorial stone on 9 November 1875 by 'Pastor Rev. D. Bloomfield James in commemoration of the foundation of the old chapel in High Street in 1573'.

Looking back on these years, the *Congregational Yearbook* states that Daniel did his best work at East Hill, the church being one of the strongest and most energetic in south London. It talks of his intellectual gifts and remarks how he was alive to the best thought of his age, adding that he was primarily an emotional man, who could communicate his passion to a rare degree. Apparently, he didn't laugh much but people often 'felt the touch of rising tears as he played with unerring fingers on the chords of pity and sympathy and love'. It adds that he had 'one of the most wonderful voices ever given to man', its note being 'a rich baritone full of undertones and harmonies'. An admirer said that he would prefer to hear a poor sermon by him than the best from another preacher. His appearance – 'tall and spare in form with masses of rich and abundant hair' – added to his appeal. A deacon from East Hill said that during his pastorate there had never been 'one cross word spoken nor even one cross look between the pastor and his church'. The family line of outstanding Nonconformist ministers was as strong as ever.

Clara had three more children: Muriel (born 1871), Norman (born 1872) and Daisy (born 1873). Clara's seventeen-year-old sister Ada was also living with them. With the expanding family, by 1873 they needed to move to larger premises and found a palatial townhouse at 11 Pembridge Villas on Wimbledon Park Road. Daniel always worked hard as a minister, and as a result of his delicate constitution, frequently made himself ill. Holidays were vital and the Jameses usually found time to take their annual summer break at Cwmbwrwch Farm. In 1876, however, when Stanley was six, it is unclear whether they made the trip or visited Lemuel, who was locked up in Usk prison.

I suspect that Daniel did not concern himself unduly with the minutiae of his children's upbringing, preferring to leave that to Clara. He was a passionate man but also, it seems, intensely private, finding the practicalities of day-to-day fatherhood irksome. And who knows what kind of impact his uncle's imprisonment had on the young Stanley? It must have affected him in some way. It is never mentioned in either of his autobiographies or in any of the family's letters. Perhaps he was ashamed.

A young Stanley, born in Bristol and brought up in London

Daniel was a restless soul, just as in adulthood Stanley would turn out to be. Neither of them would ever rest on their laurels or be content with the status quo. Intellectual and emotional upheaval was part of their make-up and, more than once, a physical move to another church was an indication of inner problems. Either that, or the ever-active headhunting tactics that Congregational churches employed in finding replacement pastors played a part in unsettling them with offers elsewhere. Or perhaps Daniel relished a move back to his Welsh roots. Whatever the case, he left East Hill in 1878 because 'he thought his ministry was not being sufficiently effective'. Walter Road Congregational Church, Swansea, offered him a position, which he initially turned down, accepting it later when they increased the salary to £700 a year (£65,000 in 2020), an incredibly large sum for those days. He started work in the autumn of 1878.

He took over from the highly regarded Thomas Jones, which, by all accounts, was a challenge. Jones, who had left for Australia to recover from illness, was renowned as a 'poet-preacher', but my great-grandfather's oratorical skills would have been a match for his predecessor. At his recognition service in Swansea, Daniel asked his new church that 'when they saw his infirmities, to bear with them, be patient and pray for him. Some people,' he went on, 'wished a minister to be a nice dapper little man, quite willing to be shut up in his pulpit.' He did not wish to be such a man as that. His ideal was a man 'with clear thought and a warm heart and speaking forcibly what he ought'. He said he wished 'to live and labour and die in Swansea'.

As the *Congregational Yearbook* has it, while Daniel had 'a style of eloquence very different in character [from that of Jones] it was scarcely less attractive and subduing in its way'. In the early years he drew huge crowds, with the building packed to the rafters, his cohort of worshippers coming from all sectors of society, rich and poor.

Despite his earlier vow to see out his days in Swansea, Daniel's stay was short-lived. The church was deeply in debt and it was suggested that a system of weekly offering envelopes be reintroduced. It was also proposed that the pastor's salary be reduced to £600 a year (£55,000 in 2020). This insecurity wouldn't have helped but, in the end, it was a scandal surrounding a publicity poster which hastened his exit. In May 1880 the church decided to hold a bazaar and plans were put into action. By chance, the previous incumbent, the legendary Reverend Thomas Jones, was back in Swansea, having returned from Australia. The deacon in charge of organising the bazaar thought it would be a good idea to include Jones's name on the poster as its patron. He received Jones's approval but failed to raise the matter with Daniel and the posters were printed and circulated.

Daniel, despite receiving a letter of explanation and apology from the deacon, refused to consent to the placards remaining as printed. At a meeting of the subcommittee under the chairmanship of Daniel, it was decided, although not unanimously, that a new placard, omitting the name of Jones, should be pasted over the original one. Some of the deacons urged Daniel to assure Jones that no discourtesy had been intended by altering the poster. He said he would consider it but, in the end, did nothing and didn't raise the subject when Jones attended the bazaar in June.

The incident created awkward undercurrents throughout the congregation, while a considerable number of letters debating the issue were published in the *South Wales Daily News*. Even then all might have been resolved, but the dispute flared up again in November. As a result, the deacon who had put Jones's name on the poster resigned; nor was that the end of the affair. *The Story of Walter Road Congregational Church* states: 'During the excitement the Rev. D. Bloomfield James stated his intention to resign and not occupy the pulpit again.' A series of meetings attempted to reconcile him with the deacons but failed and Daniel's resignation was accepted on 16 November. One recalls how at his induction he had told his congregation that he was always going to say what he thought he should.

Perhaps by now Clara had become used to her husband's mood swings, but the ensuing disruption must have been extremely upsetting. It needed all her skill and understanding to keep the family together and soothe the brow of her moody husband. Stanley was nearly eleven and it wasn't the first difference of opinion he'd see his father have with deacons. The family, however, seem to have been able to hang on to their house – 5 St James's Crescent – because they were still living there on 3 April 1881, when the census was conducted. Perhaps the loyal section of the congregation who joined Daniel at the breakaway church he established made that financially possible.

The local newspaper announced it was in a large room on the first floor of the agricultural hall in the St Helen's district of Swansea where 'the revered gentleman will preach on Sunday next both morning and evening'. Daniel took half the Walter Road congregation with him, though all the deacons stayed. The agricultural hall has since been demolished, although a sign marks the original site. Soon Daniel moved his loyal congregation from these temporary premises to the newly erected iron church of St Paul's in the west of the city. According to the words of a later secretary of Walter Road Church, 'the only bright side of this unfortunate affair is that God, in his providence, converted the folly of man into wisdom, for today we have in St Paul's a strong church serving a large district'.

The *Congregational Yearbook* states: 'Here for a few years longer he [Daniel] exercised the spell of his gifts over an attached and earnest congregation, and when he left, the Church was in a flourishing condition.' A few years after that was written, the iron church was replaced by a stone structure which still stands, except that now it houses the Viswam Bar & Restaurant. Daniel stayed there until August 1883. The postscript to this story of wounded egos, hierarchies and power struggles is that Walter Road was unable to find another pastor, so they invited the selfsame Reverend Jones to accept a shared pastorate with another minister at £200 a year. He somewhat reluctantly accepted, but it was a short-lived return: in June 1882 Jones died from overwork.

* * *

Stanley was thirteen when in August 1883 his father made his move to another south London suburb, this time as minister of Christ Church, Addiscombe. The family lived near the church at Abbotsford, 39 Clyde Road, while both Stanley and Norman were day boys at Whitgift School, Croydon. Stanley was growing up fast and his father's tendency towards intensity and anxiety was already evident in him. The young boy didn't take to Croydon, which he says was something of an intellectual desert. Presumably he and Norman walked the mile or so to school, but there is no mention of jolly schoolboy japes; here was a serious man in the making.

Norman, meanwhile, whose nickname at school was 'Jumbo', cheekily recalls in *The Autobiography of a Nobody* (published 1947) how his lifelong dislike of teachers started at this time: 'Even now the sight of a teacher brings me out in a rash... Possibly in my case either the method of teaching was of such a nature that it failed to draw out what was in the pupil, or possibly there just wasn't anything to draw out.' Already we see how different the characters of the two brothers were: Stanley earnest and intense, Norman flippant and jocular. None of that was ever really to change.

Stanley did look back and analyse his father's time in Addiscombe. 'It was unfortunate perhaps that he should have been lured to London and should have spent the major part of his ministerial career in the suburbs,' he writes in his second autobiography, *Becoming a Man*. 'He was ill-fitted to struggle against the philistinism of those to whom he was called to minister and his sensitive nature suffered much and made it difficult for him to mingle freely with others.' He added that his father took no physical exercise and spent most of his time preparing his Sunday sermons.

Daniel's fourth church, recently built in Canning Road, Addiscombe, had opened only the previous year and had seen a number of temporary ministers. During Daniel's six years at Addiscombe, an extension, consisting of a lecture hall and schoolrooms, was erected. The architect was John Sulman, who later made his name in Australia as the architect of many municipal buildings in Sydney and Canberra. The church itself was knocked down in January 1971 and the land sold off for flats but the hall – now known as Clyde Hall – still stands. On its facade there is a plaque marking the placing of the foundation stone and yet again, as at East Hill, my great-grandfather's name ended up on the inscription for being the incumbent pastor at the time, 22 May 1886.

In the meantime, with his father settled at his new church, the sixteen-year-old Stanley describes how his 'omnivorous and indiscriminate reading' was rapidly steering him away from the career as a Congregational minister that was being mapped out for him. He writes: 'I was given money for lunch. But this I frequently spent on acquiring copies of the poets published in a cheap series by Messrs Warne & Co. The voluntary fasting involved does not seem to have troubled me.'

He not only lapped up English classics, but devoured the plays of the dramatist Aeschylus. 'I had previously read Shelley's *Prometheus Unbound*, and *Paradise Lost*, but the effect of Aeschylus was like nothing else,' he comments. 'I wrote verse myself – mostly in Spenserian stanzas... some of it was tolerable enough to be printed in the school magazine.'

He would also have been aware of the cultural shocks that were being felt in every sphere of life at that time. William Morris was preaching the gospel of socialism, Matthew Arnold was attacking organised religion – both orthodox Christianity and Nonconformism – while Thomas Huxley was criticising the whole nature of belief from a scientific standpoint and Darwin's views on evolution were gaining traction. Although these pioneering ideas made an impression on both father and son, the picture was complex, of course. Daniel, while being liberal in outlook, was nevertheless traditional in other respects, frequently delving into Cardinal Newman's writings to seek inspiration for his own sermons. He often quoted the poet Robert Browning while at the same time being an admirer of the controversial American pulpit orator Henry Ward Beecher, brother of Harriet Beecher Stowe who wrote *Uncle Tom's Cabin*. John Keble, a founding member of the Tractarian Movement which sought to recover the Catholic heritage of the Church of England, was another among Daniel's eclectic mix of guiding lights. Stanley himself had been named after Arthur Stanley, the Dean of Westminster. There was a fervour of ideas which my grandfather happily soaked up.

Despite his growing intellectual misgivings about religion, Stanley found it impossible to make a clean break with his father. He never ceased to find Daniel's emotional preaching and 'the mystical and poetic spirit of his Welsh blood' alluring, and he marks this time as having a huge influence on his future career. He writes:

Unwittingly, for there was but little intercourse between us on such matters, he preserved me from flying off at a tangent... It would have been strange if I had not felt drawn to follow my father's footsteps... Even more than hereditary influences and parental wishes, my fate seemed decided by the fact that my father was entirely ignorant of that outside world in which, had I elected to adopt some other career, I should have had to make my way. His lack of practicality would have made it impossible for him to launch me in any other profession or business but his own. For my part, I had given so little thought to any alternative that, when I began to realise the limitations of the Nonconformist pulpit, the thought of having to find an opening for myself was terrifying.

Stanley found it difficult to establish simple schoolboy friendships or have fun, something that his younger brother, with his easy-going take on life, had no difficulty in achieving. An inability to relax was starting to reveal itself; it was to be a recurring aspect of Stanley's make-up for the next thirty years.

* * *

It is no surprise that a friend of Daniel's whom Stanley describes as a 'poet, mystic, preacher, novelist and a mediator between traditional Christianity and its modern variants' should become a hero of his. The man in question was the Scottish writer of children's fantasy novels and a member of the Church of England, Dr George MacDonald. From time to time he was a guest of the Jameses, staying the weekend, preaching on the Sunday and delivering a lecture on a Shakespeare play or the poetry of Coleridge or Shelley on the Monday. With his silvery hair and long white beard and a tartan shawl thrown over his shoulders, it's easy to see why Stanley looked up to him. The family read and reread his novels. My grandfather recalled the occasion when MacDonald gave the family a case containing a collection of his fairy stories, along with his poems. 'It was through him that I first caught a glimpse of our Lord's personality,' he writes. 'I owe it to him that, at a comparatively early age, the Gospels came alive as the story of a real man.'

Modestly, Stanley doesn't mention the prize he won at sixteen for his essay, 'Shelley Compared With Keats'. William Wood, archivist at Whitgift School, helped me locate it and sent me a copy. The essay is mature for a teenager. It is learned, scholarly even, perhaps precocious, with perceptive insights into some of Shelley's familiar and much-loved poems, as well as lesser-known ones. He praises Shelley for his lofty ideals, and one can't help but imagine that Stanley saw in the poet a template for his own visions. In the essay he writes:

Could Shelley have attained the perfection of his soaring aspirations, the timeworn customs and the habits of centuries would there and then have been buried in the dust of the ages; tyranny and oppression in social and religious life would have been overcome and trampled under the feet that they had for time out of mind chained and bound; slavery and cruel wrongs would be obliterated from the face of the earth and perish everlastingly, and man would once more be free, ruled but by Love.

But even here he wags his ideological finger at Shelley, adding, 'There is one blemish. "Love is God," says Shelley: why not alter it to "God is love?" and then the single spot would be gone.'

Despite Stanley's growing disenchantment with organised religion, his father's theological voice rings loud and clear. True, there is nothing groundbreaking in Stanley's treatise, but we can detect the embryo of ideas that were to later inspire – and hound – the adult man. Given the intellectual, psychological and sexual turmoil that was to dominate long periods of his adult life, it might have been expected that he would gravitate towards this most romantic of Romantic poets.

By way of conclusion, Stanley writes: 'We are told that he visited the sick, comforted the dying, and gave his money to the poor... A man who could thus spend his life for others, who wrote for the benefit of humanity, certainly deserves a better name than infidel.' No wonder my grandfather admired him. For many of my adolescent years, Shelley was my favourite poet, too. On long walks I used to recite his poetry to myself.

In December 1886 the school magazine printed 'The Statue', a sixty-line, blank verse poem describing the pain of lost love written by Stanley in the style of Keats. It was described by the editor as 'certainly one of the finest things yet seen in the magazine'. A short quotation from the beginning demonstrates its merit and maturity:

An ivied church! – a ruin of past years –
Like a lone sentinel, stands o'er a cliff,
And silent gazes on the sea below.
But 'midst its crumbling ruin, and the gloom
That ever rests within, there stands a form,
White-sculptured, of a youth of noble mien,
And while around decay and darkness reign,
In vain they touch the snow-white marble youth.
And this the legend that the fishers tell
To strangers who inquire the sculptor's name.

William Wood also sent me clippings of Stanley's sporting prowess. He played rugby, his name appearing on the First XV team sheet as a back-row forward. He appears in the report of a cricket match in which, batting at number four, he was out caught for nine. But I can't quite imagine his father cheering on his son from the touchline.

~ 3 ~
BREAKING AWAY

My search for Worple Road Congregational Church, Wimbledon, in books or on the Internet came to nothing. So, I walked for over a mile down the existing road looking for signs of the church where Daniel became minister in 1889. It was nowhere to be seen. Only when I scoured old maps at the Surrey History Centre in Woking did it become clear. It turned out that this imposing church with its towering spire, just round the corner from Wimbledon station, had long since disappeared, replaced by a Sainsbury's supermarket. In searching for places from the past, I was staggered by the number of supermarkets now situated where Nonconformist churches used to be. And the wearing out of shoe leather was not something I'd been anticipating when I started to hunt for my ancestors.

The church was at the heart of this fashionable and prosperous suburb, and among its congregation were some big hitters on the London business and cultural scene – Daniel's new posting was just about as prestigious as it got in Nonconformist circles. Significantly, too, his appointment came at a time when the Congregational Church in particular was attracting those sympathetic to the most progressive movements of the day. His congregation liked Daniel immediately and he quickly gained a reputation for being 'a preacher and a scholar, a gifted and great-hearted pastor, the first preacher of Wimbledon and the acknowledged equal of most of the popular preachers of the day'. He received his highest salary to date, ensuring that Clara and the family were well provided for. Under the previous pastorate of Walter C. Talbot, Worple Road boasted a large congregation, but Daniel's vibrant preaching attracted even more worshippers, who were likely to have given his liberal ideas a more sympathetic ear than the Addiscombe church had. Nor was he forgotten: he was regularly asked to officiate at his former churches, not least at the reopening of Castle Green Chapel, Bristol, after it had suffered a devastating fire.

Among the influential people at Worple Road was the campaigning journalist, author, social reformer and medium, W. T. Stead, who is also recognised as the pioneer of investigative journalism. Both his and Daniel's liberal outlook meant they would have seen eye to eye on many issues of the day and Stead seems to have been a personal friend of the Jameses. An intriguing paragraph in his 1891 book *Real Ghost Stories* points to an intimacy that stretched beyond ecclesiastical walls. Recalling true stories of extraterrestrial happenings, he records a story that Clara had told him. Apparently, her mother Elizabeth, her aunt Charlotte and a Miss E. of Bideford, Devon, were at school together in Teignmouth. The last two girls formed a great friendship, and promised whoever died first would come to the other. In about 1815 Charlotte was on the landing of her house when she saw Miss E. walking up the stairs. Charlotte was not at all frightened as she was expecting her friend and called out: 'Oh, how glad I am to see you.' A few days later it transpired that Miss E. had died that very same evening.

Stanley probably knew Stead, too, and would have been intrigued by the more spiritual remarks of this unusual journalist. In two separate pieces of writing Stead was to foresee tragic accidents at sea, one involving an iceberg. Despite having had these uncanny foresights, Stead himself was on that fateful *Titanic* voyage in 1912, and drowned.

W.T. Stead, the pioneering journalist, worshipped at the Reverend
Daniel James's Wimbledon church and was a friend of the family

The family home was Caerleon, 5 Crescent Road, which to this day is
a handsome, red-brick villa with a bay window frontage in a quiet cul-de-
sac leading up the hill towards Wimbledon Common. Here lived Daniel
and Clara, Muriel, aged nineteen, Norman, eighteen, and Daisy, seventeen,
as well as Clara's parents, Thomas and Elizabeth Pulsford. Between 1887
and 1893 Stanley hardly lived with the family.

He had left Whitgift School in December 1886, without passing any external
exams, Norman having left over a year before. Attaining qualifications didn't
have the same importance then as it does now, but nevertheless it does seem
to have been an abrupt departure. He had shown intellectual promise and
university would have beckoned. It is clear from *The Adventures of a Spiritual
Tramp* (1925) and *Becoming a Man* (1944), his two autobiographies, that at
some point Stanley entered an especially turbulent phase of his life during
which he managed to fall out with his father and enrol for – and resign from
– at least five educational institutions, both as a student and as a teacher.

In his two autobiographies, he is vague about what he was doing at any
specific time, preferring to dwell on the state of his soul and its metaphysical
struggles. The sequence of events is hard to unravel. But it is not too fanciful

to surmise that the all-pervading theological atmosphere in the Wimbledon house emanating from both the James and Pulsford sides of the family was more than Stanley could bear. We can also assume that John Pulsford, particularly when he was preaching in London, would have stayed with the family and that Stanley knew and spoke to him.

In the early days of his rebellion, Stanley buried his head in romantic and radical literature, but later he needed to remove himself physically. In the event, those Nonconformist influences worked both positively and negatively on him, undoubtedly helping to shape his future religious life. For now, they provided extra fuel for the smouldering revolt that was engulfing him, which quickly drove an ideological wedge between him and his father. He was finally emerging from Daniel's shadow and, symbolically, he was already signing himself 'Stanley B. James', thereby rejecting his father's wish for the family to use the name Bloomfield.

His brother Norman, meanwhile, went straight to Amersham Hall, Caversham, a 'school for the sons of dignified gentlemen'. The principal was a Reverend Ebenezer West, who funded the building of Caversham Baptist Free Church. Stanley also has Amersham Hall on his CV, but that may have been as an assistant teacher rather than as a pupil. He certainly writes about a school he taught at without giving it a name. 'The character of this school may be gathered from the fact that it was known locally as Dotheboys Hall [the name Charles Dickens gave to an excessively cruel educational establishment in *Nicholas Nickleby*],' Stanley writes. 'The Head was a pimply-faced, brown-bearded individual who frequently officiated at the Baptist Chapel to which it was my duty to take the boys. When he preached, he wore black cotton gloves, and he preached unctuously.'

On 1 October 1887 Stanley entered University College, Aberystwyth, and took a course whose subjects were English, history, Latin, Greek, chemistry and mathematics. We don't know why he went so far away to study or what the purpose of the course was, though he may have been preparing for the Congregational college in Bangor, further up the coast, to train to be a minister. Whatever the reason, it seems to have been a period of intellectual expansion. He writes:

I well remember reading Emerson's essay on "Self-Reliance" for the first time. It was during a country walk one spring morning.

Primroses peeped from the dried leaves. The Welsh hills rose up around me. I sat down by the side of the road and pulled the book from my pocket. It was an intoxication... Some nameless fear had been exorcised. I rose up, drew a breath, and determined, at all hazards, to be myself.

At one point he writes about poor exam results, the reason for his disappointing grades being his preoccupation with studying books outside the syllabus rather than out-and-out laziness. He was unable to 'give his mind to dead languages or mathematics', subjects which were central to his course at Aberystwyth. Other reasons for his restlessness were 'the spirit that was abroad in the 1880s' and, not least, a love affair which 'made steady application difficult'. He never says who the woman was.

Walt Whitman, poet of democracy and individual freedom

It was Walt Whitman, the American poet of democracy and personal freedom, who provided the spiritual ambrosia that his soul craved. 'Here were cosmic vision, large spaces, a faith in and charity towards the universal man,' he writes. 'It was this development of my manhood, I would have said, which was the prime obligation... There is a catholic man and a natural law and it is this natural law in all its catholicity and not some arbitrary and external code which sets the standard of conduct. To be a man, then, was the goal, not compliance with puritan taboos but growth in normality.'

But Stanley quit Aberystwyth before the end of the course, finding it impossible to study any longer. For want of anything better to do he enrolled on a Congregational ministers' training course at Western College in Bristol, where his father had trained. He writes: 'I had no other means of earning a living except that which the Congregational ministry offered.' But he was soon to give up this course, too, finding the discipline of the training too irksome, and thought that, once and for all, this was his last attempt to make a career out of the pulpit. To make ends meet he lurched with reluctance towards teaching again, landing a job at a small school in north London, which he describes as the dreariest thing he had ever done.

The bleak and desperate note of those troubled years, however, was lightened by a venture into acting. While teaching, he found time to take elocution lessons designed to set him on a path towards the theatrical profession. 'I had a good voice, a certain measure of experience in amateur theatricals, and a considerable amount of self-confidence,' he says. He claims to have had some success, so treated this experiment with the utmost seriousness. Indeed, throughout his life, he loved to act and seems to have had a nice line in comic improvisation.

He was asked to fill in for an actor who had been forced to cry off from his leading role in Henry Arthur Jones's *The Middleman* at a theatre in Newport, Monmouthshire, in 1891. He had twenty-four hours to learn the part – but when the evening came, he froze as every word vanished from his mind. The prompter's voice was heard and the actors tried their best to rescue the situation, but the performance was ruined and the next morning he took the train back to London, his tail between his thespian legs. In passing, Stanley remarks how charitable his fellow troupers had been, just as they are in J. B. Priestley's *The Good Companions*. The ignominious failure put an end to making acting his future career. What came next was a second attempt to train for the Congregational ministry, surely in desperation. He entered another theological college as a lay student, but this proved to be a cul-de-sac, too, and within months he had left.

These disappointments failed to put an end to his spiritual quest; it was merely driven underground. He acknowledges that there were long periods of agnosticism during which 'the Wayfarer merely drifted on the stream of circumstances, taking the line of least resistance'. Along this tortuous path of indecision he befriended a Unitarian minister with whom he had lodged during the holidays. He was an American from Boston and it was in his church there that one of Stanley's literary heroes, Ralph Waldo Emerson, delivered some of the discourses that made the New England philosopher famous. Stanley even preached for his new friend, the tolerant Unitarian outlook making it possible for even a raw, lost youth to stand in the pulpit and talk. He must have made an impression because he was told that funds had been made available to send him to Manchester College, Oxford, to train for the Unitarian ministry.

Responding enthusiastically to the idea, Stanley says he resigned from the school where he was teaching at that point and moved to lodgings in Richmond, where his friend lived, in order to prepare for the examination. The 1891 census, taken on 5 April, does indeed show Stanley, aged twenty-one, living at Bath House, 35 London Road, Twickenham, but as part of another school with twenty-four other residents. He is described as an assistant schoolmaster under the headship of James Blackman, who was married with six children.

Shortly after this he moved again to other digs in the district – 2 Clarence Villas, St Mary's Grove – and it was here that he met fellow lodger George Julian Harney, Chartism's *enfant terrible*, a Marxist who was always on the radical side of the movement. Then aged seventy-four, he was still writing articles for the *Newcastle Chronicle* and, according to Stanley, reading Byron voraciously. He was an activist who had always advocated the use of physical force and enjoyed riling his conservative comrades by flaunting the red cap of liberty at public meetings. Harney had befriended Karl Marx and Friedrich Engels so it was perhaps no surprise when Stanley met a tall, rangy figure in the half-light on the landing one day. It was none other than Friedrich Engels, aged about seventy, visiting his revolutionary English friend.

Above left: George Julian Harney, Chartist and militant Marxist
Above right: Friedrich Engels was a frequent visitor to Stanley's
Richmond lodgings

No surprise either that, as the time for the examination approached, Stanley stalled and called off the enterprise. The same old inhibitions which had gripped him over training for the Congregational ministry afflicted him with Unitarianism, too. He baulked at the prospect of being moulded along Oxford lines and felt a chill at this brand of Nonconformity's lack of regard for emotion. More fundamentally, he was now questioning the very nature of religious belief. He was rapidly reaching an impasse and looking for a way out.

* * *

Stanley's very own existential drama was about to receive another Ibsenesque twist, but this time it was a turn of events that was out of his control. It emanated from his father and his deteriorating relationship with a section of the congregation at Worple Road. Without this fresh ruction, father and son might have been able to mend their bridges, but the ensuing disruption to family life was too far-reaching for any kind of reconciliation.

Paradoxically, Daniel's very success at the church contributed to the crisis. Once more, as in Swansea, he clashed with the deacons, who, feeling their authority threatened, became jealous of the admiration he was attracting. At a special meeting called to discuss the issue, the deacons said they found Daniel too impractical and too dictatorial. They complained of not being consulted and at times when their views differed from his he in turn felt he was being thwarted. The result was that the deacons felt paralysed. Daniel stopped attending meetings and almost all communication with the deacons ground to a halt.

Other controversies contributed to a perfect storm that sparked a massive ecclesiastical bust-up. Some deacons complained that the Sunday school was not receiving the attention it should. And the finances, as ever, were unhealthy, despite the large and growing church roll. Perhaps the finger can be pointed at Daniel here as on more than one occasion he said he wanted nothing to do with the monetary aspect of the church. In his defence, he complains of not being 'attended to by the deacons' and states that only one of them had been loyal to him.

At the same time, the congregation itself was splitting into two – those old timers represented largely by the diaconate, and the newcomers who sought a stronger voice in church affairs. It was from this new but significant grouping that Daniel found the sympathy and support he craved. It all came to a head with the annual election of deacons in December 1892, with the newcomers mounting a campaign in which they demanded greater representation. But they lost, and promptly complained that the voting system was stacked in the ruling party's favour.

Was it rigged? There is no way of knowing, but the schism was complete. Eighty-four members quit and sent in their letter of resignation, with Clara, Muriel and Daisy among their number. On 18 January 1893, Daniel resigned, his letter to the secretary stating: 'My dear Mr Barrie, will you kindly inform the church that my ministry among them will terminate on the 29th of this month and I hope to preach my last sermon on the evening of that day. With best wishes for your future spiritual welfare, I am yours truly, D. B James.'

The text he chose for that last sermon was from the First Epistle of Peter, Chapter Two, Verse 17: 'Honour all men, love the brotherhood, fear God, honour the king.' The most prestigious post of Daniel's career lay in pieces at his feet.

The *Surrey Comet* records on 21 January: 'Anything but peace and concord has been the result of the resignation of Rev. D. Bloomfield James... and whatever may be the merits of the dispute... certain it is that a breach has been caused which it will take years to heal.'

And the *Christian World* notes that Daniel's resignation had brought about a 'fierce and unseemly controversy'. It goes on to say that Christians from other denominations in Wimbledon were joining together to try to persuade him to stay on. Meanwhile, letters containing more heat than discretion were appearing in the press and the deacons who opposed Daniel were receiving considerable abuse. The *Surrey Comet* published a letter from an Anglican who asks what the Congregational body could be thinking of to allow such a state of things to exist. The contributor says he was aware of the frequent differences that occur between Congregational leaders and their pastors. He asks why the services of 'this splendid man' could not be retained for Wimbledon? 'Is there no way of keeping amongst us such a power for good as Mr James?'

The final, remaining act was to establish another church around Daniel, which had always been part of a longer-term plan by the newcomers' faction. For the time being the breakaway group, with my great-grandfather revitalised and at the helm, held meetings in a nearby hall, but the rumblings of discontent from the other group continued. One member accused Daniel of being 'unfaithful to the church as a whole', while another claimed that the minority were seeking revenge and wanted to wreck Worple Road, additionally warning that a new church based on one man was dangerous and risky. Having condemned the setting-up of a rival body, the deacons hoped the breakaway group would realise it was wrong and return to the original congregation. Well, that never happened, and the two churches went their own ways. Nevertheless, the rupture was felt keenly on both sides. In February the remaining membership agreed 'to arrange some mode of parting that would be kind and friendly on the part of the church'.

So much for the church documents, which point to the more temporal reasons for the rift. But it's left to Stanley, reflecting on the episode some fifty years later, to offer a possible deeper, doctrinal reason: 'In one sense [Daniel] was more traditional than his Nonconformist brethren... On his shelves stood [Cardinal] Newman's sermons. When his broad views created trouble in the Wimbledon congregation… he hived off with a large following and built another church where he could give freer expression to his views.'

In setting up another church more in keeping with his vision of how worship should be conducted, Daniel eventually found some peace of mind, particularly given the fact that he received support from Clara and others who broke away from Worple Road. But, despite that, the ructions could not be just shrugged off; clearly they had a lasting effect on the family's equilibrium and perhaps none of them fully recovered.

* * *

It is at this point, in March 1893, that Stanley's younger brother Norman assumes centre stage and unwittingly determines his brother's fate for the next six years. Until now he has been in the shadows, the light-hearted jester playing second fiddle to the tragic hero. In a very different way to Stanley, Norman was to make his mark upon the world, but for now we can see him trapped, uncertain of his future and overwhelmed by the oppressive religiosity of the Wimbledon home.

He had been working as a tea trader in the south London suburbs but now sought a more exciting occupation. He shared his brother's restlessness. Many years later, after he had achieved fame in the political arena and as a journeyman journalist, in *The Autobiography of a Nobody* he describes the way the family had become exasperated by his inability to settle to any task, and how different he was from everyone else in the family – and outside it. He made himself out to be a misfit – more shades of Stanley. He writes: 'I am sorry to say that my parents, though they were kind in a pitying way, never took to me, and though I tried to emulate them, and though my brothers and sister did their unpleasant best to inculcate in me respectable thoughts and manners, they never succeeded.'

Apart from a feeling of genuine sadness and confusion that Norman captures here, what is strange is his reference to his brothers and sister. According to the accepted version of the family tree, Norman had one brother and two sisters. Surely a slip of the pen.

He relates how the local MP, an acquaintance of his father's, was called on to help find the incalcitrant boy a job. The man in question called round and was plied with several glasses of good port before being introduced to Norman. The idea was to ease his way into the civil service but very quickly the MP frowned and adjudged that Norman's unusual character would debar him from that particular career. Instead, the family opted for the last refuge of the nineteenth-century, middle-class, difficult son – the colonies. His ticket to Canada was bought, and he was given money for expenses – 'not too much, of course... The word "dissipation" was much in vogue those days, and the family took wise precautions to see that I could not dissipate myself too early in life.' Meanwhile, contact was made with three other young men from different families whose parents also 'thought that their offspring would be better off in the colonies, or at least that their families would be better off with them in the colonies', according to Norman. And so, on the appointed day, four young men travelled to Liverpool by train to embark on their new life.

Quite when Stanley decided to go too is unclear. Norman makes no mention of Stanley travelling with him on the boat, although he briefly describes the other three. Stanley says: 'My brother... was on the point of emigrating to Canada, and I resolved to accompany him. The decision was a sheer gamble prompted by despair.' Throughout his book Norman never mentions Stanley once, although their paths frequently crossed in Alberta and they ran a shop together for a while. Stanley almost certainly did accompany his brother but, for whatever reason, Norman chose not to include him in his narrative.

Their lifestyles couldn't have been more different. Norman writes: 'I think it would be a refreshing change if someone who had never done, said or written anything remarkable would write an autobiography that would be a plain, unvarnished tale about nothings. I cannot think of anybody more suited to this task than myself.' One can't help wondering whether he is deliberately cocking a snook at his elder brother's writing with its high-minded preoccupations and self-regard.

It's worth noting Stanley's bleak feelings on leaving England: 'Cutting the umbilical cord that bound me to my native land proved a more painful thing than I had anticipated. It was a forlorn emigrant who waved goodbye to the little group of relatives – and to one who was not a relative – at Euston.' Was the 'one' the woman with whom he'd had a relationship in Aberystwyth four years previously? He continues:

No convict on the point of being transported to Van Diemen's Land could have felt more hopeless of the future than I. It was a kind of death, but a death in which there was no prospect of a resurrection. Faith was dead; ambition, too, had succumbed... My exile did not even hold out the possibility, which sustains other emigrants, of making a colonial fortune... It is scarcely possible to exaggerate the sense of desolation with which I set sail for the new world.

Comparing himself to a convict being transported overseas seems extreme. Would Norman have mocked his gloom and told him to pull himself together? And it's hard to see how Stanley would have joined in the high jinks the boys got up to in Liverpool before embarking on their all-in package to Winnipeg on 23 March 1893. They nearly missed the boat when they were arrested by police and taken to the local constabulary after one of them made a rousing, drunken speech on the steps of City Hall. But when the police realised they were leaving the country, they were marched to the wharf and guarded until a steward assumed responsibility for them. I wonder if the orator was Norman himself, limbering up for his future career as an Alberta politician. I wonder, too, if by then Stanley was carrying a copy of Whitman's poems in his pocket, as he was to do later on a day-to-day basis. If so, as the Atlantic rollers crashed against the bow of the *S.S. Parisian*, he might have read:

Afoot and light-hearted I take to the open road,
Healthy, free, the world before me,
The long brown path before me leading wherever I choose.
Henceforth I ask not good fortune, I myself am good fortune,
Henceforth I whimper no more, postpone no more, need nothing,
Done with indoor complaints, libraries, querulous criticisms,
Strong and content I travel the open road.

Those inspiring words might have had the power to revive even his severely drooping spirits. And they might have convinced him that, at last, real adventure lay ahead.

Top left: After falling out with his father and failing to find settled employment, Stanley decided to emigrate to Canada with his brother. **Top Right:** Norman, who gave up his job as a tea trader. **Above:** The brothers sailed from Liverpool to Halifax on the *SS Parisian* on 23 March 1893, arriving 11 days later. Credit: Norway Heritage Collection, Borge Solem

GO WEST, YOUNG MAN

~ 4 ~

THE COWBOY

The Atlantic crossing from Liverpool to Halifax, arriving on 2 April, took Stanley and the others in the party 11 days. The inclusive deal they'd booked took them straight on to Winnipeg by train, after which they independently made their way to Calgary and the Rocky Mountains. They knew there was little point in lingering in the east where itinerant labour was less in demand. They followed the British émigré's well-trodden route to Alberta where there were more jobs, Stanley and Norman having already read a whole raft of literature about the 'glories of Canada'. Once in Calgary, they would have found out, probably by hearsay or hanging around in bars, about any vacant jobs in the district. The group dispersed and went their own ways, Stanley heading initially to the River Bow and then to Jumping Pound, Norman to Priddis.

My sources for my grandfather's four ranching years are his two autobiographies, articles he wrote for the *Calgary Herald*, a talk he gave in New York in 1927, the Glenbow Museum archives, sections of Norman's book, the conversations I had in Alberta with five grandsons of Stanley's workmates from 120 years earlier, and a meeting with a professor. At various times in this first phase of his life out West, Stanley worked as a cowboy, shepherd, logger, bridge-builder, haymaker – and general dogsbody. My slightly obsessive search for a route map of the places he went between 1893 and 1897 was made harder by the fact that he didn't record place names accurately. Indeed, he may even have indulged in a certain amount of semi-fictionalisation. Although my research didn't produce definitive answers, it is clear that he was continually moving from job to job. He writes:

I settled down in neither one locality nor occupation. I passed from east to west, and from north to south, travelling light, and heeding not the direction so long as I was moving... I was like those people who decide their course by reference to a pack of cards or by opening a book and taking the first word their eyes fall on as the word of Fate.

I arrived in Alberta beneath wide, empty skies, a suitable metaphor for the openness and uncertainty of the quest ahead. For a few days I blundered about the foothills trying to match Stanley's descriptions to twenty-first-century locations. Slowly I began to piece together where he might have been – or at least where he hadn't been. It was only when I made connections with people – mostly modern-day ranchers – whose grandfathers had worked alongside mine that I was able to pin down various places where he had worked.

The families prominent among ranchers in the 1890s are still ranching today and I spent time with them. It was also useful to talk to Simon Evans, professor of geography at the University of Calgary, who put Stanley's adventure in context. He pointed out – in a kindly way – that my grandfather was just one of thousands of men who came from the British Isles and settled like 'flotsam and jetsam' at the foot of the Rockies. Interestingly, Stanley used the same phrase to describe the influx of middle-class British hopefuls like himself who washed up in those foothills.

My grandfather's first job was almost certainly at Mitford, a settlement that no longer exists, just west of present-day Cochrane. The already well-heeled Tom Cochrane had brought his family from England to make a fortune from ranching, but his efforts proved to be a catalogue of disasters. Not realising that cattle needed feed to see them through the harsh conditions, he could only look on as the whole of his herd died of starvation his second winter there. His ignominious reputation is today recalled in the name of the modern town, a dormitory facility for Calgary.

When Stanley arrived, hopes of establishing Mitford as the centre of a large ranching business were still high. Cochrane desperately needed a bridge by which to convey his cattle and workers, and Stanley's job was to help build a bridge across the Bow River, along with, among others, a former banker from Dublin. If Stanley thought his first position was going to be straightforward, he was in for a rude awakening. He recalls how on his first day he was given the tricky job of teamster. He writes: 'Not only because I had never before handled a team but, even more, because I was brooding over something I had read, I made innumerable mistakes. These contributed to the gaiety of the party.' He adds that he was the only one of the team who could swim. 'I was given all the jobs that involved the risk of falling into the torrent, though it was clear that, had I done so, swimming would have been of little use.'

When, on my research visit to Alberta, I read this out to Roy Copithorne, whose grandfather would have known mine, he smiled knowingly. 'The Englishmen who came over were always the butt of jokes,' he said. 'They were seen as gullible. They would have teased the hell out of him. If you were a foolish goose, there was always someone willing to pluck you.' What's more, Stanley's bridge only stood until 1897 before being swept away by violent flood waters. But the rough treatment he received didn't deter him from taking on this kind of work again. Four years later he landed a similar job building a bridge over the Milk River, just a few miles from the US border.

Ranching was, however, Stanley's main occupation. One tends to think of the cowboy as a kind of mythical being who rode the Prairies for centuries. Yet his legendary status was squeezed into just over thirty years, starting in the late 1870s and lasting until the early years of the twentieth century. My grandfather's time in the saddle came right in the middle of that era. I was able to pin down his location, which at that time went by the name of Jumping Pond, although the name changed to Jumping Pound at the beginning of the twentieth century, which it remains today. The name derives from the practice of native Indians driving buffalo off cliff edges to their deaths below, then using every bit of the carcass for their own needs. Nowadays, the Jumping Pound area runs about thirty-five miles from Moose Mountain in the south to Cochrane in the north, just where Jumping Pound Creek joins the Bow River.

A decision by W.W. Stuart to hire a photographer to record life on the ranch affords a unique opportunity to see Stanley the cowboy. Tᴏᴘ: he is in the centre foreground, mounted on his horse; Cᴇɴᴛʀᴇ: he is in the front row, the only man not wearing a hat; Bᴏᴛᴛᴏᴍ: he is on the far left of the group branding cattle. Credit: Glenbow Museum, Calgary

Among the ranchers that my grandfather worked for was W. W. Stuart, whose land was on the banks of Jumping Pound Creek. Stuart was an Englishman who came out West for his health, first travelling to Colorado, then arriving at Jumping Pound in 1886, where his brother Duncan had already established a ranch. They bought a herd of cattle in Manitoba and drove it an incredible eight hundred miles to the ranch, which was said to be the longest cattle drive in North American history. Stuart's ill health eventually forced him to give up the ranch, which was bought by John Bateman in 1905.

Now his grandson, Jim Bateman, and his partner Gayle have charge of a herd of thirty cattle that graze on the banks of Jumping Pound Creek. I went to see them, and over cups of coffee they showed me their collection of photographs from the old days. I'd already found two shots of cowboys taken in 1893 on the Glenbow Museum website, one showing a branding session, the other ten cowboys on horseback posing for the camera. I had already wondered if the only fresh-faced youth among them – the only one who didn't look like a seasoned cowboy, in fact – could have been my grandfather. Now Jim Bateman showed me a third photograph of the same group, taken at the same time. Again, the raw-looking young man lying down in the middle of the front row, dressed in chaps and with a Stetson hat balanced on his knee, raised speculation. I pulled out some other photographs of Stanley taken both before his time in Canada and afterwards, back in England. With the help of a magnifying glass Jim and Gayle compared the shots. Without any prompting from me, they chorused: 'That's your grandfather. No question.'

I conducted the same experiment with other ranchers who had roots going back to the 1890s, and they all concurred. The 126-year-old photos constituted a fantastic discovery. In the photo showing the ten cowboys mounted on horseback, Stanley appears in the foreground sitting proudly on a cayuse, a small horse, native to North America, known for its endurance. He is the only horseman in the group whose reins are not attached to a bridle but are merely slung around the horse's neck. This unusual feature probably indicates that he was not expert enough to be able to ride a horse in the accepted way, at least in his early days. With his left hand firmly placed on his hip, he is definitely posing, centre-stage. In the group photograph without horses, Jim Bateman's grandfather, John, is on the far left of the back row and Stanley's boss, W. W. Stuart, is second on the left in the front row. The photographs, by S. A. Smyth, were taken on the nearby XC Ranch at branding time when neighbours helped out fellow ranchers with the marking of their cattle, after which the good turn would be reciprocated. If Stuart was taking part, it was natural for Stanley to join in, too.

A pen portrait of Stuart in *Chaps and Chinooks* states: 'His pet aversion was the useless sons of English gentlemen who had come out to learn farming or ranching in the West. Nevertheless, he had them much about him in the open house for bachelor ranchers... at the Jumping Pound Crossing...' This disregard for emigrants and their irresponsible behaviour is echoed in a passage from the *Journal of Alberta Postal History* by Dale Spiers: 'Bachelor cowboys were the main passengers on the mail [wagons]. They would go into town for a good time and would be falling down drunk on the return trip, so [someone] had to keep an eye on them as well as the mail.'

Even though Stanley and Norman were not true remittance men, there's every chance that they were the butt of cattlemen's jokes. Greenhorns were advised [to buy] ... 'boots with a good high heel, woolly chaps, spurs two inches in diameter, a woollen shirt worn open at the neck, [with] a brilliant pink or violet silk handkerchief, and a wide-brimmed Stetson hat,' according to Mark Zuehlke in *Scoundrels, Dreamers and Second Sons*. 'The remittance men strode manfully, and, considering the large spurs, noisily, up and down the boardwalks of Calgary, swaggered in and out of bars, and generally made themselves a constant source of amusement to the hard-bitten Canadian cattlemen.'

Remittance men, often the second sons of well-heeled families in Britain, were sent out to the colonies to make something of themselves, while being kept in money with monthly handouts – often huge amounts – from their fathers. Changes in the law had made it impossible to buy a commission and the cost of living had risen, so the fathers of large families had to think of other ways to provide for their sons. Neither Stanley nor Norman fitted into this category, but local ranchers usually didn't bother distinguishing between the types. They lumped these emigrants together, referring to all of them as remittance men from England, even though they sometimes came from Scotland or Ireland. Being former public-school boys, they all spoke with the same accent, so their origins were immaterial in the eyes of the established ranchers.

Although the locals poured scorn on these remittance men, they nevertheless frequently kept an eye on the postal deliveries to check when the bulging packages of notes arrived, at which point they set about separating their owners from their monthly allowance by every means available, according to Norman. While admitting the freeloading element, my great-uncle points out that these men were invariably good company, energetic, progressive, decent and likable. They were, he says, generous to a fault, as well as being reckless, original and fearless. He concedes that they drank too much but remarks that they were far more scrupulous in their behaviour than many respectable businessmen. With the coming of the First World War the short-lived phenomenon of the remittance man died out.

Zuehlke refers to one R. C. 'Dicky' Bright, who certainly was a reckless and original remittance man, and the chances are that Stanley knew him and spent time with him as their dates and the area they lived in fit exactly. The Englishman, whose grandfather was Richard Bright, the first person to describe the clinical manifestations of the kidney disorder that came to be known as Bright's Disease, had a small homestead on the Bow River. He loved to party and drink in Calgary and guaranteed his monthly flow of money by telling his father that he was building up a flourishing ranch. In fact, he had just one horse and no livestock. The game seemed to be up when his father, becoming suspicious, paid him a visit. Cunningly, Bright quickly borrowed enough cattle from neighbouring ranches to assemble a large herd. The ranch where Stanley was working was likely to have been one of these. When his father commented on the dilapidated ranch buildings his son merely countered by saying that he was sinking all his funds into establishing the herd. His father left satisfied and the money kept on coming.

Bright's sisters arranged to come for an extended stay the following summer. He could not repeat the ruse as the particularly harsh winter had killed off thousands of cattle whose skeletons were still scattered over the foothills. As he showed his sisters round, he cursed his luck that his herd had been destroyed in this way. They were fooled. The sisters returned home to their father with their brother's tale of woe – and the money continued to flow. I am sure Stanley and Bright would have shared a drink or three at the Alberta Hotel in Calgary.

Stuart's 1890s house still stands, albeit in a decrepit state. This is where Stanley would have been fed and picked up his letters when the mail came in every Sunday evening. Just next to it would have been the bunkhouse where he and the other ranch hands slept. But if there was any lingering doubt about Stanley's connection with this ranch, an amusing extract from *Chaps and Chinooks* provides irrefutable proof. Jane Larrington, Stuart's daughter, writes about her years there as a young girl: 'I had been taught my ABCs from a young Englishman who was of no use on the ranch. He had left home because he wanted to be an actor and his parents were determined that he should enter the ministry. Eventually he gave in and returned to England.'

My grandfather's horsemanship must have improved with time, as he did take part in the round-ups and the branding that were the highlights of the ranching year. In those days, the cattle wandered freely over the foothills, mixing with the herds of other owners, their unique brands being the only form of identification. After a week or so of scouring the country, the cowboys herded in the cows and reunited them with their owners.

This work was not without its dangers. Twice Stanley was tossed by bulls and on the first occasion was gored, sustaining two cracked ribs. He was caught in blizzards. Once he got lost on the Prairie and 'experienced something of the panic that has driven men mad'. Another time, riding on the edge of an abyss, he avoided being swept out of the saddle by the bough of a tree by flinging himself along the horse's neck. Then there was always the risk, when riding after cattle, that one's horse would put its foot in a gopher hole and throw the rider to the ground, head-first. He writes of how he made butter by putting cream in an old cocoa tin, which he then tied on to the horn of the saddle. In the course of the day's riding it would be jolted into quite passable butter.

My visit to Alberta happened to coincide with the branding season and my 'fixer' Bev, a Copithorne whose great-grandfather worked with Stanley, took me to the WineGlass Ranch to see the owner's three hundred calves being marked. Five experts in the art of lassoing on horseback had been hired for the event. The calves were brought into a pen, their mothers bellowing for their young ones throughout the whole proceedings. A horseman would pick out a calf, twirl his rope and send it round one or two back legs. His horse would then walk forward, dragging the animal along the ground, whereupon a team of branders leapt into action, holding a red-hot iron in the shape of the owner's mark against the calf's flanks. Two men would hold the calf down at each end, another would dispense two antibiotic injections and – if it was male – it would be castrated. The castration took a matter of seconds and the discarded testicles were thrown into a nearby hedge for animals and birds to devour. Finally, a painkiller would be given in the mouth. The branders admitted it did hurt the calves but, after they were released, their mothers quickly located them and they walked sedately away to the adjoining pastureland where recovery was quick.

Before I headed off to XC Ranch to meet Tom and Patty Copithorne, Jim Bateman took me to see the confluence of Jumping Pound Creek and Little Jumping Pound Creek, streams which had been an almost constant backdrop to Stanley's ranching days. The ice-cold water, melted from the snow-clad peaks of the Rockies, tumbled over the pebbles, making a restful, clattering sound, just as it had in Stanley's day, 125 years before. Jim saw me ruminating and walked away, kindly leaving me alone for a few minutes. The tears that welled up in my eyes took me by surprise.

It was branding day for the XC ranch, too, but Tom and Patty found time to chat. They seemed genuinely interested in Stanley. I showed them copies of the 1893 photos and they confirmed that they had been taken on their land. They even showed me the exact spot where the stock pen had been, just above Jumping Pound Creek. Traditionally, the woman of the family lays on a spread of cakes for the workers at the end of branding day. Patty's peanut butter cakes were legendary in the region, and she let me have an early taste. They invited me to the branding; unfortunately, I had another appointment.

* * *

In winter my grandfather usually turned to cutting spruce and larch for fuel and building material. He went into partnership with an older man who had a team of horses and a sleigh and a contract for wood in Calgary. The system they adopted was to chop and load one day and drive the consignment into town the next, returning the following day. 'The work in the bush was the most enjoyable of all the physical labours – save that of riding,' Stanley writes. 'The crash of a snow-laden tree, leaving a gap through which the Rockies could be seen, was music to my ears. The swing of the axe and the resinous smell of conifers are treasured memories.' He recalls the loneliness of living in a hut by himself:

From my shanty I looked up at the frosty stars and listened to the song of a bird as it rose, died away and then grew louder than before. And as I looked out into the night, which seemed to hold its breath, there arose the low howl of a coyote, which is perhaps the most dismal sound in all nature's repertoire of sounds. My blood was chilled as I realised that for miles around there was no other human being.

During my stay I rented a cabin from the Copithornes which bordered a wild wood in the foothills. I was determined to hear the coyotes' strange cries for myself, and one night just before leaving I managed to catch the sound, rising and falling eerily on the cold Canadian night. I took the sound back with me to England.

Out in the ungoverned West, where winters were bitter, one's accommodation could suddenly become someone else's. Stanley describes how, coming back one evening with his fellow woodsman and a sleigh full of chopped logs after a day's cutting, he saw the light shining in their wooden shanty. There was someone else's team of horses in the stable. Once indoors, they met two men who had taken over occupancy of the hut and thrown their bedding on the floor. He comments wryly that he and his mate had done the same some weeks before on finding the vacant accommodation – but at least the place had been empty.

On occasions it was all hands to the pump as the North-West Mounted Police called on everyone to help put out a forest fire. My grandfather wasn't so concerned with the urgency of extinguishing the blaze before too much timber was destroyed; he comments on the 'volumes of smoke and sparks, the glare being reflected in a little lake held in a saucer-like hollow beneath. As a background stood the mountains unperturbed, and behind them an evening sky, rosy with sunset.'

A summer of sheep herding provided Stanley with one of his happiest periods in the foothills. He clearly relished the isolation involved in looking after two thousand sheep. He remarks that the sight of another rider on the horizon was 'like the appearance of a ship to sailors tossed on some derelict raft'. He lived in a shepherd's wagon, so small that a passer-by remarked that there was no room for a mosquito and the resident to be inside at the same time. A ranching museum I visited contained one of these basic, four-wheel contraptions and I imagined my grandfather spending weeks on end living in it. The most important – and most risky – part of being a shepherd was keeping the coyotes at bay; they were particularly partial to mutton.

While relishing the isolation and the chance for contemplation that this life afforded, he writes of the longing for civilisation that a passing train could induce in him. He often used to stand on the track dreaming of the cities and the life of the mind that the metal rails could connect him to. I asked my modern-day ranchers at Jumping Pound where he would have stood. Without a doubt, they said, it was on the Merino Ranch, where W. W. Stuart had kept an experimental herd of this breed of sheep before deciding that they weren't suitable for the terrain and switching to cattle ranching. Long-term, handed-down memories like this were commonplace in southwest Alberta when I was there. I decided to drive out of Cochrane, along the Stoney First Nation track, to see if I could locate the area. I soon reached the Merino Ranch and there, just beyond a field of grazing bison, ran the railway track. This side of it was a wide stretch of pastureland. This was almost definitely where Stanley worked as a shepherd during that long, hot summer.

The wide, open spaces of the foothills and the time he spent alone sometimes matched Stanley's solipsistic but happy mood, as it did during that summer of shepherding. But occasionally the emptiness of the landscape reinforced his loneliness. He recalls how he used to scan faces in the hope of finding the friend he needed. Looking back years later, he wants to help the young man he had been who was trying to find his feet in the world. 'As I observe his plight, his wretched follies, his worse-than-follies, I cannot but love him. It looked as though there was nothing to do except to be the football kicked hither and thither between the goalposts of birth and death.' There is despair here, depression even. On the run from his father's Nonconformist way of life, he had found nothing to replace it.

Part of that loneliness was due to the fact that he was largely encountering only men; there were quite simply very few women on the ranch. He comments ruefully that the scarcity of females was, to some extent, remedied by the education department which ended up acting as a marriage bureau. When a vacancy occurred at the schoolhouse, an advertisement would appear for a new teacher, 'woman preferred'. The young schoolmistress would no sooner settle down to her duties than one of the cowboys would start paying her attention and later the wedding would take place, and soon after an advertisement for her replacement would appear in the press.

My grandfather, who sometimes described himself as half English, half Welsh and half North American, had no desire, unlike his workmates, to make money quickly. Consequently, he refused to apply himself to any form of labour. He says he never became a good rider (although on another occasion he says he did master the skill) or sheep-herder, hinting that sometimes he deliberately appeared stupid so that his real self could hide behind the mask. He admits that he was regarded as lazy and lacking in staying power. Here, I think, one can detect that sense of elitism and separateness from the goings-on around him that would be a constant feature of his life. But he was also able to embrace the formlessness of his existence. He writes:

For all practical purposes, the cult of Mammon was our only religion... No national tradition, no great heritage of culture, no loyalty to an ancient Faith, toned down the rawness of our life or served as a refining or harmonizing influence. A more heterogeneous gathering it would be difficult to discover. We came from all lands, all trades, all grades of social life. Near me lived one who had been a Parisian clown. Not far away was a settler who had been an organist by profession. Ex-soldiers were numerous. The man with whom I lived for some while had been in former days a London coster. Not only was I an exile; I had come to a country where all were exiles.

Elsewhere he adds that among their number was a Russian count. There were happier times when the clouds lifted and he achieved satisfaction in the physicality of his outdoor existence. He describes how he relished the freedom from all ties and how being both a spiritual and actual tramp became an ideal. He even suggests that this vigorous life bore him in good stead in years to come:

The physical development which a rough, open-air life had assisted was to prove of permanent value under future urban conditions. I was tanned, broad and inured to all the vagaries of the weather,

able to sit a bucking cayuse, to plow, milk and wield an axe. When
a photograph of myself, taken shortly before my departure from
England, was sent to me, I looked at it in astonishment... Such
was the change wrought by the West even after a few months...
In both a spiritual and physical sense [the ranching experience]
had been the rack on which I had been stretched to man's-size.
That is why I loved it. There were other reasons for loving it – the
camaraderie of the range and the shack sing-song, the grandeur of
the amphitheatre formed within the embrace of the mountains and
forest-clad foothills.

He found time to retire alone to his bunk to smoke his pipe and to read poetry. He read anything and everything he could get his hands on. He'd brought favourite books out with him – mostly poets – but he says that these writers, being largely of the 'indoor' variety, appeared artificial and often unreadable. In one of his frequent moves, he left them behind in his shack. One day he rode over to see Norman, only to find him out. He recalls how he turned over a number of battered dime novels that he found lying around. One particular book caught his eye. 'It was real literature,' he writes. 'My thirsty mind absorbed page after page greedily. Not for many years did I learn that I had recognised one of the masters of modern English – William Hale White, who wrote under the name Mark Rutherford.' The book he had been reading was *The Revolution in Tanner's Lane*.

One winter, on the other hand, he read and reread Shakespeare and brushed up his French. Another time he had to content himself with reading a pile of back copies of a magazine called the *Family Herald*. Then there was always his beloved Walt Whitman, a copy of whose poems was a permanent fixture in his pocket as he rode the ranch. The Roman writer and stoic Epictetus, 'who had learned to oppose his human pride against the humiliation of servile conditions', according to Stanley, provided some solace, too. 'It was the only creed that made any appeal to me,' he comments. 'I had his work with me constantly.' Herbert Spencer's agnosticism appealed at first and he read him voraciously. Eventually, however, he found him too depressing and he flung the book out on to the grass and wondered later if a cowboy had picked it up and read it. A cowboy's opinion of the philosopher Herbert Spencer would probably be unprintable, he guessed.

~ 5 ~
THE LOCAL CORRESPONDENT

Stanley always needed to write: it was in his bones. And it was after only a few months in the foothills that his literary urges kicked in and he started penning pieces on spec for the *Calgary Herald*, not knowing whether the editor would accept them. Based on the ranch at Jumping Pound, he turned himself into the district correspondent, with both serious and light-hearted reports of the goings-on of this growing rural community.

Tracking down these pieces proved surprisingly easy, although his name seldom appears alongside a piece. Having read masses of his writing, I am familiar with his different styles. What seldom appears is a straight piece of objective reporting: that is not his way. Instead, we get either a mischievous aside, an acerbic comment about the vagaries of human behaviour, or an overblown, sometimes senticious pronouncement, which reminds one of the prize-winning essay he wrote at Whitgift School when he was seventeen.

The easy contributions to detect are obviously those with his name at the end – Stanley B. James. These tend to be notifications of upcoming social events, including performances of plays he himself had written. Then there are the anonymous pieces that comment on the pressing issues of the day in the district, in which strict objectivity is not always achieved or even the aim. Finally, when he wants to put forward an even more opinionated view, he reverts to the letters to the editor format and uses an amusing byline. There are even poems which bear his unmistakeable stamp.

The pressing issue of the day was irrigation and more of his articles are concerned with this topic than anything else. Many settlers between the rivers Bow and Elbow wanted to try their hand at arable farming, but were restrained by the short ninety-day growing season that the harsh climate allowed. The poor quality of the land and the fact that it was too dry in the summer and too wet in the winter added to the challenge. A plentiful supply of water, it was argued, could increase the chances of success. Locals in Jumping Pound, Springbank and Spruce Vale lobbied local and national politicians to grant them the necessary licences to dig trenches which would divert water away from the Elbow and Jumping Pound Creek to irrigate over 21,000 acres. Stanley reports on the numerous meetings, held in different schoolhouses. An outspoken band of landowners in Jumping Pound didn't want the project, let alone the heavier tax burden that would follow its implementation. They were ranchers, not arable farmers, and not interested in changing.

Over the next two years, decisions were taken, then reversed, then changed back again until everyone's divergent views were accommodated. The objectors reached a compromise whereby their tax burden was less irksome than it was for those in favour of the project. When Stanley wanted to promote controversial views or ridicule someone whose ideas were diametrically opposed to his own, he employs the pseudonyms 'Irrigation', 'Alpha' and 'Persecuted Jumping Pond'.

Roy Copithorne showed me the dam that had been built on his land in the 1890s to contain the waters of Jumping Pound Creek. There were still rusting, broken flumes from those days lying at the bottom of the stream. He also pointed out the one irrigation channel that had been built across acres of land between the creek and the Elbow. But for all the talk of the need to introduce an irrigation scheme, the project was never fully realised. The drive towards crop farming died away and ranching became virtually the only activity.

In a talk that he gave many years later on a lecture tour to New York, Stanley said that on one occasion he had crossed the line with a personal jibe that was stronger than usual. I have tried to find the offending article but failed. This is his own reminiscence, thirty-two years after the event:

'There was a meeting concerning irrigation, presided over by a chairman of portly appearance. I wrote that the chair was filled to overflowing. [He] was said to be looking for me but he did not find me, or I should not be here this evening.'

Over the four-year period in which he wrote there were frequent references to flooding, usually in May or June. Bridges collapsed and fields were submerged, small ranchers suffering dreadfully as a result. On one occasion, a visiting government inspector made his boat available to the locals. Stanley's articles call on landowners to repair their bridges 'without delay' so day-to-day commerce could recommence. A particularly invasive flood in 1897 saw all the bridges at Jumping Pound and Mitford – including the one that Stanley had helped build in 1893 – collapse and the irrigation flumes and gates get badly damaged. Tree trunks swept down from the Rockies and blocked the flow, despite Stuart's valiant efforts to divert them away by assuming the part of a lumberjack. On another occasion, a sporting tiff broke out between the cricketers of Millarville and Calgary, when the men from the country were unable to travel to the game because of rising waters. The churlish city boys judged this to be no excuse.

When vast numbers of cattle died from blackleg after eating a poisonous plant, Stanley's article recommends that they be inoculated with garlic to counteract the debilitating effects. How efficacious this would have been is unclear. He frequently seeks to lighten the tone with satire. Shortly after the outbreak of blackleg, he writes: 'Another disease has attacked the ranchers themselves, I mean Clondicitis.' The Clondike – or Klondike – was one of the main places where gold prospectors headed.

There are, of course, reports about the district the authorship of which is impossible to know. The chances are it was Stanley but, as I scoured the electronic pages of the *Calgary Herald* in a newspaper archive, I couldn't be certain. For example, I learned that the building of skimming stations in outlying areas meant that farmers, large or small, could be paid in cash for their milk, which was then transported to creameries and turned into butter. Every report records healthy profits. A government inspector, returning after a tour of the dairies in Denmark, suggested that Alberta butter would soon be good enough to sell to the English. 'The Crescent Creamery got their first cream today from the Jumping Pond Separator and will soon have another lot from the one at Spruce Vale,' a news brief announces. A new cheese factory in Calgary also boomed. Even coal was discovered in the region, with Mr H. Sibbald verifying that there was 'a vein of considerable thickness' on his land, which 'he intends working himself'. On my visit I saw the still unmined seam of coal running through the cliff face.

Hunting coyotes and wolves, in a bid to control the killing of cows and sheep, was a regular weekend sport. Meets were frequently organised and everyone who could ride was expected to take part, the men proudly recording the amount of booty they collected. One entry in the *Calgary Herald* states that local riders were expected to attend the next meet at Stuart's ranch at 11 a.m. on Saturday. But two weeks later in the paper Stanley turns protector of wildlife by writing a humorous piece about an imagined emergency meeting of endangered coyotes. In the invented fantasy, the animals pass the motion that:

> *Jumping Pond is becoming intolerable, the number of dogs and the sporting instincts of the community being in complete antagonism to our interests as coyotes; and further this meeting desires to put on record its especial condemnation of the Copithorne Bros, who encourage and abet said dogs in their depradations [sic], and also of Mrs R. Copithorne and Mrs Stuart who lead the men on in their iniquitous course of coyote murder.*

The motion was passed unanimously, followed by the coyote national anthem, which, in Stanley's words, goes:

The coyotes sit by the bloated steer
Beneath the moonlit sky,
And howl, till the far-off foothills hear
And answer the dismal cry.
Yo – hoo – hoo!
Yo – hoo – hoo!

The toothsome beef is three weeks dead,
Good for the fangs of whelps,
And the rancher sleeps in his bunk or bed,
Nor wakes at the coyote's yelps.

Yo – hoo – hoo!
Yo – hoo – hoo!

The rancher sleeps in his bed or bunk,
As though his sleep were a swoon
But the coyotes feast on three weeks' dead
And howl to the ghostly moon.
Yo – hoo – hoo!
Yo – hoo – hoo!

In another report giving notice of a future meet, in the interests of impartiality, he lets a family of coyotes have their say:

Translated from the Greek. 'Why,' said the young coyote to his mother, 'dost thou tremble and wherefore weepest thou?' 'Because, my son, next Saturday a great hunt is devised against us by our enemy, man, at Jumping Pond and the meet is at T. A. Hatfield's, six miles east of the post office.' 'Then,' asked the cub, 'why not consort with our cousin the timber wolf and tear them with our teeth and rend them with our claws?' Smiling pensively at her son, the mother replied, 'Even so! But as soon as thou sightest the foremost hound thou wilt be the first to forsake thy mother's side to seek safety on a vain flight.'

Just like any good newspaper diarist, Stanley sometimes made something out of nothing. In July 1897 he reported an incident in which a Springbank settler had been driving home with his wife when they were ambushed in the dark by what appeared be two highwaymen. Two of the Jumping Pond ranchers had purchased some cattle in Calgary, and while resting the stock halfway had picketed their horses near the trail. The horses had got across the trail and the ranchers feared for their ropes and when they heard the rig approaching rushed in to stop the procession, one grabbing the horse's head and the other the wheels of the rig. No revolvers were used but the travellers got a scare. Stanley concludes: 'Moral: don't stay so late in town.'

In rapid succession he wrote two farces which were performed in the Jumping Pound schoolhouse by cowboys and ranchers, who also took some of the women's parts. The first one was called *The Widow's Suitors* and he reports on his own creation: 'The affair was a success in every particular.' The second one was called *Does Your Mother Know You're Out?* and it, too, was received with 'enthusiastic applause'. The author, he wrote, was to be congratulated on gathering together such a talented company. Mrs Mickle in the character of Bella Masham surprised the audience with her 'vigorous and thoroughly earnest acting. No less appreciated were Messrs W. Gibson and W. W. Stuart as Private O'Hannagan and Joe Johnson.' He recalls that the brogue of the former and the Yankee drawl of the latter [Stanley's boss] seemed to come naturally. 'Nor must Mr James be forgotten,' he continued, 'though he acted somewhat more in the spirit of burlesque than were the other characters, it was no less satisfactory.' He concludes by remarking that once the farce was over, the floor was cleared, supper served and dancing commenced. Apparently, no one went home until five o'clock the next morning.

Jumping Pond Concert.

Although the weather up to a late hour on Friday afternoon was sufficiently severe to prevent people coming from a distance. The school house was comfortably full when the programme was commenced. Every item was received with enthusiastic applause. Indeed it would be hard to say which of the number of artists received most favour. After a short interval the curtain, which had been lowered at the close of the concert, was raised on the scene of the farce, "Does your mother know you're out?" This little piece (the author of which is Mr. Stanley James) went merrily from start to finish. Mr. James is to be congratulated on having gathered together so able a company. Mrs. Oliver Mickle, in the character of Bella Masham, surprised the audience by her vigorous and thoroughly earnest acting. No less appreciated were Messrs. W. Gibson and W. W. Stuart, as Private O'Hannagan and Joe Johnson. The brogue of the former and the Yankee drawl of the latter seemed to come naturally, and greatly heightened the effect of their respective parts. Nor must Mr. James, Reginald de Raynes, be forgotten, though he acted somewhat more in the spirit of burlesque than were the other characters, it was no less satisfactory. Mrs. Stuart's few well-spoken lines brought this amusing little farce to an end in good style. The farce over, the floor was cleared, supper served and dancing commenced. The company did not separate until near five o'clock Saturday morning.

Stanley's review of *Does Your Mother Know You're Out?*, the farce he himself wrote and in which he acted in February 1895. Credit: *Calgary Herald*

Thirty years later, Stanley reflects:

I have scribbled a good deal in my time, but I never wrote with more satisfaction to myself than when I fathered a play. It wasn't a limelight affair. Nor did it call for the make-up box, but I am proud to say that it won the approval of the audience, a large part of which had never been in a theatre and therefore, in their judgment, did not employ conventional standards but laughed only at that which appealed to their unsophisticated sense of fun.

On my visit to the area, I was shown the spot, on a crossroads on the route south out of Cochrane, where the old schoolhouse had hosted Stanley's two little plays. In the 1890s it would have been in the centre of the Jumping Pound community, which numbered far more people than it does today.

News briefs give a sense of the ebb and flow of local life: winter was the time for 'bachelor dances', the entrance money raised going to good causes. No doubt it was a rare opportunity for cowboys to meet local women, and vice versa. There was the usual record of births, marriages and deaths – as well as branding and round-ups at regular times of the year. A Mr W. J. Wade died when his team of horses backed over the riverbank and crushed him. And the newly married and 'legendary hostess' Mrs Fraser died suddenly at twenty-one, just as she and her husband were starting to make a going concern of the Collins Ranch they had just bought.

One short sentence in the *Calgary Herald* mentions Stanley's brother, Norman. On 13 March 1895, this appears at the end of Jumping Pond Notes: 'Norman B. James paid a visit last week to his brother Stanley.' News must have been hard to come by that week.

In *The Autobiography of a Nobody,* Norman tells us that he worked on a ranch in Priddis, which is about twenty miles southeast of Jumping Pound, so the brothers would have been able to see each other from time to time. It's worth dipping into Norman's account because he provides a different insight into the day-to-day life of a cowboy.

Norman landed his first job through the manager of the Calgary hotel where he was staying who introduced him to a rancher who needed some help. This was probably a Mr Hone, who ranched in the Priddis area. Like Stanley, Norman was called on to do a range of jobs, for which he earned

$10 a month (£250 in 2020). In his book he pokes fun at his initial inability to perform these tasks. He cites an episode in which he mounts a cayuse for the first time:

I climbed on to a horse that I was told had been 'gentled'. It appears that was a flexible word and didn't mean quite what I thought it did. Maybe he was, but I never really got a chance to find out the truth of the statement. The horse... seemed to think that unity is strength, so bunched all his four corners together before going up in the air and lighting just about where he started. Unfortunately, I lit first. I tried to grab the horn but somehow the horn wasn't there just at that time. So, I sat down for a while and let the busy world go by.

One day he was instructed to collect some milk from a neighbour on horseback. All was well until the return journey when the lid of the can fell off, the clatter frightening his horse which then reared. 'Up he went, and up I went, and also up went the milk. I beat the milk to the ground by a scant second. In fact, the milk never did reach the ground. I caught it on its way down.'

Norman was friends with Charlie Priddis, who gave his name to the tiny settlement, which consisted of a post office, a church and a handful of buildings. He recalls how when he first met him, Priddis was getting on in years. He had a small, grey moustache and a goatee beard that tried to give him an air of staidness by which nobody was fooled. Priddis, Norman says, was the most delightful, lovable and irresponsible character he had ever met. He used to collect the mail from Calgary in his horse and cart, cracking the whip while shouting: 'Make way for Her Majesty's Mail'. So reckless was his riding that people invariably had to go back and pick up the mail and parcels that had fallen off the wagon. Despite the chaos, remittance envelopes generally turned up sooner or later. My great-uncle says that Priddis was never known to do a mean act or say an uncharitable word, and was always the first to help in an emergency.

Norman describes the camaraderie among the settlers, which from time to time turned into raucous parties – even free-for-alls after which everyone was good friends: 'There was one particular log shack that we used to frequent... It belonged to two brothers... [who] owned a few cows, a fair supply of money, and the main asset – two banjos, at the playing of which they were far more expert than they were at cattle ranching.' When attending one of these parties, they had to bring their own chairs which they tied to the back of the saddle. They would retrace their steps the next morning, perhaps with the chair missing a leg or two.

Once a month the young settlers attended church, either the tiny white one in Priddis or the new one in nearby Millarville. Norman says that he helped construct this, which was personally funded by the Reverend William Webb-Peploe, copying the vertical spruce log structure of his own house and built in record time. It still stands today, so I made a point of visiting and admiring this beautiful little church. Norman describes Webb-Peploe as 'a tall, thin man with a flowing brown beard, a delightful voice and a quiet kindly manner, and a natural dignity that endeared him to all of us… I don't know what qualities it takes to make a real saint, but he had them all.'

After the Sunday service they used to troop over to the vicar's house to take tea with him and his wife. Despite knowing his congregation's failings, the great man never preached at them. Norman says that his talks were clear, logical and earnest and cut through all the idle banter that the cowboys used to indulge in at the bunkhouse. His sermons were heartfelt chats from a man who loved his fellow-man. 'May his memory live long among those who were privileged to know him,' Norman concludes.

These sweet words have all the more impact because in Norman's writing such notes of reverence are hard to find, his style being predominantly jocular or satirical. This paean of praise to Webb-Peploe is included in the book *Our Foothills*, a historical compilation by members of the Southern Alberta Pioneers.

These passages from *The Autobiography of a Nobody* paint a humorous picture of ranching life, a foil to Stanley's more serious narrative. Norman also had periods of drifting. He joined lumber, mining and hobo camps, road and construction gangs, ran a general store in Lethbridge, worked in an editorial office and acted on stage, experiences which paralleled those of my grandfather.

* * *

Stanley usually sent his reports to J. J. Young, editor of the *Calgary Herald,* by mail. On one occasion in early 1897 when he delivered his weekly report in person, Young offered him a position on the paper. Bored by ranch life, judging by his own comments, Stanley leapt at the opportunity of what would have seemed like creative work. He was to learn the job of editing, work as a staff writer and deputise for Young when he was absent, researching the mining industry and identifying potential new business opportunities for himself.

The population of Calgary was then only about five thousand and Stanley claims there were just two stone buildings in the town at that time – the railroad depot and the Hudson's Bay Company store. But it would have been impossible for him to resist the lure of the town's relatively bright lights. He writes: 'I should never again see that vast panorama... and that no broncho [sic] would ever again feel my weight... A certain phase had been worked through, certain experiences endured. Never again should I be for so long a period the bondslave of manual labour.'

On his last day before moving to Calgary to take up the post, he climbed a nearby hill and looked down on the area that had been home. Bill Bateman drove me up in his four-by-four truck to the place in question – now known as Bateman's Hill. Together we stood where Stanley had stood 122 years before. Far to the west was the cloudy outline of the Rockies, to the east the flatlands of the Prairies. Bill, a gentle, dignified man, alert to the power of personal histories, stood in silence and let the mysterious passage of years sink quietly into my soul. After all, his grandfather had worked side by side with mine.

In those days the *Calgary Herald* was a daily paper, requiring two columns of local news, with a weekly edition for outlying districts. It meant Stanley – apparently being the sole gatherer of news – had to do the rounds of the drinking saloons, not only in Calgary but in the rural areas. 'I soon acquired the habit of drinking with all sorts and conditions of men which might have had serious consequences,' he writes. 'Even as it was, I drank far more than was good for me.' One of those drinking dens was undoubtedly the Alberta Hotel, which boasted the longest bar between Winnipeg and Vancouver at 125 feet, quite long enough for Stanley to engage in several different conversations over the course of an evening, and to earwig others when perhaps he shouldn't have done. The hotel's outside appearance is much the same today. I, too, sat in the hotel's cavernous interior and listened and watched as smart-suited business folk discussed fluctuations in the value of oil shares and potential markets in real estate.

The bar at the Alberta Hotel, Calgary, where as a reporter, Stanley
eavesdropped and chin-wagged to glean the latest gossip

Stanley also attended inquests and court sessions, interviewed visiting
celebrities and covered theatrical and other shows. He recalls how settlers
frequently paid their subscriptions by offering the paper a sack of potatoes
or a few pounds of butter. He remarks that the pettiness of the local news
made the standard of journalism poor, while the advertiser reigned supreme.
He tells us, however, that he produced an eight-page supplement aimed
at the growing number of gold prospectors heading for the Klondike
fields in Alaska. Its purpose was to persuade them to make the journey
through Calgary rather than use the better-known route through British
Columbia. I found this impressive document in the archives of the Glenbow
Museum. My grandfather's special edition contains informative articles on
the benefits of following the Peace River, avoiding the dangerous rapids,
while recommending the best camping spots. The pages are crammed with
the advertisements of clothing retailers and ironmongers. Overall, it makes
impressive reading, but unfortunately it didn't persuade prospectors to

abandon the established route further west. In passing, Stanley comments in *Becoming a Man* that he had been tempted to join that army of gold diggers and head north, but that he declined to do so because he was enjoying his brief flirtation with 'literature' so much.

The special Klondike gold rush supplement, conceived and edited by Stanley in 1897.
Credit: *Calgary Herald*

One piece of work that was beyond any doubt his own – he refers to the episode in both autobiographies – is the article entitled 'Those Babies' published on 27 February 1897, which I found in the *Calgary Herald* archives. It's an amusing tale rather than a news piece or feature. But the story has an added frisson because my grandfather claimed it was read by the writer Owen Wister who incorporated it into his novel *The Virginian*. It does indeed appear in chapters ten and eleven of the novel, which itself provided the inspiration for no less than three feature films, as well as a long-running TV series. One might contend – at a stretch – that no lesser screen legends than Gary Cooper, Lee J. Cobb and James Drury, all of whom acted in versions of *The Virginian*, spoke words inspired by Stanley. I was excited because I thought I might be about to indulge in a significant piece of literary detective work. But did what amounted to a charge of plagiarism stand up to scrutiny?

The story was that a dance was given in a certain town and those coming from a long way off brought their children with them and placed them in a back room until the end of the party. Some of the cowboys, somewhat worse for wear and up for some pranks, had the idea of changing the clothes and the places of the sleeping babies. When the dancing concluded in the morning, the parents picked up their sleeping children and drove off in their sleighs in the possession of other people's babies. When the parents discovered the mistake later, they were outraged and drove furiously around the district in an attempt to get shot of the wrong'uns and recover the right ones. The tale is signed 'VAG', short for 'Vagabond', a *nom de plume* Stanley used on a number of occasions.

It's a good story. Unfortunately, on closer examination, I discovered the plagiarism claim doesn't stand up. In February 1893 – a month before Stanley arrived in Canada – Wister records the story in his Texas journal. Wister, who heard it from a man called Jim Neil, writes: 'Neil admitted that he had heard the story down at San Saba… I think that if the thing did not actually occur, somebody thought of doing it while they were actually at a dance with a pile of babies in sight.' We have to conclude that Wister's own notes were his main source. The truth is that this story was in common currency at that time, something that was regularly narrated round campfires on ranches in the West. When I relayed the story to a couple of old timers in Cochrane, they nodded and confirmed that it was a well-known tale. That was a false trail you sent me on, Stanley.

Contributed poems also helped to fill those column inches, their literary merit seeming to be less of a consideration than the amount of space they occupied. Some are dated before Stanley became assistant editor and were among the contributions he sent in from Jumping Pound. 'Hockey in Verse' is one such. Signed 'S_____s' (an abbreviation of Stanley James), it lists the ice hockey players of Millarville who clashed with rivals Dewdney (now Okotoks) one cold day in early 1896. It's dated 3 February. Each verse is devoted to describing the hockey skills of the village team. The last verse is devoted to the poet himself, who apparently fell on to his back a lot during the match and became a laughing stock.

I found three more poems by Stanley. Their style and rhythm match others written by him, and that light-hearted, rollicking meter is something of a trademark. There can't have been many poets writing at that time in the region, let alone any who would have had the chutzpah to turn their work into contributions to the *Calgary Herald*. One is entitled 'The Sucker's Lament', which I haven't included because it is of no great merit. The other two are romantic in tone. They concern women in general, or rather a longing for them.

Her Bright Eyes So Sparkling

Believe me, fair reader, if all the dear charms
Of the maidens I've met in my day
Were all placed together and close to my arms
The Albertan's would surely hold sway
For a heart that is beating and pulsing for thee;
For a heart that is loving and true.
To the maid of Alberta whose charms I can see
In her bright eyes so sparkling and blue.

If all the dear maidens of lands I have seen
Were to place their dear hearts at my feet,
I would spurn them and turn to my Alberta Queen
With fond kisses so loving and sweet.
That no doubt would arise in her dear little mind
That my fond love was thoroughly true.
Aye as true as the beauty I always shall find
In her bright eyes so sparkling and blue.

The longing for beautiful women continues with 'The Cowboy's Plea', a variation on the old ballad 'The Cowboy's Lament':

A cry from the cowboy comes to us,
A sorrowful, pitiful wail.
It is wafted on gentle breezes,
Or borne on the powerful gale.

But wherever, wherever we hear it
'Tis ever and always the same,

Oh, for some charming woman
To wear our euphonious name.

The females in sunny Alberta
Number not as forests' leaves,
And the market is 'short' on the former,
And 'long' on men, and the beeves.

Now, while you are importing cattle,
Give heed to our modest request,
And bring in a train load of women
Whose pedigrees rank with the best.

Working at the *Calgary Herald* enabled my grandfather to widen his circle of acquaintances and to enjoy a fuller social life. One of those he was closest to was a Scotsman whom he calls Bob Macdonald in the first autobiography and Alec Gordon in the second. While I was in Calgary I tried to establish if the drunken, stony-broke and utterly unscrupulous journalist he describes was none other than the legendary Bob Edwards, who in 1902 was to publish and edit the *Eye Opener* newspaper. In *Poverty Gulch*, Stanley refers to this unusual publication in which investigative journalism sits side by side with scurrilous gossip. It was hard to pin down Edwards's whereabouts in the late 1890s, let alone whether he was in Calgary. But he was certainly in High River, which is not far away.

Macdonald/Gordon certainly believed that the journalist was not responsible for the veracity of his copy. 'The friendship was an event,' Stanley writes. 'It introduced me to a type of man of which I had seen little, the cosmopolitan Bohemian and travelled journalist. He was a fellow loafer who had acquired a skill in the art of loafing to which I could not pretend.'

Some facts don't fit, however. Stanley writes that Macdonald/Gordon was old enough to be his father and that in later years he met him again in London, where he was down on his luck and soon to die in abject poverty. This did not happen to Edwards, but my grandfather was easily capable of conflating events and personalities to suit his narrative. I haven't determined the truth, but there is no doubt that Stanley relished the unruly company of anarchic, intelligent and dishonest men. Joining these two in digs was an impecunious lawyer who made a point of taking a circuitous route into town to avoid his creditors. Then there was the deaf architect who, on meeting you in the street, held up his hand to his ear and said: 'I don't mind if I do; a little Scotch, please.'

One day in late summer 1897, J. J. Young returned to the paper after a spell looking after his mining concerns, and promptly fired my grandfather. The reason seems to have been connected to a leader Stanley had written which criticized the misleading pamphlets being issued to lure miners from Great Britain to Alberta on false pretences. He had claimed that, after a short spell of work, the men invariably found themselves unemployed, a state of affairs that the editor was reluctant to acknowledge, perhaps because of related business interests. Admirable journalism, it seems, but it was too much for the boss to stomach and Stanley was sent packing. As Stanley admits, there may have been other reasons. He had in fact done a reasonably good job and perhaps Young felt threatened by the young man's talent. Whatever the cause, the next phase of his itinerant life beckoned and his time in the foothills was over.

~ 6 ~
RIDING THE RODS

The sharp shadows lay long and low across the flat landscape under a cloudless sky. I looked east to the limitless horizon of the Prairie, its grasses swaying in the gentle morning breeze, and west towards the outline of the Rockies, their still snow-capped peaks sparkling in the early sunlight. It was the loneliest spot I had yet encountered in following my grandfather's footsteps across southern Alberta. It was these featureless plains that he'd wandered across, without any real purpose, after being fired from the newspaper. Walt Whitman's open road it certainly was. He would have been less sure about being 'strong and content'. As for me, I was happy just to have entered this lost world of his, if only briefly.

On leaving Calgary, Stanley reasoned that it was impossible to return to life on the ranch. He'd heard that a trainload of cattle bound for England was leaving Lethbridge – 130 miles to the south – in the next few days and a cattleman was needed to accompany them. He bought a train ticket as far as Fort Macleod because that was as far as his money stretched. He then walked the remaining thirty miles or so to Lethbridge, only to find that the cattle train had already left. Penniless now, dejection set in.

He knew of a temporary haymaking job in High River, which he'd passed through a hundred miles to the north two days before. There was nothing for it but to retrace his steps and follow the railway line back. He describes how he walked nonstop one day and one night and well into the next morning. At one point the weekly train from Fort Macleod to Calgary slowly passed him on a slight upgrade. The guard beckoned him to jump on, but Stanley failed to take in his meaning until it was too late: he'd missed the chance of a ride. 'Night came and still I walked... though I think if such a thing be possible, that now and again I dozed as I walked.' He was too afraid to take a rest because of the rattlesnakes. But an old timer I told this story to was sceptical: it was too cold for rattlesnakes in Alberta, he said. Arriving exhausted at the farm, Stanley was hired by the owner for three weeks of haymaking but first he had to catch up on his sleep – all eighteen hours of it.

I lingered in High River, dropping into the Museum of the Highwood, to see if it housed any documents relevant to my research. The curator looked through lists but there was no record of Stanley, his seven or so years in Canada falling between the census years of 1891 and 1901. High River had once been a strategic junction, but these days it was no longer served by the railway and was of less administrative importance. I stayed one night and the next morning and looked for the farm where Stanley had harvested hay. I knew it was just north of the town, but a couple of unlikely shacks was the best I could manage. It could have been almost anywhere. Giving up, I turned south, following Highway 2A, my map marking the now disused railway that Stanley had walked up, but now there was only a raised bank of gravel, sometimes covered with scrubby grass. I took a photograph of the route of the track which he'd walked along.

The now disused railway line from Calgary to Fort Macleod that a penniless Stanley walked along after being fired by the newspaper. Credit: the author

With the haymaking over, this time having enough money for the full fare, Stanley returned to Lethbridge, which was a burgeoning coal mining town. With a business partner, his brother Norman had opened a shop there whose sign announced: 'Cosmopolitan Store: Knick-knacks and Novelties'. Apparently one day a woman asked, looking from one to the other: 'Say, which of you fellers is Knick-knacks and which is Novelties?' I found their advertisement in the *Lethbridge News*, published in the run-up to 1898. 'Now is the time to buy your holiday presents and make your friends happy,' it states. 'Our store is filled with suitable and useful articles for both great and small, at prices to suit all pockets. We have no time or space to mention half the pretty things, so you will have to come and see for yourselves.'

For a while, Stanley helped out at their already successful retail outlet. Not surprisingly, though, the customary restlessness kicked in and he broke away to create an outlet of the business that was altogether more entrepreneurial. Not far away, the Crow's Nest Railway Pass was being built and a large number of relatively well-paid navvies had their camp at the end of the line, but nowhere to spend their hard-earned cash. Stanley borrowed a wagon, a team of horses and a bell tent. He loaded up supplies of tobacco, mouth organs, braces, handkerchiefs and notepaper among other things, and pitched his tent in the centre of the camp. Very quickly trade became brisk and profits grew. But even that left him unfulfilled. He found the temptation to join the railway workers impossible to resist and temporarily worked as a teamster. 'These men were as jolly a gang as ever I fell in with,' he writes. 'Big, brawny men, with an abundance of high spirits and good humour.'

Lethbridge had gained the reputation for being a rough and rowdy place where young men outnumbered women several times over. Add to that a considerable amount of money in men's pockets and it was no surprise that prostitution was rife. Brothels sprang up in the river gorge away from the town until all attempts at modesty were abandoned and the women moved up into the town itself. On payday the saloons, brothels and gambling joints came alive as cowherders, coal miners, farmers, labourers and railroaders thought nothing of spending their entire pay in a matter of days. There is no reason to suspect that the James brothers were any different from the rest.

Towards the end of his time in Lethbridge, Stanley met a man called Harry, whom he refers to as 'very likeable, if not particularly scrupulous'. Originally a baker's assistant from Toronto, he had been earning a precarious living in the Rockies as 'a professor of phrenology, palmistry and other weird cults'. When Stanley encountered him, he was selling a kind of pink powder guaranteed to cure all ills.

Seeing that Stanley had 'the gift of the gab', Harry proposed a business partnership in which my grandfather would be the salesman and he the supplier of the miraculous potion. Unfortunately, this potentially lucrative business venture never materialised because another plan came to the fore. Harry was tiring of his time out west and wanted to return to his wife in Toronto. He, too, was relatively penniless so he suggested they both jump a freight train and head east as hoboes. Here was more cheap adventure, so my grandfather readily agreed to the idea. Stanley had clearly had a few weeks of fun in and around Lethbridge, but now he was saying goodbye to Alberta for good. Norman, on the other hand, stayed, soon to marry a local woman before going into farming in Youngstown.

Stanley's first experience of being a hobo had been an unpromising one: he had missed the ride the guard offered him on the Fort Macleod to Calgary train. In another search for work, he had crossed the border into the United States and travelled to Great Falls, Montana, but on finding no newspaper work there, with empty pockets he rode the rods on a train back to Canada, his first episode as a hobo. He hid out at the bottom of an empty coal truck until the freight train reached Lethbridge. The writer Jack London would, in tramp parlance, have referred to him as a 'gay-cat' – in other words, a greenhorn hobo.

On the appointed evening Stanley accompanied Harry down to the freight yards. Following in Stanley's footsteps, I too went there, naively asking a Lethbridge resident where the station was, then wondered why he looked at me so strangely. Later I discovered not only that passenger trains don't service Lethbridge but there isn't even a station. I parked my car by the railroad track.

Harry was an old hand at hoboing. In the growing darkness, their pockets stuffed with food and drink, they ducked and dived behind wagons to avoid being seen by the crew of the train they had earmarked, then sat down on the brake beam beneath a truck and waited. Harry's knowledge of the workings of the railways meant he was sure the train was bound for Toronto. With the temperature dropping fast, Stanley's 1897 transport of delight whistled, and the train pulled out into the pitch-black Prairie night.

Riding the rods involved perching on a narrow metal structure running parallel with the axles while holding on to the gearing overhead. At first, Stanley had the sensation of being hurled, bound and helpless, through space. The men's feet were so low down that if they'd been dislodged by the movement their legs could have slipped on to the track and been dragged along at 50 mph. But Stanley settled and even slept, waking to the sight of a frozen Prairie dawn with telegraph poles sweeping by against a whitening sky. Suddenly, for some reason, out in the open miles from anywhere, the train juddered to a halt. The guard walked up to the engine to speak to the driver and saw four legs dangling under one of the trucks.

According to London, a hobo never quite knew how he would be treated if discovered. In the east the railway officials, being more urbane and well versed in the ins and outs of unemployment, tended to be more lenient. Out West they were stricter and sometimes violently dislodged vagabonds from their perches and kicked them to the ground.

Harry and Stanley were thrown off. The pair followed the line of smoke on the northern horizon and in the evening came to a small depot where they were given a meal and informed that another freight train was expected. This proved to be a train of closed trucks, but they managed to climb inside one and lie on top of the coal. A few minutes into the journey another hobo called out from the darkness – they were not alone; indeed, the truck was full of them. The next day the train went into a siding and stopped. They were forced to wait for another ride, which turned out to be the mail express. They ensconced themselves in the tender only to be trodden on by the fireman who, unconcerned by their freeloading, asked if they had any whisky. Unsure of their position among the lumps of coal, they jumped off and took another freight train, walked along the top of the trucks and hid in an empty meat truck – presumably the refrigeration was turned off – in which they lay tightly packed for two nights and three days.

They broke the journey at Winnipeg and took advantage of the Salvation Army shelter. The final leg was in the hay box of a truck carrying horses where they were forced to lie on the brake beam again. Eventually they reached Toronto after a journey of two weeks, evaded the prying eyes of a detective in the freight yards and headed, coal-stained, hungry and tired, for the warmth and comfort of Harry's home. Despite the hardship of life on the rails, one gets the impression that Stanley wouldn't have missed it for the world.

It was a short while after Stanley's adventure – on 20 March 1899 – that the Welsh writer W. H. Davies was riding the rods from east to west to join the thousands of men prospecting for gold in the Klondike. Jumping a train in Renfrew, Ontario, with his companion, Three-fingered Jack, he slipped and his right leg was crushed beneath the wheels. Doctors amputated it just below the knee and he spent the rest of his life with a wooden leg. The event heralded his return to England and spawned a life of writing, which was to produce *The Autobiography of a Super-Tramp* in 1908. Stanley called his first autobiography, published in 1925, *The Adventures of a Spiritual Tramp,* knowing the Davies book, of course. It was the renowned artist Dame Laura Knight, with her interest in marginalised communities including gypsies, wanderers and circus performers, who brought the two together in the late 1920s, and W. H. Davies became a close friend of my grandfather after the two erstwhile vagabonds spent a pleasant evening at her house comparing notes about the vagrant life.

W.H. Davies, the Welsh writer and hobo, who lost a leg while jumping trains

Norman also mixed with hoboes in North America, an experience he describes in his autobiography. He reflects more deeply than Stanley does on what kind of men these were. Generally, his dealings with them were positive, although he remarks that there were some rather unsavoury characters among them. He admits that they weren't above stealing items on a regular basis and would be regarded as untrustworthy when measured against society's more orthodox standards. On the other hand, he is amazed by their learning and knowledge of the world, something he says that 'would have made our leaders squirm' with embarrassment. He is impressed, too, by their code of ethics, which men in the business world could have learned much from. He writes: 'We call them parasites, but… they asked very little from the poor or each other… They were a genial lot, and their wit was at least equal to that of any platform orator to whom I ever had to listen.' Like his brother, Norman needed to break away from the narrow confines of his early years, and the untutored life of the Prairies provided that opportunity. He goes on: 'I have met men and women who were… vicious through and through, and they are not always members of the so-called criminal classes either, but I have found that when you dig down deep you find a man or woman who is decent, kindly and friendly at heart.'

This was the journey that took Stanley out of the West and symbolically impelled him back towards the east and eventually Europe and a reconstituted life of the heart, spirit and mind. In fact, he was to write about – and recall in his public talks – those few weeks for many years to come. The freedom of the railroad and the lack of ties to anything that might be called civilisation suited him perfectly. He hadn't yet thrown off the shackles of his puritan upbringing and riding the rods represented the alternative lifestyle he was eager to carve out.

~ 7 ~
STARS AND STRIPES

Rested, watered and fed – and on his own again – Stanley set about looking for work in Toronto, which even in those days was a bustling, entrepreneurial metropolis compared to Calgary. The money machine and, according to him, a resulting soullessness, was operating unchecked. Stanley jumped headlong into this maelstrom of profit-driven activity and looked for something lucrative in journalism. He picked up a job that involved selling advertising space for a new publication which was destined to fold within weeks. Once again at a loose end, he loafed around the offices of the *Mail and Empire*, enjoying the company of journalists, hoping that something would turn up.

He looked up his old pal from the *Calgary Herald*, Bob MacDonald/ Alec Gordon, and found that he had fallen happily in love with a fellow journalist who had cured him of his excessive drinking. The new couple introduced Stanley to a group of their bohemian friends in Toronto, and my grandfather seems to have gravitated towards them as a protection against what he regarded as the philistinism of an alien city.

Nothing journalistic came his way, but another idea for the next big adventure did. Washington was recruiting an expeditionary force to sail to Cuba and Puerto Rico to mount a campaign against the Spanish forces. So, by scraping together the fare, he took the train to Buffalo in the hope of joining the ranks of Roosevelt's Rough Riders in the Spanish-American

War. Unfortunately, he arrived on a Friday and it was already too late in the day to enlist. With two days to wait and fifty cents in his pocket, he faced a bleak weekend. He describes how he went for a swim in Lake Erie and then spent the last of his money at a coffee stall, rediscovering the camaraderie of the down-and-outs. He slept in the porch of the public library and the next day, driven by hunger, made for the Salvation Army shelter, remembering how it had been a lifeline back in Winnipeg. He couldn't afford the price of supper or a bunk bed but managed to scrounge something to eat and somewhere to sleep by offering to scrub the floor for one of the workers.

Despite the continuous snores in the dormitory he managed to sleep. But the next day was no better. He says he was far more lonely than he had been in his sheep-herder's hut along with his horse and dogs. But this time the purposelessness of his existence made it even harder to bear. If he had vanished, no one would have known and he wouldn't have been missed. But he found some solace in the company of a woman he met in a park, the first he had spoken to for ages. They talked only of trifles, but he was grateful for the company. They met again and they kissed goodbye. 'One does not forget little things like that,' he comments ruefully.

Stanley entered another period of intense soul-searching which this time smacks of desperation. Perhaps he was aware that he was approaching thirty, an age at which those cossetted bankers of Toronto were likely to be married and carving out their chosen careers. He clearly felt cut off from the conventional ebbs and flows of the temporal world. In *Becoming a Man,* he writes: 'Peter Pan put down in the midst of the traffic at Ludgate Circus would have been scarcely more benumbed.' He goes on to try to reason why this is. 'A shrinking sensitiveness from the noisy vulgarity of the crowd played its part... An inability to appreciate the value of material things, a lack of ability in dealing with practical affairs were contributory causes.' But he adds another cause by harking back to his Bible-reading days and argues that being steeped in the life of the prophets necessarily throws up obstacles that make the pursuit of imperial, commercial and cultural ambitions impossible. Every cloud has a silver lining, of course:

Therefore, the Wayfarer was able to find in successive failure a
certain compensation and, while outwardly bemoaning his fate,
derive from it a measure of satisfaction. Sleeping in Salvation Army

*shelters or in public parks and hobnobbing with tramps round a
street coffee-stall, he had visitations that brought him a refreshing
and unexpected sense of freedom and joy. The very method adopted
to escape from 'the world' brought one into closer contact with
it. Idealism was balanced by a counteracting realism... The more
you sought the company of the saints, the more you found yourself
associated with the riff-raff of this world.*

Monday came and Stanley went to a recruiting depot to sign up, but was
promptly turned down for dental reasons. He reflected that it was easier to
get into the States than it was to get into the army. The next day he made
another application at a different centre, making sure he kept his mouth shut
– and no dental deficiencies were detected. However, he was told he had a
weakness in one eye. The kind, inspecting orderly invented a ruse in which
he advised Stanley to take away the eye chart, study and memorise it and
return in a few hours' time. This he duly did, by which time another orderly
was on duty and he passed with flying colours. He was unable to join the
Rough Riders, because they had no depot there. Instead, he signed up with
the 13th US Infantry on 13 June 1898. His army papers state that he was
twenty-six and a half, when in fact he was twenty-eight. His complexion
is described as 'ruddy', his occupation as 'farmer', his character as 'good'
and his height 'five feet, five and a quarter inches'. The next phase was
about to begin.

* * *

Revolts had been occurring against the alleged maladministration of Spanish
rule in Cuba without any kind of US intervention for a number of years, but
the stakes were raised by the media in the late 1890s. Newspapers belonging
to Joseph Pulitzer and William Randolph Hearst used yellow journalism
to agitate for war. But that was the last thing the business community
wanted as the economy was just recovering from a deep depression, so
they lobbied against it. What's more, firms had commercial interests in the
Caribbean, particularly in tobacco and sugar markets. Theodore Roosevelt,
however, maintains in his autobiography that the main cause of the war

was a humanitarian one: 'It was our duty, even more from the standpoint of national honour than from the standpoint of national interest, to stop the devastation and destruction.'

The tipping point was the mysterious sinking of the armoured cruiser *USS Maine* in Havana Harbour on 15 February 1898. It was the trigger that the press were looking for and they blamed the Spanish for an act of treachery. The pressure on President McKinley to take revenge and support the Cuban cause reached fever pitch, and he demanded a Spanish withdrawal. On 21 April the US Navy began a blockade of Cuba. Only later did an American commission disprove that Spanish agents had had anything to do with the sinking, but inevitably the countries slipped into a war which lasted a little more than ten weeks.

The first part of his training complete, Stanley gathered on the parade in Fort Porter with his company, before marching off to board the train to Atlanta. The American Expeditionary Force was on its way. With a bulging rucksack on his back, a rifle in his hand and the Stars and Stripes banner flapping above his head, Stanley listened to the parting words of the colonel, then they were off, though any thought of imminent action would have to be put on hold until they had undertaken more training in Atlanta. Initial feelings of warmth towards the gentler pace of life in the South dissipated when Stanley witnessed ugly scenes between whites and blacks. In a shop he saw the man behind the counter refuse to serve a man referred to as a 'nigger'. And he saw a white man draw his gun on a black youth simply because the youth had teased his dog and hadn't stopped when asked to do so. These events made a naïve Stanley reassess any idealistic notions he might have had about the Southern States.

Soon the troops were off again, this time propelled by a wood-fired train through the Florida pines, hung with drooping moss, to Tampa. Here, the burlesque element of Stanley's adventure started in earnest. The soldiers were wearing thick blue uniforms totally unsuited to hot-weather campaigning in the Caribbean. They were issued with thinner clothes, which were hastily distributed without any attention to measurements. Stanley was given a size far too large for his frame and when he put it on, he writes, it made him look like one of those shuffling figures Charlie Chaplin impersonated.

At various times during his stint under the Star-Spangled Banner he wondered whether his decision to sign up had deeper significance. Writing in 1925 – by then a confirmed Catholic – he asserts that the subconscious mind of Puritan America, with cultural memories of the Inquisition, made it easier to believe the stories about the alleged atrocities of Spanish rule circulated by the newspapers. For him, though, as a soldier from the other side of the Atlantic, it was more complex. At bottom, of course, he had joined up for something to do, to earn a crust without having to think about it and to add another adventure to his growing portfolio. But, in his more analytical moments, he states that his initial motivation had an English aspect to it: he was taking up arms against a cruel, tyrannical Catholic power which had been the enemy of England since the Reformation. Just as it did for those idealistic young men who joined up in 1914, reality quickly made its presence felt. Stanley's war experience was of a completely different kind to that of those tragic men – indeed he hardly tasted military action at all. Rather, his dose of reality took the form of observing the contrast between his own comrades – the men from the northern states – and the representatives of the old faith and culture of Europe. 'The rawness and assertiveness of the one and the quiet dignity of the other clashed in my mind and the conflict created a distinctly unpleasant impression and made me quite consciously uneasy,' he writes.

The days of drilling on the burning sands in Tampa done, the men were shipped to Cuba, where they saw the remnant of the Spanish fleet beneath Morro Castle and the smokestack of the *Merrimac* sunk by Lieutenant Hobson midway across the Santiago channel. Their sojourn in Cuba was short-lived and they were soon sailing on to Puerto Rico. Drawing near the island at dawn the gunboat accompanying them opened fire and the men were ordered beneath deck to receive the first real ammunition many of them had ever handled. The conflict had started – what there was of it. On another occasion at Guánica, minutes before entering combat some of the men were still receiving instruction on how to use their rifles.

Phyllis, Stanley's first child, told me that her father had been a war correspondent in the conflict. She claimed his lecture 'Cowboy to Pulpit' told of life on a Canadian ranch followed by his time as a newspaper correspondent with the American army in the Cuban War. At first, I was sceptical because I could find no hint in Stanley's own writings that he had added the role of journalist to his duties as a private. He could, of course, have been his rather vague self at this point in the narrative and forgotten to mention it. Or he might have wanted to cover his tracks because reporting on the campaign would probably have been prohibited. Which paper would he have written for? He had been sacked by the *Calgary Herald* and failed to make any impression at the *Mail and Empire* in Toronto. It looked unlikely. But later I found three pieces of evidence that he had indeed been a war reporter.

The first clue was in a 1905 article in an Exeter newspaper reporting on a talk he had given about his life; in it he refers to his time as war correspondent for a Toronto newspaper. Then I found a 1908 article which confirmed this. Finally, before he took up his post as pastor at Trinity, Walthamstow, the May 1906 issue of the *Trinity Record* published a short article introducing its new incumbent. It states: 'An opening appeared for him to go to the front as correspondent of a Toronto paper in the Spanish American War, but this could only be done as a soldier, so Mr James volunteered.' According to this, he enrolled as a soldier in order to carry out his duties as a journalist, rather than writing reports because he found himself in a position to do so. Unfortunately, I have found no record of his reports. I wonder if his despatches from the front were as much of the comic opera variety as the descriptions in his books.

Yankee wiliness prevented the soldiers from having the wool pulled over their eyes while on a march across inland Puerto Rico in pursuit of the Spanish foe. At a crossroads and unsure of which way to proceed, the commanding officer asked a priest who happened to be standing there which road the Spaniards had taken. The priest pointed to the left. The order was given to proceed to the right and in half an hour they had caught up with the enemy. Stanley records that the episode was taken by his fellow US troops as an example of the duplicity characteristic of those of a Catholic persuasion, outmanoeuvred by the superior intelligence of the North American.

Then there was the white cow incident while Stanley was on outpost duty. He describes how in the course of the night the soldier next to him fired at what he swore was the enemy advancing under cover of darkness. The panic spread, and soon the whole line of outposts was spitting fire into the night. So serious was the attack thought to be that the order was given to retire. However, no enemy followed up the retreat and, in the morning, an old white cow was found riddled with bullets, mistaken in the night for an attacking formation of white-uniformed Spaniards. When, however, Stanley and his men faced a real enemy, he describes how while everyone around him was mad with the lust of battle, he was gripped by a deep inhibition. Desperate not to kill anyone, but at the same time not wanting to be discovered by his fellow soldiers to have a silent gun, he aimed his bullets over the heads of the enemy, intentionally missing them. Was this the first demonstration of his pacifist beliefs?

The first Catholic sparks may have begun smouldering here, too. He was taken with the cool inner courtyards of the haciendas, the way the men strolled around looking elegant in their white duck shoes and greeted each other with dignity. He noticed how the people walked in and out of the churches appearing to be at ease with God. All these things had a restful effect, he says, and he feasted his eyes on these scenes of antiquity. 'That Spanish colonialism was corrupt and inefficient to the last degree became evident in several ways, but one forgave it as one forgives a demimonde, for the beauty it showed even in decay,' he wrote.

Poster depicting the Americans taking revenge on the Spanish for allegedly sinking the *USS Maine* in Havana Harbour

But the fighting he witnessed was sporadic and the comic opera elements far outweighed the serious business of war. He recalls how as his company marched through San German in pursuit of the Spanish force they were greeted by the townsfolk with not only waves and cheers from balconies and sidewalks but with wine and cigars, too. Months later in New York with the war over, he was rifling through an old newspaper and spotted a photograph of the same scene, complete with acclaiming crowds: the date and location were the same but closer inspection revealed that the army receiving the gifts was Spanish. Both sides in the conflict had been subject to the same warm welcome from the good people of San German – in 'sublime impartiality'. It's just that one welcome took place two hours ahead of the next.

Stanley, ever one with an eye for the women, even found time for a bit of low-key romance. It was at Ponce in Puerto Rico when he performed washing duties for some of his comrades. He went to the river to do the laundry, but a young girl spotted his amateurish efforts and offered to carry out the job for him. When she had finished, she took them away to dry and he followed and waited. This, over the ensuing days, became a ritual, along with a visit to her brother-in-law's house where she lived, and a chat in broken Spanish. One day the brother-in-law played the part of matchmaker and proposed marriage. Stanley never knew if it was with the girl's consent. 'She was indeed quite a nice girl,' he writes. 'But I lost my nerve. Being unprepared… for a matrimonial adventure, yet desiring to save the lady's feelings, I pleaded a wife in America… bigamy was out of the question.'

An armistice was declared in Puerto Rico on 12 August that year with victory for the invaders; the struggle for Cuba ended at about the same time, culminating in the Treaty of Paris on 10 December. But Stanley's own struggle was just about to begin: he fell seriously ill. The US army suffered far more fatalities from disease than from the fighting – 281 were killed in combat while 2,061 died from illness. By the time the conflict was over in Cuba, seventy-five per cent of the expeditionary force were unfit for service, yellow fever and dysentery being the main causes. Puerto Rico was no different.

Stanley paints a picture of the conditions the men faced during their efforts to subdue the enemy across the challenging terrain of the island. The first problem was unsafe food:

Some contractors must have made fortunes by supplying inferior tinned meats and other food-stuffs; thousands of tons were thrown overboard as being unfit for consumption... On one occasion, owing, it was said, to the panicking of pack-mules under fire, we were without food for the best part of 24 hours. It was also the rainy season and the men's dog-kennel tents were swamped by torrential downpours and they would wake up lying in pools of water. When the men fell ill there were no medical supplies available, not even quinine. I had prided myself that I was the only man in our company who had not at some time fallen out.

But when the armistice was declared, he promptly collapsed as the army was in the middle of the island and heading back to the coast. He staggered behind, plied with cups of strong coffee by villagers. At one point he asked the driver of an ox cart for a lift, which was refused. In what – ironically – might have been the only time my grandfather aimed a rifle in anger (although it was empty), he demanded a ride and he got the transport he needed. He reached the coast and then had to wait weeks for the promised hospital ship, there being no nursing facilities at Ponce. Instead, he shared a gin warehouse, which served as temporary barracks, with the other men. He says he weighed a staggering five stone instead of his normal ten. He was given little hope of recovery and was put on the danger list. 'Even in this condition I still did police duty at night, sharing the deserted streets with land-crabs,' he recalls. When the ship eventually arrived, he had to be carried on board. Although he doesn't state as much, the bald truth is that he came perilously close to death.

He was transferred to New York and spent the winter slowly recovering in different military hospitals. He never says what the diagnosis was, but he was likely to have been suffering from dysentery, or possibly yellow fever. He was officially invalided out on 22 March 1899. Visitors brought him books, all of which – except one – he eventually abandoned. The volume which held his interest was the New Testament, to which he turned indolently at first, but then persevered with because it brought with it a kind of healing. 'Something clean and sweet and restorative emanated from this little book. I chronicle no dramatic experience, no emotional outburst, no cataclysmic penitence, but just that sense of a re-creative Presence,' he writes.

Feeling much recovered, he then had to quickly make some practical decisions. At first it appeared that the obvious solution was to return to the foothills of the Rockies, the only place where he still felt at home. But after finding some acceptable accommodation in New York, he decided to stay put and set about looking for work. He had been given an introduction to the editor of the *Brooklyn Eagle* and, on meeting him, was given an assignment to tease out a story based on sparse information contained in an item in the personal columns of that day's paper. It involved some kind of domestic tragedy and he set out to investigate, crossing Brooklyn Bridge to locate the address, until his sensibilities around respecting others' privacy made him baulk and he called a halt to his quest. 'Something of the literary prude in that, if you like,' he writes. 'Not a little of the prig, I'm sure. I had neither the heart to go on with the business nor the courage to go back to the *Eagle* office and report my inability.'

Reading this episode reminded me of my own first day in journalism on the *East Grinstead Observer* in August 1974. I was given an assignment by the chief reporter and told to go and interview someone and 'get the story'. I cannot remember what the circumstances were, but I flunked it rather than intrude into someone else's affairs. Yet the reason for my apprehension had more to do with shyness than with any moral disquiet: Stanley was altogether more confident than I was. Another difference, however, is that I did go into the office the next day and ended up spending most of my working life as a journalist.

Stanley counted up his money and found that his payoff from the military was generous enough to cover the cost of a passage back to England. He spontaneously decided to book the boat for two days' time without any idea of what he would do on his return. While on the one hand he had pleasant feelings of anticipation about seeing his family again, on the other he was aware that he was returning empty-handed, a failure. But he knew that the rather bookish and dreamy young man had learnt self-reliance. He writes:

'Life itself took precedence of what is written about life, facts had become to be of more importance than comments on facts. My mind was filled with pictures of stock-yards, crowded side-walks, rifles cracking in the thick growth of Puerto Rico plantations, ocean liners steaming up New York bay, the sound of sirens and hooters

*signalling sea traffic from all parts of the world, dejected prisoners
of war, lumbermen in the bush, cowboys corralling cattle, judges
sitting to try cattle-thieves, goldminers with their huskies and laden
sleighs setting off for the Far North, negroes working in the cotton
fields of the South, editors reading proofs, down-town restaurants
and cafeterias where sailors of many nations, hefty workmen in
blue overalls and crooks of all sorts came and went, saloon-keepers
serving drinks and prostitutes on the lookout for a chance client.*

The door to the kind of belief – Catholicism – that he eventually embraced
had been opened, but he allowed it to shut again. But he did experience
euphoria in sailing away from America with his back to the Statue of Liberty,
the ozone of the Atlantic really did penetrate his being, and the spirit of
Europe once again coursed powerfully through his veins. The adventure
wasn't over: it would still be very much part of his life. But now it would
be an adventure of the mind and soul rather than of the body.

SUBURBAN STRUGGLES

~ 8 ~

THE PRODIGAL'S RETURN

I am sure Stanley on his return in 1899 at the age of twenty-nine managed to locate Daniel's breakaway church more easily than I did when I was pounding the pavements of Wimbledon in search of my ancestors. I googled Christ Church and discovered that there was a place of worship of that name on Copse Hill, yet it announced itself as Church of England. The building at the top of the hill with its stately tower and spire was impressive, even though it was draped in scaffolding. I met the vicar, but the name 'James' meant nothing to him, nor was there any record of a minister with that name in the booklet he lent me. Nonconformist and Church of England folk in those days went their separate ways, so they would never have shared a place of worship. Phone calls to secretaries of other places of worship in the area gave me no fresh insights. It all became clear when I visited the Surrey History Centre in Woking. There I found the minutes of Christ Church, Alwyne Road, with my great-grandfather's name signing off countless meetings. I had been looking in the wrong area, but perseverance had paid off. Old maps showed where it had been – very near Daniel's first Wimbledon church in Worple Road – before becoming a United Reformed church and eventually being knocked down.

Before Stanley left for Canada he was fully aware of his father's rift with half his congregation and the plan to set up the new church. In the end, Daniel's suggestion that they use a plot of land next to the post office was eventually adopted. The name Christ Church – again suggested by Daniel – was agreed on and the tender of £3,697 (£400,000 in 2020) for the new building was accepted.

A friend of mine lived out his first twenty years in Alwyne Road, almost opposite the church. He remembers it as a 'rather unattractive, red-brick thing at the end of the street', which his eyes rested on when he opened the curtains in the morning.

It is hard to know to what extent Stanley had stayed in touch with the family during his six-year absence in North America. Always jealous of his independence and intent on carving out his own life, he didn't see himself as part of the Wimbledon set-up. Despite that, he is unlikely to have made a complete break and at least his mother would have written to him from time to time. He is bound to have known, for example, that Clara's parents, Thomas and Elizabeth Pulsford, had moved out of Caerleon to live in Ruthin, North Wales, where they died in 1895 within months of each other. His younger sister Daisy had married William Sutherland at Christ Church in 1896. William was deputy headmaster of King's College School, Wimbledon, and the couple now lived close by in Worple Road. But Stanley probably didn't know that in that same year, his father had been accused of plagiarising from a book entitled *Shakespearean and Bible Characters,* written by the Reverend James Bell. It appears from an article in the *Dundee Evening Telegraph* that I stumbled across on a newspaper archive website that Daniel admitted he had drawn on a passage from the book. Bell responded: 'It is deliberate plagiarism. Is Mr James aware that he is liable to an action at law for infringement of copyright? His retreat into silence will not avail him.' The outcome of this odd little altercation is unknown.

* * *

My research also threw up an extraordinary coincidence. I knew that my cousin Rosemary's husband, Simon Ely, had had relatives in that area of south London. One of them had owned and run a department store in

Wimbledon called Elys and it still thrives today. I saw the name 'Ely' on more than one occasion when I was trying to disentangle the scrawling handwriting of the secretary in the two churches' minutes. There was a George Ely and a Joseph Ely. On feeding the information back to Simon, he told me that they were half-brothers, at least one teetotal and both religious, and that Joseph was his grandfather. It seems that while Joseph stayed with the original congregation and took over his half-brother's duties as clerk of Worple Road church halls, George followed Daniel to Christ Church.

It is not too much of an exaggeration to say that the new church was built around Daniel. There were 102 people on the roll, the total being comprised of followers from Worple Road and others from the nearby Presbyterian church, with Clara on the women's committee. The new premises opened on 26 September 1894. 'In a rather special sense the church was identified with his [Daniel's] personality,' writes Stanley.

The liturgical character of its worship and even its architecture, reminding one far more of Anglicanism than of traditional Dissent, were due to his preferences. In the vestry were exhibited photographs of those heroes whom his eclectic taste had canonised: Newman and Faber side by side with George MacDonald and Charles Kingsley, and even George Eliot and Darwin had places in this strange collection.

Even at Worple Road, the Anglican *Book of Common Prayer* had been in use while surplices were worn by officiating ministers, and these traits continued at Alwyne Road. In many ways, these were outward manifestations of a revolt against Puritanism's tendency towards dourness. They could also be seen as a change in the social position of Nonconformity: aping the rituals of the Establishment was a way of gaining respectability. Nevertheless, Daniel had been lending his support to Herbert Asquith's Disestablishment Bill for the Church in Wales, which took until 1914 to become law.

The most significant change in Stanley's absence had been his father health, which was rapidly deteriorating, making it difficult for him to continue working. He was described as being in 'a state of nervous prostration' and was found to be suffering from Bright's disease. Stanley stepped in and read the lessons for him, then preached for him too, which much to his surprise found favour with the congregation. Although he doesn't mention it, with this course of action, Stanley must have gone some way towards healing the previous division between himself and his father. On 18 July, at a special meeting, Daniel was given six months' leave of absence, and in November he had his stipend reduced. The family had also probably moved from the relative spaciousness of 5 Crescent Road to 60 Alexandra Road, a smaller house a mile away but nearer Christ Church.

Daniel vowed to return to his position on the first Sunday of the new century. Stanley, meanwhile, continued to fill his place. There is no record as to whether Daniel fulfilled his New Year's commitment to preach, but by 27 March 1900, 'the pastor was presiding' again. The recovery did not last long though, and by 29 May he had fallen ill again, never to recover. On 26 June, the monthly meeting of the deacons gave Stanley an extension, only for Daniel to pass away two days later.

The James household must have suddenly become a quiet and desolate place for Clara and the already fractured family. Stanley was finding his feet after his Prairie adventures, Muriel was working as a kindergarten teacher in Addiscombe, Norman was settled in Canada and Daisy was living with her husband. Daniel's funeral was on 2 July, after which he was buried in Gap Road Cemetery, Wimbledon. I found his grave, which had been damaged but, unlike others around it, was not smothered by ivy. The cross had fallen off its plinth and its shaft was lying on the ground, broken in two. The inscription reads: 'The Rev D. Bloomfield James who passed to a higher life – death cannot conquer love... in ever faithful and undying love'. Local masons have now repaired his grave.

Daniel died young, at fifty-nine. It was left to the *Congregational Yearbook* of 1901 to give him a fitting memorial. Part of his obituary was included in a book entitled *Eminent Welshmen*:

Daniel Bloomfield James [came], as so many eloquent preachers have done, from a good old farming stock, to which calling he was brought up, till his mind turned irresistibly to the ministry as his vocation... He was thoroughly Welsh in blood and temperament, but his training was almost entirely English, and though he spoke a little Welsh, he could never preach in that tongue... From the beginning of his ministry it was clear that a fresh and striking personality had emerged, and that here was a preacher of no mean order. Physically, temperamentally and spiritually, there was an impression of distinction made by all his utterances. Crowds soon flocked to hear him, and men listened eagerly to his glowing eloquence.

With such gifts, it is surprising that Bloomfield James did not take a more commanding rank among the great preachers of the age. The reason was not far to seek. The orator's temperament is almost always an unstable quantity, and Mr James had the defect of his qualities in a marked degree. He was painfully shy and retiring, keenly sensitive to criticism, and unable to stand the occasional rough handling to which preachers, like other public men, are sometimes subject. As years passed, he retired more and more into himself, and when broken health came upon him, he was liable to periods of deep melancholy. But he was ever a gentle, tender, and most lovable man... After two years of partial inability (though he never resigned his charge, the personal devotion of his people continuing to the end) he steadily sank, and died on 28 June, rejoicing in God his Saviour... many there are who look back to his influence over them as one of the purest and most helpful in their lives; and thousands would have been glad to pay the last tribute of a tear at his open grave.

* * *

Stanley seems to have performed his allotted task adequately enough for the deacons to offer him the position for another six months and only in October did they start thinking about recruiting a replacement. A proposal that he should be offered the post permanently was defeated by nineteen votes to fourteen. Nevertheless, the minutes for 15 January 1901 state that Stanley was due to preach again on 24 February.

Having not long departed from military action in the Caribbean and the dust of the Prairies only recently brushed out of his hair, Stanley found suburbia hard to contend with, let alone the burden of administering and giving spiritual sustenance to a prestigious body of Wimbledon believers, many twice his age. Despite his assertions that the Bible had renewed its impact on him in the ward of the New York hospital, there is no evidence that he had abandoned his agnosticism. He acknowledges the bravura of it all. 'I can only wonder at my nerve,' he writes later. 'The mental throes which accompanied the preparation of those first sermons are indescribable... my thinking apparatus was rusty and almost unworkable... [but] it was in the spirit of adventure that I mounted the pulpit. Pulpiteering evoked a native strain.'

He lists some of the topics on which he preached: the Dreyfus Case, the Boer War and the ethics of Jesus. It was a chance for him to express himself after seven years of ruminating on the problems of existence and he leapt at the opportunity of unburdening his soul. 'Sunday by Sunday,' he writes, 'I inflicted my impressions of life, totally devoid of any really disciplined thought and altogether without authority, on a congregation of respectable suburban folk, who fondly imagined, I suppose, that they were fulfilling some obligation in listening to me.' But he was surprised by just how much reciprocity there was with his audience: 'Like most lonely people, I imagined that my private thoughts were unshared by anyone else. I did not realise that the waters of the invisible time spirit had washed up against the bases of the Rockies and penetrated even to the Prairie shanties in which I had my dwelling.' His thoughts and feelings raced ahead and he convinced himself that he had finally found his vocation – that of a Congregational minister – although he had entered it through the back door.

But in more sober moments he realised that he was walking on shaky ground. He had no qualifications and no system of belief – apart from his spirituality – to back up his utterances from the pulpit. And he was running out of themes. If there were no current events to ruminate on, he would turn tentatively to the Scriptures in an attempt to eke out some cogent lesson from the New Testament. But, just as he was on the point of mining this rich, more conventional seam, he encountered objections from the young men in his congregation, who favoured the distinctly secular approach of the new Brotherhood movement and PSAs (Pleasant Sunday Afternoons, a late-nineteenth-century gathering of men who sought to take part in an edifying exchange of ideas along with tea and biscuits). 'The gulf of sheer secularism is always yawning beneath the feet of the Nonconformist preacher. Nor is there any wall to safeguard him. The Church merges imperceptibly into the world, the supernatural into the natural,' he writes.

In his perceptive way he foresaw most of the pitfalls inherent in being a Congregational minister. One major difficulty arose from the fact that the personality of the pastor was all-important in a way that it was not in Church of England or Catholic circles. It was not the minister's office, but his natural abilities, personal attractiveness and force of character that told, just as it was his ability as a preacher and not his functions as a priest that drew congregations, he observes. Only a strong man could escape these psychological dangers, while what he called 'an unlovely professionalism' was apt to characterise his manner. Meanwhile, the pose of the public speaker and the habit of listening to his own unchallenged voice tended to ruin him as a conversationalist. Added to these difficulties was the possibility of undesirable relationships almost forced upon one by the human need of a confessor. It was surprising, he concludes, that so many men in the ministry of the free churches escaped as they did. That last sentence was indeed prophetic, but it would be another sixteen years of ministry before it would bear fruit in starkly secular fashion. Stanley was to be one minister who did not 'escape'.

He was not the type to get nervous at the thought of preaching: 'The egotism of the pulpit was in my veins.' But what held terrors for him were social occasions when he was expected to mingle and make conversation. The reaction he experienced was so extreme that he describes it in terms of a 'paralysing panic... I had no conversation. I did not know what to do with my hands and I was painfully conscious of my feet.' No doubt a modern-day psychoanalyst would be able to proffer a view as to what was going on. But he persevered and tried to fit in to those suburban ways, while at the same time remaining sceptical that any unbelieving Wimbledon souls would be shown the light as a result of his endeavours.

* * *

There was another reason for his steadfastness: he was engaged to be married. He had met Jessica Heley, my grandmother, when she accompanied an aunt on a social visit to Clara sometime in 1899. The attraction seems to have been instant, although Stanley says that on that first meeting he teased her. He writes in his diary that evening: 'Met Miss Heley.' I have in my possession three pocket-books written by Oliver Wendell Holmes, which were Stanley's first presents to his new love. These light-hearted essays are entitled *The Autocrat at the Breakfast-Table*, *The Poet at the Breakfast-Table* and *The Professor at the Breakfast-Table*. On the inside cover of each Stanley declared his love for her. They seem to have become engaged very quickly although the marriage wouldn't take place until 1 October 1901.

Jess Heley around the time of her engagement

Jess, as she was known, was nineteen and hailed from Wing in Buckinghamshire. She was the seventh of nine children born to Thomas Somes Heley and Annie Rolls, who was a distant relative of the family of

Charles Stewart Rolls, pioneer of the Rolls-Royce car manufacturer. Her relatively well-off family of farmers and millers were part of the village establishment, going back to at least the 1720s. She was 'buxom and cheerful' and seemed 'the quintessence of English womanhood' in Stanley's eyes. But he is loath to analyse too much, concluding that 'it was enough for me that she was – herself'. Jess, meanwhile, would have seen a handsome man of twenty-nine, presumably in good health again after recovering from his illness in Puerto Rico, bursting with enthusiasm and ideas.

There were three stumbling blocks that the love-struck couple had to surmount. Firstly, although he was living in his comfortable family home, Stanley himself had no money. He told Jess that his capital amounted to two-pence halfpenny. He comments: 'It was indeed a perilous journey on which I was asking this nineteen-year-old, country-bred girl to accompany me. And I knew myself too well to believe that the future would be one of halcyon peace. Was it quite fair to take advantage of her inexperience?' The second, related problem was that he had no permanent job. Before he met Jess he had half intended to return to North America and had certainly not been contemplating settling down to life in England.

The last problem was that she lived forty miles away in Buckinghamshire. The only way of seeing her was to jump on his bicycle, ride across London and navigate the highways and byways towards her little Chiltern village, which he did every Sunday after his duties were over. He remembered with fondness those dark rides through the countryside, the gradual breaking of the dawn, and the occasional chats with policemen on night duty. Not the least of his pleasures was the warm welcome he received on arrival, quite apart from the relief he felt at being away from suburbia. Together Stanley and Jess rose to the challenge and romance blossomed. Judging by their photos, they made a handsome couple.

Stanley still needed a job, so he did the rounds preaching at Congregational churches that had a vacant pulpit, hoping that one of them would offer him a post. Eventually he landed a job as pastor at Teignmouth Congregational Church in Devon, preaching his last sermon at Christ Church on 24 February 1901. Stanley writes that 'influence at court' eased his passage into his first real ministry, which he commenced on 5 May 1901. What that meant in practical terms was that his mother pulled a few strings. The names of her uncles, John and William Pulsford, although both dead by this time, were still highly regarded on the Congregational circuit. And assorted members of the family still lived in nearby Newton Abbot, so it was no surprise when the James compass swung west. According to the 1901 census taken on 31 March, Clara and Stanley were living near each other in central Teignmouth. Clara appears to have been in some kind of sheltered accommodation attached to St James' Church, 'living on her own means'. In his will, Daniel had left her effects to the value of £1,469 1s 6d (£155,000 in 2020); this ensured that she was comfortable for the remaining twenty-five years of her life. Stanley lived on his own for the first five months at 8 Den Crescent, an elegant set of buildings with a sea view, a few yards from the front. It is hard to imagine that Clara did not dip into her legacy to ease her son's way.

The Congregational church itself, designed by the respected architect John Sulman, is one of the finer Nonconformist buildings. It stands on a small, triangular island site between the railway line and two busy streets but manages to dominate its surroundings. Sulman had just returned from Italy where he had admired the architecture of Tuscany. It was natural for him, therefore, in his first project on his return, to ape the style by designing a lofty yet pretty Italianesque church. It was to be one of his last projects before moving to Australia where he was the chief architect of many notable public buildings in Sydney. Sulman's firm had also designed the hall attached to Christ Church, Addiscombe where Daniel had been minister fifteen years before.

John Smith, the church leader at Teignmouth in 2019, showed me around. Soon I was looking up at my grandfather's portrait in the vestry. His dark, handsome features, with a substantial mop of black hair, stared out from behind the glass, and I imagined I saw a piercing, challenging look in his eyes – perhaps a challenge thrown down for me to perform to his standards in writing this book. Urbane, twenty-first-century women, when I show them my copy of this particular portrait, tend to express their admiration with an intake of breath. He undoubtedly had a magnetic appeal. He was attractive to and attracted by women. I told Mr Smith this and he sagely replied: 'The spiritual and the sexual are closely related and sometimes one cannot distinguish one from the other. They are the opposite sides of the same coin.'

The wedding at the Union Chapel, Burcott, on 1 October, was a 'pretty' affair, according to the *Leighton Buzzard Observer*. 'The bride wore a dress of white China silk, veil and orange blossom and carried a shower bouquet.' The reception was held at her home, The Chestnuts, after which the bride and groom left for London. She gave him a picture; he gave her a gold curb bangle. Her mother Annie gave them household linen and a dinner service, Clara gave them furniture, his sister Muriel silver salt cellars and Norman, who I assume was still in Canada, must have instructed someone to buy a tablecloth to give them on his behalf. The happy couple must have been nicely set up for their new home. Stanley moved out of his bachelor digs and rented Lucerne, 8 Lower Brimley Avenue – now Lucerne, 15 Lower Brimley Road – with Clara now only five minutes' walk away in her lodgings in Higher Brimley Road.

The Union Chapel, Burcott, Wing, where Stanley and Jess married on 1 October 1901

It was to be one of the most peaceful and contented periods of Stanley's life, proving that even he – with all his restlessness – could relish havens of calm, partially removed from the maelstrom of external events and the teeming ideas that coursed through his brain at most other times. 'The Tramp was, for the time being, repressed,' he writes. Children followed in rapid succession – Phyllis in April 1902, Bob in October 1903, Jessie in March 1905 and Eric in May 1906. It was five years of quiet home life 'into which broke the cries and laughter of children'. I have one grainy and indistinct photograph of him with a woman, who must be Jess, and the children, on the sands of Teignmouth beach, with the gable of Clifton House in the background. At Christmas 1904, Stanley was the officiating minister in his own church at the marriage of his sister Muriel to Leonard Milton, an accountant.

His unofficial initiation at Christ Church, Wimbledon, must have stood him in good stead, not least because he was able to redeliver the more successful of those sermons, albeit to a different kind of worshipper. But he still wasn't qualified. It was quite within the rights of an individual Congregational church to choose whomever they wanted as a pastor; they had complete autonomy and could in theory have chosen anyone. They had chosen Stanley, but that did not mean that he was recognised by the Congregational Union of England and Wales.

This he set about rectifying by studying the required modules – systematic theology, Christian evidences and New Testament Greek. Having passed, he was ordained, according to Stanley, by a neighbouring minister. But judging by the poster advertising the event on 19 February 1903, which I discovered in the Teignmouth archives, there were no less than six men of the cloth involved in his ordination. Stanley writes:

This ordination consisted in the reading of a profession of faith drawn up by myself, and of a statement setting forth my conception of the Christian ministry, the asking and answering of a series of questions previously agreed on by my ministerial neighbour and myself, a statement from him that my declarations and answers were satisfactory, and an extempore ordination prayer.

There was no reference to priestly functions in any part of the proceedings. In that way he became a fully recognised minister of the Congregational body. Yet he comments that he had mental reservations, that something deep inside him did not accept this particular creed as forever binding. 'It was an interim religion,' he writes. 'Thus did I, with a smattering of knowledge, and an undisciplined mind, but with a fairly facile tongue, take upon myself the duties of the most sacred and responsible of all callings.'

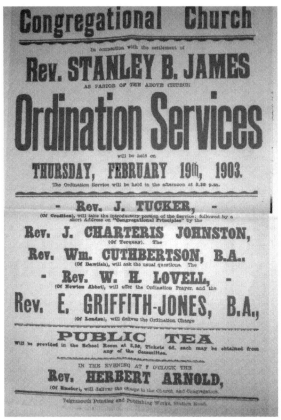

Stanley's ordination took place four years after he started
working as a minister. Credit: Teign Heritage

Jess holding Jessie, her youngest child at the time, with Phyllis and Bob, in 1905

The historian Clyde Binfield, a leading authority in all matters Nonconformist, wrote about both my great-grandfather and grandfather in 'Collective Sovereignty? Conscience in the Gathered Church'.

[Congregationalism] was certainly a religion which pandered to the pulpiteer. Given the tendency of younger ministers to desert objective revelation for the psychology of religion, and given the occupational hazard of succumbing to the brief and bright style in vogue at Brotherhoods, [Stanley] James shuddered at the secularism which yawned insistently at a preacher's feet.

For Stanley, this dualism saw him attempting to reconcile conventional evangelical mission with reading the *Hibbert Journal*, a liberal quarterly Unitarian magazine which focused on the religious issues – the psychology of belief among them – that were occupying radical Christian minds at that time.

In the eyes of the good folk of Teignmouth he seems to have done plenty of valuable work in the town, with the congregation more than doubling. Just as he had in Jumping Pound, Alberta, he set up a literary society which held weekly meetings, where members read from the classics and contemporary works, sang their favourite songs, debated topical issues and listened to speakers. Among the subjects covered were the merits of living in the countryside versus the town, and whether socialism was practicable. They heard talks about *Punch* magazine, the growth of coal gas and several by Stanley about life on the Prairie or fighting for the US army. The meeting on 11 September 1903 debated 'Women's Suffrage', with Stanley in the chair. A Mr Courtier was strongly in favour of women being allowed to play a larger part in politics but Mr H. C. Full wasn't. The motion was defeated by thirty-three votes to six, with 'most of the ladies deciding the issue in the negative', according to the *Exeter and Plymouth Gazette*. A more light-hearted evening was on offer when the group staged a mock parliamentary debate. My grandfather took the part of the prime minister who wanted to introduce a 'teeth bill', which made it compulsory for everyone over twenty-one to be provided with false teeth. The motion was heavily defeated.

On the religious front he headed various ecumenical committees, urging unity between different denominations. He set up a PSA group which attracted regular attendances of 160 men. Again, he often regaled them with stories from the Rockies. There was the Young Men's Mutual Improvement Society, to which he lectured on 'New Zealand Football'. When the secretary of the football club said he would welcome any clergymen to their games, Stanley replied that he would be ready to kick off whenever he was asked. There was a group called Christian Endeavours, an evangelical mission conducted at the Congregational church in Exmouth, a special service taken at Buckfastleigh, a concert arranged to raise funds for the church's ailing finances, and the awarding of prizes to Sunday school high achievers. On 7 November 1903 the church asked him to continue with his ministry, which he agreed to – but not for the full three years that they desired.

Stanley's politics of engagement were starting to take shape. He supported the local Liberal candidate and set up a branch of the Passive Resistance League, of which he was secretary. He was a manager on the board of Teignmouth School and hit the local headlines in March 1904, along with other Nonconformists in town, for non-payment of the education element of the local rates. His case was heard at the petty sessions in Teignmouth, but I have been unable to discover the final outcome. Like so many others, he was objecting to the Conservative government's idea for a new education bill which would financially favour Church of England and Catholic schools over and above Nonconformist ones. The bill became an act and was passed, so the cause was eventually lost, coinciding with a relative decline in the fortunes of the Dissenting Movement in the early part of the twentieth century. Interestingly, in August 1904 Stanley preached at East Hill Congregational Church in Wandsworth, where his father had been pastor in the 1870s.

During the summer of 1905 a deacon from Trinity Congregational Church in Walthamstow, East London, was taking his annual holiday with his family in Teignmouth. One Sunday he attended Stanley's church for morning service and was impressed by what he saw and heard, particularly by the sermon. His church happened to be looking for a new minister at the time, so he reported back to the diaconate, recommending my grandfather for the vacant post. Stanley was invited to preach in Walthamstow, the first time being on 22 February 1906, and again on 11 and 16 March. He made a favourable impression and was offered the post by a majority of ninety-five to five at a church meeting. He accepted, the lure of a larger salary and the pressure of having a growing family to provide for being prime motivators for his decision. He writes: 'Without hesitation... I accepted the invitation and set my face towards the problems presented by a crowded East End neighbourhood. The pulse of self-confidence beat strongly.'

For his remaining months at Teignmouth the church continued to thrive and when he finally left, the congregation universally regretted his departure. At the farewell gathering on 22 May, reference was made to the respect that the young people had for him, and to the fact that during his pastorate more than sixty new members had joined the church. He was presented with an inscribed gold watch, a chain and a cheque. The *Trinity Record* [Walthamstow] states: 'A notable feature of the evening was the reference made by brother ministers to the help Mr James had been to their churches, and on behalf of the Shaldon church, the Rev. W. Scott presented Mr James with two volumes "for remembrance".' The church of a vibrant London suburb waited expectantly, little aware of the challenges and controversy that Stanley's appointment was about to unleash.

~ 9 ~
REVOLUTION IN THE PULPIT

An unremarkable, unattractive, steep-roofed, grey-brick building on the edge of what is now called Old Walthamstow greeted Stanley and the family when they arrived in this northeast London suburb in June 1906. But what was to occur inside those walls over the next ten years certainly could not be described as unremarkable. My grandfather would turn an orthodox Nonconformist church into a hive of activity and place of experimentation that embraced most of the important social and spiritual movements of the age.

The Jameses purposely took their annual holiday before arriving so that Stanley could devote the rest of the year to Trinity uninterrupted. He joined a church that was in rude health – at least as far as membership was concerned, with about three hundred members on the roll. After his first day of preaching, the *Trinity Record* comments: 'The services were most impressive, for while the preacher avoided anything sensational, both sermons showed that he felt the great responsibility and importance of his position.'

His salary was £275 a year (£29,000 in 2020) and the family of six plus a domestic nurse lived in a large house – 118 Grove Road – five minutes' walk from the church. Trinity had started out in 1861 as a loose grouping of people worshipping in each other's houses, Walthamstow in those days being on the edge of the Essex countryside. Later that year they built 'The Ark', a rickety wooden structure on a site in Orford Road, followed by a brick building adjacent to it. The church grew in numbers so rapidly that by 1869 they had moved into a larger building – today's solid stone edifice at the junction of Orford Road and West Avenue.

Top: Trinity Congregational Church, Walthamstow, at the time Stanley became minister.
Above: The family home at 118 Grove Road

Stanley made an impact with his powerful preaching, and before long the number of members rose to over 350, with four hundred at Sunday school. After an obligatory trial period, he was asked to continue as pastor, and on 5 July a special ceremony was held in his honour. My grandparents were welcomed, music was performed and strawberries and biscuits – 'a popular innovation', according to the *Trinity Record* – were served. Stanley expressed the joy that he and Jess felt at being at Trinity. He was asked if he would miss the Devon scenery. In response he said that ministers were 'in search of human scenery, and there was more beauty here, for there was more material for work'. He found the work suited him entirely, so much so that he felt that the church had been made for him. This rather arrogant assertion echoes the way he had described Christ Church, Wimbledon, as having been built specifically for his father. Donations had reduced the church's debt of £200 to £100 (£21,000 to £11,000 in 2020) and he hoped this marked the beginning of the end for the fund-raising initiative. Meanwhile, soon after the Jameses left Teignmouth, Clara moved to Little Canford, Dorset, to live with Daisy and her husband William Sutherland in their house on the banks of the River Stour.

Stanley felt energised by Walthamstow's dynamic atmosphere. He set up a cycling club and revitalised the existing literary and debating society. He started a Christian endeavour society to promote a Christian life among young people, to encourage healthy interaction and bring them closer to a sense of God. There were other groups for youngsters – a gym, and social and needlework clubs – which altogether made up a thriving evening institute, and he was not averse to cajoling members to become more involved in the running of the church and to make a greater effort in welcoming new members. Trinity had probably been the first Congregational church in the country to bring in deaconesses, even if the reason behind that initiative was pragmatic rather than ideological. A former treasurer was profoundly deaf and only his wife could make him hear, so she was needed at business meetings. She did a good job, and the committee were minded to recruit more women. Stanley's congregation was a mix of young, old, traditional and radical believers.

He had to wait until October for his formal recognition. No less than two national politicians spoke at the ceremony. Joseph Compton-Rickett, a Yorkshire MP, spoke fondly of Daniel James and related how Stanley and his own son had been boyhood friends. 'Mr James has qualified for his work by travel and knowledge of the world,' he said. 'We are all apt to bind a man down to his pulpit utterance; religion is humanity on tip-toe reaching after an ideal, and we ought not to place the minister in the matter of his daily life above the layman.'

The second politician was Sir John Simon, Liberal MP for Walthamstow from 1906 to 1918, who was later to become one of only three people to serve as home secretary, foreign secretary and chancellor of the exchequer – along with James Callaghan and Rab Butler. He was to resign as home secretary in 1916 in protest against the introduction of conscription for single men in the First World War. Those pacifist leanings would have triggered a meeting of minds with Stanley, who was to embrace the cause with enthusiasm about the same time. Sir John was a constant presence at Trinity throughout, supporting a number of craft fairs as the church attempted to extinguish its debt. In addition, two deacons from Teignmouth attended the recognition service, saying that they were very sorry to lose their pastor and if Trinity was not satisfied with him, they would have him back tomorrow.

Stanley, in reply, said he wished Trinity to be a large-hearted church for all classes. If he found a member of the church giving the cold shoulder to anyone, he would have a warm time at the speaker's hands! Speaking of his removal from Teignmouth he said it was because he felt he was in a sort of backwater there and wanted to get back into the midstream current; the area was something of a magnet for many who supported the radical causes that were gaining currency in the early years of the century. It couldn't have been a more positive start for my grandfather and the family: the congregation's enthusiasm for their new pastor seemed boundless.

Stanley began to spread the ecclesiastical net wider by making links with radical churches. The social reformer Florence Booth, wife of Bramwell Booth, second general of the Salvation Army, had been preaching at various churches about her work 'rescuing' prostitutes in the East End. She explained to the genteel folk of Walthamstow that poverty was so rife that girls as young as thirteen were selling themselves or being sold for money. She started the Salvation Army's first rescue home for 'fallen women', the prototype for hundreds of similar institutions around the globe. One worshipper was so moved by her sermon that they gave a gold chain to the collection.

Internationalism was the order of the day, too: a system of exchange between German and English ministers was established and a local doctor received regular financial support for her medical and missionary work in India. So far, Stanley seemed to be the model, eager young pastor, exhibiting the right mix of traditional worship and lively engagement with contemporary issues. What's more, on at least two occasions he returned to Teignmouth to conduct a wedding and a funeral. The local paper records that the congregation there received him warmly.

* * *

One day a hastily scribbled and near-illegible note came through the letter box. The writer wanted to know whether the Mr James he had seen in the local paper was none other than the person he had known in Calgary and Toronto. Stanley jumped on his bike and sped round to the address. There he found Robert MacDonald/Alec Gordon, his journalist friend, knee-deep in newspapers in an otherwise bare room furnished only with a chair, a table and maps of the colonies. He had turned himself into a leading commentator on all things colonial and was contributing to a wide range of journals. After warm greetings all round, he brought Stanley up to date on his life. He had followed his beloved, intrepid war correspondent to Cuba and after a long search had found her stricken down with fever in the back streets of Santiago. He had nursed her back to health, whereupon she returned to Canada and promptly married another man. It was all too much for him to take and he turned to his former alcoholic ways, then sailed to England to try his luck there. Soon after arriving, he had been contacted by an editor in Toronto asking him to write a book about the Canadian railways which involved travelling back there. The problem was he was so poor he didn't have enough money to pay for his passage. Stanley invited him to stay with him and a week later his friend, boat ticket in hand, set out for Canada. Stanley later received a cablegram from Ottawa saying his friend had been found dead in one of the city's hotels.

How much this sad episode and the consequent turning back of his mind to his wanderings of ten years previously disturbed Stanley's equilibrium is hard to say. But from this point on, the old restlessness returned. He writes:

The novelty of the new position was beginning to wear off. Into my study would sometimes come unbidden a youth wearing a sombrero and spur, or a disreputable-looking tramp or the same figure clad in the uniform of an American infantryman. They brought with them a sense of large spaces of easy freedom from conventions and rough honesty that were somehow disquieting... It was not easy to reconcile these unkempt intruders with a suburban ministry and increasing professional associations... What place had a bohemian newspaper man or the night-moths of a Buffalo coffee-stall to do with our tamed urban folk?

Yet, he says, the man in the study deserved compassion because, after his uninvited visitors had disappeared, he would be left with the uncomfortable feeling that he was trapped. What's more, there were moments when he was conscious of denying his real self and he even began to suspect his own honesty. The conflict, like all his conflicts, went on under the surface. But, above all, he knew that the satisfaction he had found in his work was ebbing away. He was restless and his restlessness was starting to affect the quality of his work. He felt he was swimming in a choppy sea and, when the waves lifted him up, he could see no land.

This self-preoccupation speaks volumes about the type of marriage that was developing. Caught up in his own spiritual concerns, Stanley devoted little time to the four children and not much more to Jess, who was expected to bring them up without any help from him. My research unearthed letters from people at Trinity which seem to suggest that about this time Stanley was spending an increasing amount of time in the houses of single women in the congregation, often leaving Jess to return home alone after meetings. It was even said that at one stage he was contemplating going to live with the Thomas sisters, who were members of the congregation. By 1914 this indiscriminate visiting had become a feature of his ministry and becomes a central concern of my book in later chapters. In photographs taken at this time Jess and the children are always pictured without him, but they look well dressed, which suggests that Jess was doing a good job of managing the money, of which it has to be said there was enough. But she looks tired. And I learned that she always had a bottle of brandy to hand in case the stress took its toll on her heart.

Relief from the feeling of staleness that Stanley felt was creeping into the life of the church came in the form of a burgeoning religious movement known as the New Theology, the creation of the Reverend R. J. Campbell, minister at the City Temple in Holborn. It was a movement away from orthodox or fundamentalist theological thought that aimed to reconcile modern concepts and discoveries in science and philosophy with theology. A member of the Independent Labour Party (ILP) – the first manifestation of the Labour Party – and a supporter of women's suffrage, Campbell pointed 'to the unequal distribution of the means of human existence on this planet'.

A fiery, white-haired preacher of magnetic power, Campbell had attracted audiences of seven thousand to his first Sunday services as minister at the Holborn church in 1903. His undeniable allure was enhanced by his face appearing on postcards of the time alongside actors and celebrities of the day, and his legendary sermons were instantly published and distributed around Britain and America. An astute *Daily Mail* editor recognised this phenomenon and highlighted Campbell's campaign of revolt against established dogma while emphasising Christianity's social obligations. The widely held view was that he was a visionary who could combine all the forces of revolt in the religious and humanitarian world. He launched an organisation called the Progressive League, enlisting the support of the more spiritual and idealistic elements of the ILP.

At first, Stanley had opposed the movement, joining in a chorus of conservative opposition to its tenets. But now he joined the Progressive League, finding in its beliefs the excitement that his mind and soul craved. 'R. J. Campbell's defiance and the enunciation of a Christianity conscious of its social obligations rather than the City Temple minister's theology made a strong appeal to me,' he writes. 'Here was an opportunity... to escape from the dilemma that had faced me. The compromise would enable me to continue in my profession, but would also allow me wider latitude.' The City Temple became a mecca for theological rebels and it was not unknown for men in pubs to debate the concepts of immanence and transcendence almost as naturally as they did free trade and protection, or football. So, Stanley was in good company. Muriel Lester, the Christian revolutionary based in Bow, and Dr William Orchard, later of King's Weigh House – two people who would play an important part in my grandfather's development – were also devotees.

The new movement provided Stanley with the kind of distraction that he craved both for himself and his congregation. The onus in the Congregational church, he loved to point out, was on the minister to preach on subjects that his audience found interesting. It that sense he was in much the same position as the editor of a daily paper who depended on sensational stunts to boost circulation figures. Once these stimulants had been provided, he says, the preacher was little more than an organiser of Sunday entertainments. 'It was on this downward path I began to slip. Here was a stunt of the first order… The journalist got the better of the Christian minister.'

The pulpit where Stanley challenged his congregation with sermons about the New Theology

The Congregational Union allowed individual churches to operate more or less as they liked, with the members and minister deciding on the content and direction of worship and activities, so Stanley was immune from any potential strictures emanating from a higher authority. But he could not escape the censure of his own congregation. When he made it known at the pulpit that he was a supporter of the New Theology, there was instant controversy. True, many of the worshippers supported his stance, welcoming a liberal statement of Christianity and an acceptance of Biblical truth in accordance with modern scholarship. But the more conservative elements, including most of the diaconate, could not be placated. They tried to persuade Stanley to resign, but without success; then they resigned *en masse*.

Like father, like son. Daniel had walked away from two churches after disagreements with the deacons; now Stanley faced a similar situation. Advertisements in the church magazine were cancelled and then publication discontinued altogether. The remaining members faced an uphill struggle, not least in grappling with financial problems. The secretary, G. W. Steward, was pressured into resigning but remained loyal to my grandfather (there is a brass plaque to his memory in the existing church; Stanley didn't get one). As a symbolic act, Stanley gave himself a pay cut and reorganised the church, and for a while numbers swelled.

Although Stanley's own narrative of this time suggests that all was doom and gloom, there were light-hearted moments. The drama group performed plays by Henrik Ibsen and George Bernard Shaw, as well as less serious productions. Stanley took the opportunity to tread the boards again, receiving positive feedback although sometimes, having failed to memorise his part sufficiently, he improvised outrageously. In Ibsen's *The Pretenders*, for example, he read the entire part of the dying bishop beneath the bedclothes. At other times, he mischievously introduced stage subterfuge on the night, which caused the less experienced actors to panic. By way of revenge for a particular transgression, they devised a prank, introducing a new character to the drama to put Stanley off his tracks. But, impromptu, he handled the new element with aplomb. Other events included a Charles Dickens fair, which realised £153 (£16,000 in 2020) for repairs to the church, and picnics in Epping Forest, while the City Temple organist gave a recital and the literary society continued to flourish.

Perhaps, given Stanley's adherence to the New Theology and the importance it attached to the alleviation of hardship, it was only a matter of time before he declared himself a socialist and joined the ILP. He writes: 'It was natural that, having graduated in the University of Destitution, I should throw myself into the social movement. It was not for nothing that I had stood… with waifs and strays at coffee stalls… Revolt against my bourgeois surroundings was, under the circumstances, almost inevitable.' A group of church members who were already party members – among them the young and attractive Eva Slawson, who would become a leading actor in Stanley's story – led the way and he followed.

The discipline and rigid economic dogmas of the socialists, espoused by the likes of Sidney Webb and H. G. Wells, filled a gap left vacant by a church that was now tilting towards the undogmatic and even ungoverned. Attachment to the ILP also provided Stanley with the opportunity for developing powers of leadership, as well as for addressing open-air gatherings. He took to standing on the corner of both Hoe Street and High Street, Walthamstow, making passionate socialist speeches. More than once, on my research trips to the district, I imagined him standing there trying to make himself heard above the rattling of the trams.

More people – up to that point extremely loyal members – resigned from the church and joined other Congregational bodies. Apart from running away on ideological grounds, had they also detected a more provocative element in Stanley's addresses? He admits to adopting a teasing tone with which he sought to shock the more timid worshippers. He was also aware that the church, by abandoning previous theological positions that were relatively traditional, was now rudderless. He quickly tried to correct the imbalance by returning to some kind of orthodoxy. Whereupon, in turn, the more radical elements accused him of betrayal.

Certain progressive Christian thinkers exerted an influence on Stanley's thinking at this time. One such was Tolstoy with his non-violent resistance, simple life philosophy, striving for ethical perfection and adherence to the literal message of the Gospels. The Russian novelist's disdain for organised religion and patriotism, as well as his denunciation of materialism, were significant points of connection.

Towards the end of 1908 the *Christian Commonwealth* published a feature about Stanley, focusing to a large extent on his adventures on the other side of the Atlantic, but also making reference to the state of play in the East London church. It states:

The Rev. Stanley B. James has made a place for himself in Walthamstow, and a very distinct place it is… The bold words which [he] has preached have made him the centre of a somewhat fierce controversy… [He] is gathering around him a devoted band ready to stand shoulder to shoulder with him in the fight for God and humanity, for social and spiritual regeneration.

The *Walthamstow and Leyton Guardian* reprinted the article on 11 December, the day before my mother was born.

*   *   *

Among the postcards in the James family collection is a photograph of Dorothy Minto, a famous actress who had a string of prominent roles to her name. In the head and shoulders close-up she looks glamorous, alluring even. The reason for this arresting picture being in the archive is a mystery. She personally handwrote and sent the postcard to 'Mr and Mrs James with my love and a Happy Christmas 1908'.

The actress Dorothy Minto, friend of the James family

So, who was she exactly and how did my grandparents know her? The photograph is of her playing Flora in *The Duke's Motto* in 1908. She'd already starred as Sylvia in George Bernard Shaw's *The Philanderer*, Juliet in *Romeo and Juliet*, and the suffragette Ernestine Blunt in *Votes for Women!* by Elizabeth Robins – the first suffragist play to be performed on the London stage. My grandfather espoused suffragist causes and often preached in support of women's emancipation. Perhaps he and my grandmother went to the Royal Court to see *Votes for Women!* and went backstage to congratulate Minto – and that was the way they connected.

After seeing her in *Votes for Women!*, the reviewer from *The Clarion* – male, I assume – became all aflutter. 'Most fascinating of all the fascinating figures in this fascinating tableau,' he purrs, 'is pretty little Dorothy Minto as a young suffragette, a sweet and comely maid in neat, shop-girl attire, with a wisp of nut-brown hair straggling in attractive carelessness from under her toque. A wonderfully winning little figure in her childishness, her daintiness, her utter unconsciousness of self... So gracefully naive, so girlishly frail, so free from affectation and coquettishness.' The language is overblown in the style of the time. But, even conceding that stylistic inevitability, the review shows little regard for the suffragist themes the play explores.

When Minto, by then a member of the suffragist Actresses' Franchise League, sent that Christmas greeting, she had been married a year to a fellow actor and had a baby daughter by him. By 1913 she was living with another actor and in 1914 her husband filed for divorce, but he was killed at the Battle of the Somme. In 1921 she married and in 1927 there was a skirmish with the lord chamberlain who felt it necessary to inspect the pyjamas that she was wearing in P. G. Wodehouse's *Good Morning, Bill*. They were said to be a 'tight-fitting, black lace, filmy affair'. After scrutinising the costume, her admirer adjudged them fit for public viewing. The couple had no children and in 1928 her husband divorced her on grounds of infidelity. The National Portrait Gallery has numerous photographs of her.

Other possible, less innocent, reasons for the connection do come to mind. Minto was seemingly free with her favours. Although there is no evidence that her habitual infidelity touched Stanley in any way, with the benefit of hindsight it is possible to speculate: could this episode have been the first of other far more significant dalliances with women that would preoccupy my grandfather over the next ten years?

~ 10 ~
EAST ENDERS

At the time of that Christmas greeting from Dorothy Minto, one would have hoped that the Jameses were doting on the birth of their new daughter, 'little Kitty' – my mother, born 12 December 1908. Catherine Muriel James's entry into the drama reinforces the inescapable view that, to Stanley, his wife and children were largely walk-on parts in his own one-man show. My mother got no mention in any of his writings or letters, either at her birth or at almost any time afterwards. That meant I had little domestic material to draw on and it left me wishing that I had questioned her and her brothers and sisters more before they died. I wanted to know what those early years were really like. They were undoubtedly tough but just how tough? I had a suspicion that they were far more challenging to all concerned than has generally been acknowledged.

Given the lack of material about the family, one of my sources early on in my research was, of course, the Internet. My search regularly threw up references to my grandfather's books but nothing else of any import. It was becoming clear that I would have to make do with what my mother had once told me about her father: that he was a 'good husband and father'. I had virtually given up any hope of finding out anything more when one day I varied the search and googled 'Stanley James Rockies'. This time I was directed towards a book called *The Match Girl and the Heiress* by American

126

historian Seth Koven, published in 2014, more specifically to pages 321-22. When I read the contents, my jaw dropped open. I stared at the computer screen, unable to believe what I was reading. I stopped breathing.

Shaken, I read again: 'The signatory who most egregiously violated the spirit of their Christian revolutionary vow was Stanley James.' This vow was for the voluntary poverty manifesto. I read on: 'A man of roving ways and unsettled religious convictions, he had been a cowboy in the Canadian Rockies and a rail-riding hobo in the American West.' It had to be my grandfather.

When he returned to Britain, he assumed his father's Methodist pulpit in Wales, married, and started a family. He eventually drifted to London, apparently without his wife and children, where he worked for the Fellowship of Reconciliation, sometimes edited the 'Crusader' and delivered stirring pacifist socialist sermons to his Nonconformist Walthamstow congregation. He also grotesquely abused his ministerial authority to seduce idealistic vulnerable female congregants.

I was suspended, motionless, my brain whirring. If this was true, it had shattering implications. There was more: 'The diaries and letters of three lower-middle-class women, Ruth Slate, Eva Slawson, and Minna Simmons, record in painful graphic detail how James preached from his pulpit the "religion of love which must unite all" while using a small private room in the church to have sex with some of them.' There then followed an extract from a letter written by Minna to Ruth, in which she recounts how my grandfather seduced her.

I tried to focus. Did this mean that my grandfather was not the paragon of virtue, the man of faith, that my mother and many others had made him out to be? I needed to know. I emailed Seth in the US. Much to my surprise, he replied almost immediately: 'I tracked your grandfather quite extensively... He was a fascinating, restless, intelligent, passionate man with a keen sense of social justice and injustice... I have no doubt that it must have been shocking to read about him from the excerpt of my book. Best wishes, Seth Koven.'

I steadied myself. The author had clearly made some mistakes. Stanley had not assumed his father's Methodist pulpit in Wales – it was a Congregational pulpit and it was in Wimbledon. He moved to Devon and married; he came to London later but he didn't 'drift': he was appointed minister in Walthamstow and he came with Jess and the four children. About five mistakes already, then. How reliable was the rest of it? What were Koven's sources? How trustworthy was this historian? Did Stanley grotesquely abuse 'his ministerial authority to seduce idealistic vulnerable female congregants'? Did he use 'a small private room in the church to have sex with some of them'? Luckily, the answer lay close to hand. And it came in another book.

Koven's sole source for this background on my grandfather came from *Dear Girl*, edited by Tierl Thompson, which examines the lives of Ruth, Eva and Minna – all of whom knew my grandfather and were beautiful – through their letters and diaries. I immediately ordered it from Amazon. Here, in the actual words of the three women, would lie the facts. Unlike *The Match Girl and the Heiress*, this would be a trustworthy source. I was about to unravel the truth. I devoured the book from cover to cover. My largely uncritical view of my grandfather did indeed change dramatically, but the resulting image was far removed from, and infinitely more complex than, that of any sordid vestry scenes portrayed by Koven.

Ever one to explore all the options, and preferring face-to-face contact with the author if possible, I managed to track down Tierl Thompson. I told her by email what I was up to. To my surprise – and relief – she agreed to meet, even though *Dear Girl* had been written more than thirty years ago. We met for coffee at the British Museum and shyly shook hands. We eyed each other up. She was softly spoken but made every word count. 'It must have been a shock to you to find that out about your grandfather,' she said. 'But he has a lot to answer for.'

I knew that Thompson had been in the vanguard of women's politics in the 1980s: what the tabloid press would call a hard-line feminist. She had never seen a photograph of Stanley before. I showed her some. 'My God, he's handsome!' We chatted on, carefully. We liked each other and arranged to meet again.

Thompson's book had started out as a play of the same name performed by the Women's Theatre Group in 1983–84. The material also formed the basis of a seventeen-minute radio dramatisation broadcast as *Friend to Friend* by the BBC on 25 July 1984. So, Stanley's name (he was referred to in the play as 'Mr James') had been heard on the radio and none of the family had ever known.

The source for Thompson's book were ten boxes of material – mostly letters and diaries written by Ruth Slate, Eva Slawson and Minna Simmons – now housed in the Women's Library of the London School of Economics. She had had unique access, through a family connection, to Ruth's hoard of papers accumulated throughout her life. For months, Thompson processed these documents in the basement of Ruth's former house in Blackheath, London, some thirty years after her death. *Dear Girl* constitutes a selection of the hundreds of documents that exist. My grandfather is mentioned forty times. But because Thompson was focusing largely on the relationship between the three women, Stanley plays a minor part. I was intrigued to know if there were other references to him – perhaps some letters written by him – in the collection. I made arrangements to join the LSE library and spent many days meticulously researching the boxes. What I found fundamentally changed the nature of the book I would write. I was no longer relying on his own books and odd scraps of photos and papers. Old journalistic intuition told me that this was a 'story' that had to be told for a general audience, not just as a record for a few family members to pore over in years to come.

* * *

So, who were these East End women? Minna does not come into the picture until later, but Ruth and Eva had become close friends in the early years of the century, frequently attending the same political meetings and suffragist rallies, and going to hear the same speakers. Ruth, who was a clerk in a grocery firm, lived with her parents at 90 Carlyle Road, Manor Park, and Eva, who was illegitimate, lived with her aunt at 175 Albert Road, Leyton and worked as a shorthand typist at a legal firm in Hoe Street, Walthamstow. The railways and tram service were well developed so the women, both in their late twenties, could meet frequently, despite often being worn out by their humdrum jobs. Neither was in the best of health and both were far from well off. They were brought up along strict religious lines in the Nonconformist tradition but gradually lost patience with orthodoxy. Theirs was a passionate friendship and the record of their lives is contained in their diaries and letters to each other. Each was adventurous in her own way, driven by the desire to seek a better life not just for themselves but for what they saw as the downtrodden in society at large. Sex and gender issues were also a preoccupation, a source of worry even but, constricted by the mores of the time, the women remained inexperienced.

Eva Slawson, whose diaries recorded in detail the goings-on at Trinity

Ruth Slate, one of Walthamstow's Christian revolutionaries

Ruth and Eva often met at Liverpool Street station and spent hours enthusiastically exchanging ideas – usually earnest ones about radical political campaigns, feminism and social justice. Ruth writes in her diary on 30 January 1909: 'There is a certain Congregational minister, a much persecuted man, whom she [Eva] has recently been going to hear who I think must be a very remarkable man.' Eventually she went along to Trinity herself and writes: 'I liked Rev. James greatly and wished I could record something of his sermon.'

Clearly, Eva was already taken with Stanley's preaching and for many years she regularly reported back to Ruth on the content of his Sunday sermon. In a letter written on 7 April 1909, we get an insight into Stanley's version of radical Christianity:

[Mr James] said if he wanted to pull down the little cottage of faith in which he had dwelt for so long, it was because God had been building for us a glorious palace, hung with masterpieces. If he wanted to take the mystic halo from the head of Christ, it was because he wanted to make him more real and human to us and to clear away the harmful mists. He could not now teach us that God made the world in six days because we now know from science that those days were immense periods and that God is still making this world. It is cowardly, said he, to refuse or to fear to read God's wondrous book of nature. He who knew himself to be in communion with the eternal was absolutely free to wander through all the realms of science and knowledge sure that the truth would finally be made clear to him.

Shortly after that, Ruth writes in her diary about Fenner Brockway knocking on her door. He was a member of the Progressive League and a friend of Stanley's, as well as being a future anti-war activist and Labour MP for Leyton. He was there to persuade her to join the ILP and, since Eva was already a member, Ruth had no hesitation in signing up.

In 1910, Walthamstow was forced into a by-election after its MP, Sir John Simon, was appointed solicitor general, an anomalous tradition dating back to the eighteenth century stipulating that any MP appointed to a ministerial post had to seek re-election. This largely working-class commuter suburb

(Walthamstow was poor in places but it didn't have slums) had expanded faster than almost any other urban area in the country, making the electorate one of the largest in England. The number of voters had nearly quadrupled, from eleven thousand in 1885 to thirty-nine thousand in 1910 and, for the first time, campaigning had to take place in the evenings after workers had returned from their jobs in central London.

The by-election coincided with a recent court case – the Osborne Judgement – which had centred on Britain's labour laws and whether unions were justified in automatically collecting levies from their members specifically to fund the Labour Party. The case had been brought by Walter Osborne, a porter at Clapton railway station and branch secretary of the Amalgamated Society of Railway Servants, who had argued that unions did not have that right because the money was used to pay socialist MPs' salaries without the union members' consent. He won the case but the issue rumbled on and because he lived in Walthamstow it spilled over into the by-election, making the campaign particularly acrimonious. Osborne supported the Liberal cause and therefore backed Sir John Simon. But the ILP and the Social Democratic Federation, of which the social reformer William Morris was a member, tried to force Simon to support their more radical measures, in which they sought the reversal of the Osborne judgement. They were joined soon after by women's suffrage groups, who called on electors to keep the Liberal candidate out.

Demonstration by suffragettes during the 1910 Walthamstow by-election.
Credit: East London & West Essex Guardian Series

The James children in 1910. From left: Eric, Jessie, Bob, Phyllis and Kitty

Stanley chaired a campaign meeting in the community hall at Trinity on 13 October, while the women organised hundreds of street-corner meetings and processions. The issues at stake in the by-election in many ways made it a microcosm of the political preoccupations of Britain at the time. Nonconformist ministers – one of them being Stanley – banded together and submitted a joint nomination paper in support of Simon, who was re-elected with a slightly increased majority. His victory parade through the streets of Walthamstow was a mile long.

In October 1911, David Lloyd George was due to give a talk at the Whitefield's Tabernacle in Tottenham Court Road. Prior to the event, women's groups were urging him to give his views on the Conciliation Bill for women's suffrage, and Stanley added his weight to the cause by publishing an open letter to the chancellor in the newspaper *Votes for Women*.

Stanley's new-found political engagement meant that he was still concerning himself very little with the family, but they always took a summer holiday away together. My mother told me that they used to go to Mersea Island, in Essex, where my grandfather's sister Muriel lived with her husband, Leonard Milton. My mother referred to an incident on the beach when she was a toddler which could have had disastrous consequences for her. Her older brothers and sisters, at the end of the day, went back to their holiday home without her. Once in the house, they realised they'd forgotten her and rushed back. Luckily, she was still sitting on the sand intact, so they scooped her up into their arms and delivered her home safely. I don't know if they told Jess, or if Stanley ever knew of the incident.

* * *

Despite the growing interest Stanley was taking in politics, the church remained the hub. In late 1911 Eva writes to Ruth:

> *Mr James said in his sermon that after passing through a terrible period of agnosticism, materialism and struggle he now saw in the distance the peaks of the mountains of God gleaming in the sunlight of love and beauty. I feel I benefit so very greatly, Ruth dear, through knowing Mr James. I cannot express how healthy and uplifting I feel his influence has been.*

Minna, who was married with three children and lived at 16 Grosvenor Park Road, Walthamstow, now came onto the scene as a result of meeting Eva at Trinity services, being first mentioned in Eva's diary on 7 December 1911. There is less of her material available – letters to Eva and Ruth and poems for the most part – but when she wrote, she wrote with down-to-earth passion and vigour. In her earthiness and more elemental, headstrong nature, she was the foil to Ruth and Eva. Together the women created a powerful trio and my grandfather ended up playing an important part in each of their lives.

From 1912 we get a more rounded picture of Stanley through their eyes as they start to focus on his personality rather than the content of his sermons. In the church at large he was becoming the subject of gossip. In March, Eva writes that Minna thought that he was very nervous because at times she could feel it in his hands. Not long after, Minna tells Eva she was glad Eva hadn't been at church last Sunday because Stanley had preached one of the saddest sermons she had ever heard. And his address on 'The Spiritual and the Material' was so deep, very few people could follow him.

Eva and Stanley were becoming closer. On 12 June she writes in her diary about the time she was cooking lunch at Minna's when my grandfather arrived at the door and called out: 'Is Miss Slawson here?' In a fit of shyness,

Eva retreated to the kitchen, whereupon Minna called her back into the front room, which meant that she confronted Stanley with a pan of sizzling sausages in one hand. Flustered, she said she wasn't sure whether they were done or not. 'Mr James said he would tell me. So together we lent over the pan,' she writes breathlessly. Stanley had called about arrangements for a future church event and he sat smoking and chatting while Eva ate her sausages. He then asked her if he could walk to her office with her and she agreed. They discussed the books they were reading. Eva writes: 'Oh God, how my nature is torn: the human in me cries out, "Must I pay this price? Is it always to be mine to give – oh, how I crave to be the receiver of some deep and special love!" But this is weakness.'

All three women wrote freely because they naturally assumed their words were confidential. A twist of history has meant that I am able to draw back the Edwardian curtain and look into their – and my grandfather's – private lives. After the initial euphoria I had experienced about making these discoveries became less charged, I began to ask other searching questions about my own motivation. What right had I – or anyone else for that matter – to dwell on their innermost thoughts? It was a reconfiguration of the journalistic question about privacy and intrusion. Thompson's *raison d'etre* was clear: women's voices, particularly from the working classes, were rarely heard at that time. Her work is a unique and valuable document and the level of intrusion is negligible.

I, on the other hand, was largely looking voyeuristically at how the three women interacted with – and became increasingly intimate with – my grandfather, a minister and by now a father of five. He certainly never thought that his surreptitious visits to some of the more attractive members of his congregation would ever be documented. Unlike Thompson in her book, I was not sure that mine served any useful purpose other than it was, perhaps, interesting and that it was true. I had no real answer. I was impelled by the twin dynamics of being fascinated and telling the truth about my grandfather.

By now Eva and Minna were sitting together at church so they jointly heard Stanley's sermon on 29 June in which he preached against the militancy of the women's movement, with continual use of the word 'martyr'. He pointed out the immense powers and possibilities of the movement (of which he was a fervent supporter), but deprecated the deliberate provocation of those in authority, action he termed 'immoral'. After the service he came up to Eva and Minna and asked them what they thought of his ideas. They said they agreed with him. 'What a brave, tender, sensitive soul he possesses,' writes Eva. 'He makes his stand for the truth as he sees it.'

I wonder if my grandmother was aware of this growing intimacy between Stanley and Eva. Perhaps the disappointment of feeling that he was unable to share his thoughts with Jess was taking its toll and he genuinely sought solace from those of a like mind. Although he was forty-two, his preoccupation with current ideas and trends made the company of those much younger than himself more to his liking. Could it also have been that young, impressionable minds were more likely to entertain his challenging ideas than older members of the congregation?

Part of the reason for his frequent popping round to 16 Grosvenor Park Road to see Eva and Minna should be seen in this light, whatever other motives there may have been. On 2 July Eva writes in her diary:

Mr James was feeling the need of sympathy. He lays great stress now upon the Church, its importance and government. I said how anxious I was that as a church we should not become over-organised – we had been exceedingly free, dipping into many social and intellectual problems. Was there not a danger now of orthodoxy and over-organisation? Mr James stated that he did not attempt to please all. I had a queer feeling that Mr James (whom I love and honour) could, if he chose, be almost tyrannical... [He] said he had felt quite unable to preach on Sunday and that he had such a troublesome temper.

My grandmother was pregnant with John at this time, and Eva and Minna discussed how she would manage. The plan, according to Minna, was for the four older children – Phyllis, Bob, Jessie and Eric – to attend boarding school. Phyllis and Jessie ended up going to Milton Mount College, Gravesend in Kent, while Bob and Eric were sent to Caterham School, Surrey, both being establishments for the children of Congregational ministers. Even Phyllis, the oldest, was only eleven, while Eric was just eight. My mother Kitty was not yet five, so she escaped incarceration – for the time being. Eva was surprised by the news, saying that the children were so little. She believed it was important for children to rub shoulders with other children but that they needed the influence of home and the loving care of mother and father, too. On the other hand, she reasoned, the children being away was probably good for Jess's health.

Shortly afterwards, Stanley called 'and had a delightful little talk with Minna', commenting to her that 'there were three kinds of minister – those who frightened people into goodness, those who proved the wisdom and policy of goodness and those who made people want to be good – it was the latter he wished to become'.

Were people beginning to gossip about his continual visits to Minna's house, where he knew he was likely to catch Eva during her lunch hour? A woman in the congregation apparently asked Eva why Stanley was forever asking after her. 'I told her that some years ago he had been a very real friend to me, and I thought that accounted for the interest he sometimes showed,' Eva diplomatically replied.

On 13 October 1913, John – christened John Ivor Pulsford – was born, making it six children in eleven years. The happy occasion passed without mention from my grandfather, who clearly didn't see it as a 'spiritual event' or one that impinged on his interior life. The rumblings of dissatisfaction with my grandfather as minister continued. One member of the congregation complained that Mr James had 'gone back', adding that he must be a lonely man. Eva defended him, saying that 'I think [he] seems to be passing through a place of spiritual insight.' And in January 1914 at an evening class a woman referred to him as a rotter and said it was terrible that he should have upset Trinity the way he had. He should, she said, have started a church elsewhere. Once again Eva defended Stanley, saying that he was right to stay as he regarded his work there as part of a reformation coming from within the church.

At the beginning of February, Minna's husband Will, a lorry driver, died from consumption, leaving her virtually penniless, without any occupation. Stanley made a special visit to offer his sympathy, Eva commenting that he was always a comfort in such circumstances. On 6 March, Minna's fourth child, Joan, was born, and shortly afterwards Eva moved in with her to help out. Their friendship became deeper, and Thompson is in no doubt that it turned into a sexual relationship: 'For Eva, there was a more intense and physically passionate relationship with Minna,' she writes. 'The experience of living in what she called the "love-atmosphere" of Minna's house was exhilarating and she began to expand her ideas on physical union and relationships generally.' They shared the same bed, held each other and frequently expressed their love. Yet they seem not to have regarded it as a sexual relationship as such, merely intimacy taken to the limit. Minna had already declared herself to have 'urning' tendencies, a contemporary term – now obsolete – for a homosexual. They also both held Edward Carpenter, one of the first advocates of same-sex liaisons and a poet of democracy, in high regard, as indeed did my grandfather. With Carpenter, who has been dubbed 'the gay godfather of the British left', counting Walt Whitman among his friends, it is no surprise that Stanley and his Trinity followers should include him in their pantheon of revolutionaries.

At this point, the trio lost the presence of Ruth, who moved full time to Woodbrooke, a Quaker settlement for religious and social study near Birmingham. Having managed to procure a scholarship, she threw herself into the course, feeling her horizons rapidly expanding, while mixing with others of like mind. She kept in close contact by letter with Eva and Minna.

One evening Stanley made a surprise visit to Minna's house. Eva describes how he strode into the kitchen to see Minna struggling into a blouse and herself similarly dishevelled – she had just taken off her lace top and sleeves to wash them. They all laughed and settled down for a chat. She thanked Stanley for his Sunday evening sermon, telling him what an inspiration the whole service had been. He explained to the women how he had grown towards a more spiritual outlook compared to the strong social tenor of the early days.

'I told him I thought he had been extremely brave so to grow and develop before his people,' Eva remarks in her diary. 'He said it had certainly needed courage... this visit was the star of the day to me.'

Sometimes Stanley invited Eva into the vestry for a talk. On one occasion she records that she spent an hour listening to him talking about the books he had recently read, as well as about his life in America, particularly his time as a hobo. She asked him if he ever wished to return to North America. He replied: 'Almost always I am wishing it.' This was a man with a wife and six children, who had spent much of his time bemoaning his lonely life in the foothills. In another of those chats, he shared with Eva the idea that some cases of conversion were caused by falling in love and other influences outside the strictly religious. Was this flirtation masquerading as spiritual engagement? Meanwhile, she continued to feel that Stanley's sermons were for her alone. One of his comments made a particular impression on her: 'Let us plunge deeply into life developing all our powers, giving all – let us not count the cost.'

A sense of urgency, desperation even, became a regular feature of Stanley's preaching. He now started taking an interest in Christian mysticism, as had his great uncle, the Reverend John Pulsford. He admits in his own writing that the church was lurching towards a 'harsh secularism' and he saw this new venture as a necessary corrective. 'In my extremity I turned to mysticism and the classics of devotion,' he writes. 'The cultivation of the interior life, I imagined, might proceed without reference to dogma or sacraments and did not need the guidance of a visible and authoritative Church.'

The mystics he read and preached on were Baron von Hügel, St Francis of Assisi, St Catherine of Siena, St Teresa, Lady Julian, St John of the Cross and the contemporary Evelyn Underhill, whose book *Mysticism* was one of the most widely read Christian works in the early years of the twentieth century. For Underhill, intuition and instinct were more important than reason; and a distrust of institutionalised religion and a belief in pacifism followed. Her writings drew on the poetry of the Indian mystic Rabindranath Tagore, whose work Stanley also soaked up in intermittent bursts.

Eva herself, while welcoming much of what a mystical approach to belief offered, was unhappy with its 'lack of vigour'. And when Stanley's subject was St Augustine, she feels that 'Mr James does not give of his best... because he does not read of his subject enough – the addresses are fragmentary, disconnected and uninteresting... I am with [him] in his deepening spiritual life, but I feel that there is something wrong with the development of the church.' The growing disquiet among his followers was echoed by Minna, who marks 'Mr James's tendency to orthodoxy'.

It was the summer of 1914 and tensions were growing in central Europe. It was time to take stock. Stanley was aware that he was a very different person from the man who had stepped up to the Walthamstow pulpit eight years previously. 'Not having found any satisfactory anchorage, I was at the mercy of every wind that blew and, not altogether involuntarily, became an easy prey to the immediate environment of the moment,' he writes in *The Adventures of a Spiritual Tramp*. 'The spectre of war hung in the darkening skies.'

After reading the religious journals for several weeks, Stanley had become 'filled with disgust' at the 'timid unwavering attitude' of the church establishment towards the impending conflict. 'So far I had not heard one voice raised against this seeming surrender,' he writes.

He describes how he tried to recover the power of prayer so that he could help to avert the crisis that threatened. Meanwhile a note of passionate urgency and almost hysterical entreaty had entered into his preaching. He was like a sailor who sees a storm advancing and realises he has no chart or compasses and that the engines have broken down. He even wondered whether the suppressed Catholic in him was making it impossible for him to share in the current hysterical patriotism. But he argued that passion had to be met with passion and the refusal to join in the hatred had itself to take on a more militant character. In that way he concluded that he became an aggressive and dogmatic pacifist. But for now, he managed to keep his new conviction under wraps. It was one thing to harbour private beliefs, quite another to announce them to the world at large, particularly as a pastor. He pondered how this should play out in the public arena of Trinity.

* * *

On 1 August 1914, the Saturday before the outbreak of war on 4 August, Jess and the children travelled for their annual holiday to the Essex coast. Stanley stayed in Walthamstow for the Sunday services. Eva attended both morning and evening service and heard two sermons by Stanley in which he spoke of the possibility of God having lessons to teach all nations by the impending war. He went on to say that the world had been blessed with prosperity, but then asked how nations had chosen to use it. Answer: to build dreadnoughts and prepare for war. If the money had been spent on social, intellectual and artistic reform and advancement, he argued, how different things would now be.

At the evening service Stanley was scheduled to speak on Wordsworth's poetry. His initial thought was to abandon the idea and to speak out about his opposition to the war. But he backed off because of the ructions it might cause before he was fully prepared to face the consequences. So, in the end he did talk of 'Grasmere rather than Germany'. He admits in his autobiography that, given the impending conflict, his sermon had been a farce.

After the service, Stanley asked Eva and another member of the congregation, a Mr Jones, if they would like to come back to his house. Eva accepted, commenting in her diary: 'My heart leapt.'

Once in the house Mr James knocked up a simple supper and, according to Eva, was his old, delightful, impetuous self. He said how often he had longed for something closer, more intimate than ordinary church fellowship, something in the nature of an engagement between man and woman, or woman and woman, and man and man that could be relied upon, even though separated, for fellowship and inspiration. Why couldn't they form such a fellowship or brotherhood now – a kind of church within the church. Then, Eva explains:

Mr James said to me, 'Do you know I was just going to call you Eva – Miss Slawson seems so formal after tonight.' I replied, 'Well, call me Eva, then – all my friends, everyone, does – I should like you to do so.' Nevertheless, I was startled when, later on in the evening, looking through his books, I asked him if he would be wanting a certain volume, he answered, 'No, Eva.' I experienced such a thrill of joy, such a sense of added kinship and friendship and reverence as I shall never forget.

The three of them talked that evening about Roman Catholicism, its shortcomings rather than its strengths. Then, as they became more at ease, their impromptu heart-to-heart session became more confessional, each sharing some intimate secret about themselves – Mr Jones about his loneliness, Eva about a vision and dream she'd had, and Stanley about a woman he once knew who had been utterly 'changed by trouble'. Not only that, but Eva slips in that Stanley said he had been engaged to this woman. Who was she? Eva concludes:

I can write no more of this wondrous evening – we were upon the mountain tops. Mr James said he should think of it all as he rode [cycled] through the night about 50 or 60 miles into the country... I found Minna waiting up for me – we hastened to bed, but sleep was not for me. I sat upright in bed for a long time, gazing at the moon, and thinking of many things. Then I thought of Mr James riding through the still night and I laid me down with prayers that God would bless and inspire him and keep us all in his strength and love.

Stanley writes of this dead-of-night dash to the coast on the eve of the war:

That ride along the unlit Essex roads, past sleeping villages whose inmates must surely be dreaming of battlefields, and into the sudden glare of silent towns where lonely policemen eagerly questioned the night-rider for the latest news seems now to belong to some other life. It gave me my last fleeting glimpse of the England that is for ever gone.

During those weeks away on holiday he thought long and hard about whether he should announce his anti-war beliefs from the pulpit. The more he studied the New Testament the clearer his thoughts became. He decried the way the churches and the state were being swept along by a tide of national feeling. He felt his opposition hardening and he decided to return to Trinity utterly committed to the pacifist cause. Soon after the conflict started, he observes:

Now the environment itself was shaken to its foundations. The men who for half their lifetime had been going up to the city by the 8.45 were donning khaki and practising bayonet-drill. Food prices mounted up, and comfortable citizens learned what it was to go without their customary luxuries. Barriers of class were falling in every direction. The shibboleths of the sects sounded remote and unreal. Century-old traditions vanished in a night.

For once, the seismic changes that now beckoned were not of Stanley's making and were beyond his control. Nothing would ever be quite the same again, neither for him nor for the world at large.

~ 11 ~
ZEPPELINS OVER WALTHAMSTOW

Searchlights picked out the sinister shape of the machine of death as it moved almost imperceptibly across the night sky. The zeppelin floated over north London and then dropped its load of bombs on the houses below, killing ten people. This was the terrifying vision of the first attack by what became known as the 'baby killers' in the early years of the war. It was a new and frightening intrusion for the people of Walthamstow and the backdrop to my grandfather's story for the next four years.

Thanks to Eva, we have a direct link to the sermons Stanley made on his return from holiday. On 6 September 1914 he wondered what the result would be if a nation refused to fight and was actively kind to its enemies. Whatever the answer, he maintained that the British should back peace, not nationalism, and try to see the whole matter from a Christ-like perspective. The testing time had come to stand together for the kingdom of the future. The war was a crime and not part of a plan, as other churches believed. While Eva agreed that this was the right approach, others at Trinity were distinctly uneasy, believing that such a stance would actually encourage more aggressive military acts. Using the text, 'Wherefore come out from among them, and be ye separate'. Stanley pointed out that Christ stood outside the nationalist movement of his time.

Later that autumn, Stanley delivered a lecture that was, according to Eva, a '*tour de force*' and saw him at his passionate best. 'The whole address was marvellous,' she writes in her diary. '[He] referred to the national situation: we are the melting pot. The progress of science [has] brought the world practically under one roof but this kind of progress will never unify humanity… It must be the religion of love, the religion of the spirit which must unite all.'

The three women were regularly writing to each other with news of the war as it affected their parts of London. Zeppelin attacks were a constant source of worry, particularly to Eva living in Leyton. On another Sunday, Stanley took a visual image with which everyone was by now familiar – the searchlight – suggesting that half the danger of an evil disappears when light is shone on it. Then he threw out a challenge, asking worshippers if they were justified in allowing the evil of war to become part of life.

East Londoners lived in fear of zeppelin bombs, nicknamed 'the baby killers'

Stanley's oldest child, Phyllis – then twelve years old – remembers in the chapter that she contributed to the history of Trinity, that a resolution was sent from the church to the government against compulsory military service. The church also contributed to the Belgian relief fund and sent help to Britain's unemployed. Turning her attention to the wider effect of her father's words from the pulpit, she commented that the tenets of pacifism attracted new sympathisers, but also weakened the church, with numbers being further depleted. Finances – as usual – were at a low ebb. The deacons, who had been re-elected *en bloc* for the duration of the war, realised the precariousness of the situation but they dealt bravely with the perennial question of heating and abolished the system of pew rents.

A 'come to church' campaign was inaugurated, and a League of Young Worshippers formed.

Later, reflecting on these days, Stanley recalls how 'when an intimate friend, the son of a famous general and himself not unknown in Irish history, asked me my reasons [for adopting a pacifist stance], I replied that any stick was good enough with which to beat a dog'. He meant that given the current order of things one didn't have to be too particular about one's choice of weapon. The friend was Captain Jack White who, for a short time, played an important part in Stanley's life. Stanley says that his pacifist position had deeper motives. At bottom it was an effort to bear witness to the supranational and international character of Christianity. Identification of the national cause with the religion of Jesus Christ seemed to him to be full of danger and his attitude, while it looked towards the universalism of Christianity, was consistent with that Nonconformist tradition which had always protested against an identification of the church with the state.

My grandfather, looking back ten years later, takes the blame for being myopic about his pacifism. He said his preaching was too one-sided and it was wrong to speak in idealistic terms of love for one's enemy when the sons, brothers and husbands of the congregation were being killed. In his defence, he argued that the Nonconformist attitude of scorn towards the conscientious objector was a clear repudiation of its own principles in which liberty of conscience was of paramount importance. Every week military tribunals were considering the cases of men who refused to fight, the details of each hearing being reported in minute detail in the *Walthamstow and Leyton Guardian* along with the week's casualties.

Eva and Minna seem to have had an increasing number of discussions about Stanley, reaching the conclusion that it was time for him to go. They thought they had had the best of him and his preaching, which now lacked the quality of earlier years. They said that if he had branched out for a bolder, freer church two or three years previously, he might have retained that inspirational power, although they both recognised his struggles and difficulties. On one occasion Eva writes in her diary that she had started the day full of enthusiasm but had ended it depressed in her minister, adding that fear had come into his life. She couldn't help feeling that the church had become much more ordinary and she longed for the old days, the old fire and enthusiasm. Anything rather than charitable respectability.

In a letter to Ruth she says there was so much that was dark and difficult at that time. One day she had gone into the vestry and was startled by the suffering in Stanley's face, saying that he seemed far away from everybody while talking softly of the transcendence of Christ. He said that the crisis in the church was not only one of finance and attendance but of spirit. Spiritual atrophy seemed to have settled over the congregation. On 1 February 1915, she writes in her diary:

> *I had just begun my lunch… when a knock came at the door and in walked Mr James… He wished he could introduce more form and ritual into the church service and set prayers in which all might join, so that the people need not be at the mercy of a minister's moods. He referred a good deal to the Roman Catholic religion and with evident favour… I could not help feeling the great change in Mr James – the old dear warm personality is there, breaking through in flashes; but oh! the crust of formalism which is growing up around him! Has he not a tendency to run an idea to death? For instance, to symbolise everything would be wearisome. As to ritual – I love all that enriches and ennobles life, but it must be from a conscious desire and choice. I think if it were imposed on me, I should long to break loose from forms and ceremonies. I feel the time will come when Mr James will break away from Nonconformity. Then he will either take to the life of the tramp teacher – or will it be Roman Catholicism that will claim him? I felt very disturbed after parting from Mr James.*

* * *

Eva was reluctantly persuaded to become superintendent of the church's Girls' League and Women's Conference. Every Wednesday evening, they would typically listen to stories from her, recite poetry, sing, dance, or do gymnastics. Eva, ever modest about her abilities, was often downcast in the belief that she wasn't doing a good job. But evidence suggests otherwise: the girls loved her. She records how on one occasion, as she entered the room, 'Jessie James cried: "Oh, it's Eva Slawson", and she and Phyllis slipped their arms through mine.' Another week she writes in her diary: 'I enjoyed the League this evening – Mr James looked in upon me and his daughters (including little Kitty) were with us. The girls were darlings. I told them an Indian story and they seemed just spell-bound... at the finish the girls suggested titles for the story.' And at another meeting:

Such a delightful time at the League this evening. And my meeting proved a great success and a good gathering of girls – Winnie, Kitty and Chrissie recited and sang well. Mr James told the story of the telegraph pole, which learned to sing the song of service. I would like to see the story published.

Phyllis and Jessie are my aunts, of course. And little Kitty is my mother, aged seven. When I read this, in Eva's handwriting, in the hushed confines of the Women's Library at the LSE, I let out an involuntary gasp. Then tears started to form in my eyes. It was a palpable connection to my mother, all the more endearing for being so unexpected. This young woman for a few hours each week was guardian to my mother, and thought that what she wrote, 103 years before I laid eyes on it, would never be read by another soul. Hardly less extraordinary was the fact that she was a beautiful woman who loved my grandfather, with every indication that her feelings were reciprocated. The poignancy was double-layered by the realisation that a short distance away my grandmother was probably busy with some household chore, unaware that her husband was paying far more attention to a presentable woman in his congregation than he was to either herself or his daughters.

In June 1915 there is another insight into the James family drama. After a Sunday service, a group of worshippers went to a nearby garden to admire the early summer flowers. Just as they were leaving, Stanley ran up, saying that Jess was standing further down the road and had been taken ill. She was suffering in the last days of her pregnancy with David, her seventh baby. She recovered and David was born on 14 June.

The church services were now taking on a more ritualised flavour, frequently opening with an anthem sung by the choir, then the chanting of the Lord's Prayer. One of the congregation joked that when the change first happened, he looked around for the incense. Eva records how Stanley told her of his rambles in the Essex countryside. When she told him that she had been reading Dante, he commented that he had sometimes thought of lecturing on the life of the Italian poet but the romance was so sensual that he decided not to. On other occasions when Stanley called at Minna's house, Eva was happy to drop all she was doing rather than miss the opportunity of spending some time with him. 'Now everything might go to the four winds of heaven for me rather than forfeit a visit from Mr James,' she writes. Another Sunday Eva writes: 'I could have wept as the service closed – Mr James raised his voice to hoarseness – at the end he remarked to me: "We hardly shake hands now, do we, Eva?" Just the little intimate touch, making me feel our nearest even although my mind was clouded.'

* * *

By now, Ruth had spent two years at Woodbrooke. It had been an immensely positive experience for her, providing the intellectual stimulus and progressive vision that she longed for. Her descriptions inspired Eva, too, and in the summer of 1915, Ruth managed to secure a scholarship there for her friend. In the weeks before her departure in October, Eva shared her fears with Stanley about leaving her relatives in the Leyton house on their own. Above all, she worried that there would be more air raids, but Stanley said he didn't think there would be another one on Leyton. Leyton and Walthamstow were Eva's life and she seldom travelled up to London, unlike Ruth. She hated crowds and was worried about what the future in Birmingham might hold. She writes in her diary that she recalled her life at the chapel and all Stanley had been to her – strengthening her and her faith. On the one hand she looked forward to her new life; on the other she was worried about what challenges she would face.

She writes to Ruth: 'I had a wondrous evening with Mr James at his home – one of those rare and beautiful experiences difficult to describe. I seemed to live in another world for some days afterwards… such times are foretastes of heaven and of Walt Whitman's vision.' In her diary she gives even greater vent to her feelings:

Mr James asked me to come to his home this evening. He said that his feeling for me had been of a special nature – more like that of

*a brother for a sister. He had always felt he could come and tell
me everything. Some people and some friendships one didn't mind
passing out of one's life, but he did not wish me to pass out of his
life. He asked me to write to him and said he would write to me.
He wished there had been more opportunity for our friendship –
to meet, to know me – now that I was going, he felt all this. I felt
overwhelmed with gratitude for the gift of this noble friendship. I
spent the night in a state of ecstasy.*

At first, she found the challenging learning regime at Woodbrooke not to
her liking, but eventually she settled and flourished. She records how when
she felt worn out she would gather those dear to her into her innermost heart.
And, at the end of the day, she would think of her connection to Stanley,
recalling the talks she had had with him, of the flashes of self-revelation
which had sometimes escaped him, and the need he felt for sympathy in the
outside world. 'It may be in my power to supply a little of that, although I
am only one little atom in the big world,' she writes.

The periods of tiredness that had been affecting Eva for a number of
years were growing in intensity and frequency. It was a sign that her
undetected diabetes was worsening. Because she was immensely stoic,
she hardly ever complained, so none of her friends had any inkling of
just how serious her condition was. Her health fluctuated – one day she
complains in her diary of throbbing headaches but the next day they
cleared, and she was feeling fine. But, in the early months of the following
year, she deteriorated. Still, she writes in a letter to some friends that the
current term at Woodbrooke had meant a tremendous amount to her and
that she was growing in self-confidence. She looks forward to returning
to Walthamstow reinvigorated and ready for battle. 'There is so much I
just *long* to help in – so much evil to combat – so many ideals to try to
bring into being!' she writes.

On 27 February, however, she wrote what was to be her last letter to Ruth.
She died in Birmingham on 4 March 1916, a long way from her friends
and beloved East End. It was, of course, a complete shock to everyone.

After Eva's death, Minna wrote her friend a letter, knowing that she
would never read it. She, Ruth, Stanley and one or two others travelled to
Woodbrooke for her funeral and to collect her belongings. Minna writes:

*When we were leaving you my love, such a blaze of sunlight streamed
down from the sky – it seemed as if even the sun loved you and
wanted to shed its beams around you for the last time. We had tea
afterwards, walked round the grounds. I couldn't help laughing to see
Mr James walking round in a pair of canary-coloured slippers. We
parted from Woodbrooke and caught the train – Cecil and Mr James
nearly missed it. We were laden with your parcels and I'm sure you
came back with us. We were all so jolly and just laughed.*

Later Minna wrote a poem expressing her grief:

Dear God, didst thou need my love
That thou should take her from me?
I cannot feel 'twas good for me
To be so rent in twain,
Sometimes she seems so far away
Sometimes so near.
At times the fears so endless
At times a moment.
Abide with me sweet Eva
In death, even as thou didst in life
This is my heart's cry.

Ruth, more reflective than Minna, wrote a fitting memorial to her in the
Woodbrooke Chronicle:

*I feel my power of expression too limited to give more than a
glimpse of her beautiful spirit... Those who knew her intimately
know how her lovely faculties were blossoming out in the new
world (to her) of released energies and opportunities... The motive
power of her life was love – enriched by a profound intelligence,
and a sympathy wonderful in its depth and perception. Shy, and
fearful of obtruding herself on the notice of others, I feel that... the
little fellowship of friends she has left in London know from long
experience the power she possessed to inspire others and to radiate
a spirit of goodwill and joy in high endeavour.*

Eva's quiet influence at Trinity should not be underestimated. Over the years she had grown to be a leader of the worshippers representing the radical arm of the church, so my mother and my aunts would have been saddened, too. For Stanley, whatever suppressed romantic feelings there may have been on both sides, she was someone with whom he could share his innermost thoughts.

~ 12 ~

BURN MY LETTERS!

Eva's gentle spirit was the hidden glue that bound Trinity's band of radicals together. She was the lynchpin holding in place Ruth's idealism, Minna's passion and Stanley's deep need to be revered and loved. She had performed her part so perfectly and imperceptibly that when she died her friends not only mourned her passing but soon found that their own lives were turned upside down and more primitive forces released, with destructive power. It is only by a bizarre chain of events that the truth emerged. Ruth Slate kept all her own, Eva's and Minna's writings, including nine letters to her from Stanley. Her treasure trove of heart-to-heart confessions would have rotted away in a Blackheath basement if it hadn't been for Thompson's dedication and determination to bring them to light.

Those nine letters from Stanley to Ruth were written between March 1916 and March 1917. Can we already detect in the otherwise conventional letter of condolence on 7 March hints of more complex feelings?

My dear Ruth, just a few lines so that the silence which today seems
so silent may be broken by at least one friendly voice. I am sure
that the best memorial we can raise to her [Eva] is a fellowship
of those who in loving her have learned to love one another... So,
we must stand by each other – you and I – and all she lived for...

We shall fight side by side… I only feel that there is something very
sacred, tender, joyful in this fellowship of ours. It is Eva's gift to us.
Perhaps in a sense she died to give it to us. My love to you in all
sincerity and comradeship, Stanley.

Is this the language of what might be called an 'elite spirituality'? If
so, it wasn't the only time that he would express such a notion; he would
often return to the theme. And Minna, as we shall see later, talks about
the importance of regenerating the world with a special kind of Christian.
The word 'love' in the sign-off doubles up in an entanglement of both the
spiritual and sexual. If that is seen as far-fetched, in the next letter he refers
to Carpenter and Whitman, twin prophets of sexual liberation. The language
is so finely tuned that he always leaves a door open through which he can
slip back, in case Ruth becomes uneasy about the thinly veiled references
to physicality.

A week later he writes: 'My dear Ruth… Minna has handed me two
letters from you for which I am very thankful.' He seems, then, to be using
Minna's house as a post office because he does not want the letters sent to
118 Grove Road.

It is very, very good to have your friendship. I am only afraid that
when you know me better you may feel that you have given me more
than I deserve. But at least you have not given me more than I need.
I soak up all the affection you can bestow like a sponge. I am very
thirsty of soul and heart-hungry. Fellowship is the bread and water of
life – such fellowship as ours. Out of it is to come the man-woman and
the woman-man of the future – these new types of whom Carpenter
and Whitman wrote and whom Paul had in mind when he said: 'In
Christ is neither male nor female'… How good it would be if you were
able to live within reach of Trinity and able to co-operate actively… I
dream of a band of such co-workers, animated by one spirit, building
up together a real fellowship. I wonder if I am selfish in thinking of
you giving your services to this Church as though it could appeal to
you as it does to me. I want to commandeer you not for myself but
for something far higher and bigger. We are in Eva's hands. He has
brought us so far together. In all sincerity and affection, Yours, Stanley.

The images are bolder and more tangible: soaking up, sponges, heart-hungry. In another letter he tells Ruth what memorial they have decided to buy for Eva: it is a copy of the picture *Towards the Dawn*. He then writes:

> *By and by, one discovers that the physical presence was not as important as we thought – not as essential for the conveying of the Real Presence as we imagined. Does this sound unsympathetic? I never realised till now how much I loved her and how precious beyond words would be one touch of her hand. But such dreams are weakening. We are soldiers on the march and the order has come to 'fall in' and we must go on... Do not think yourself forgotten or useless. Your fellowship has given me strength and inspiration. One has, I find, to form around one a number of people whose friendship is a reminder of one's best thoughts and purposes. To deserve their love is a strong motive for true living. To constantly ask oneself what they could think and such and such an action is one's best defence. We carry responsibility for the whole group to which we belong. Always yours, Stanley.*

I believe these letters offer a telling insight into Stanley's true nature, away from the public utterances of his sermons recorded so beautifully by Eva and away from his autobiographies which are overlaid with a retrospective Catholic critique.

Sometimes he can only scribble off a short letter: 'How good it is to trust me with so much knowledge of yourself and your life! I deeply appreciate it and sympathise more than I can say with your difficulties. I want to help. Let this be an indication of my continued affection and interest. S.'

In May Stanley writes to Ruth, who the previous summer had passed her exams at Woodbrooke with flying colours and was now in her new job as welfare officer at the Rowntree factory in York:

> *I think you have the advantage over me in one respect. I seem only recently to have awakened to the beauty of Eva's nature. All these years I have allowed to slip by without taking the gift that Eva was putting into my hands. Few have no such regrets. You have your treasure of memories. She has been very much present with*

*us. The spirit of love seems to have been reinforced. Perhaps it
is true of her too that it was 'expedient' that she should go away
that the comforter might come in larger measure. A fellowship has
quite naturally sprung up from her grave, of which you and are I
members. That is a great joy to me – one of the great things in my
life. Such an intimate and sacred relationship I have always wanted.
Could Eva have given us any greater thing than this? But why was
it necessary that she should be taken away in order that we might
find one another? Yours, Stanley.*

Minna now worked as a private nurse, often staying overnight in people's
houses or even for an extended period, helping patients recover from illness.
Although she and her husband Will do not seem to have been temperamentally
suited, he had nevertheless provided her with an income and some semblance
of family structure. But now she was on her own with her four children
and she felt lonely.

One evening, with the Battle of the Somme just into its third week, she
had gone with Stanley to hear Maude Royden, a famous preacher, suffragist
and pacifist, speaking in central London. This was almost certainly at City
Temple, Holborn, where Royden became a pastor the following year. I
wonder if Jess knew that during his frequent evening absences from the
family home, he was in the company of attractive young women. Minna and
Stanley returned to Walthamstow and went into her house, 16 Grosvenor Park
Road. In a letter to Ruth on 15 July 1916 she relates what happened next:

*I must be frank and truthful to you and so I will tell you, dear, what
no other eye must ever see. What I now confess is with the deepest
shame and humiliation. Yet, dear, with joy, that one can feel as I have
felt, is to know the very consciousness of reality. Ruth, can you love
me after this? We had a most lovely talk. Well, dear, we went into the
front room alone and he kissed me, opened my dress and kissed my
breasts too and he said how he felt I was his. He was just going away
when he came back and pleaded with me dear to give him everything
a woman can give a man. I told him I was sure we should regret it
but no dear anything that would make me his. Well, dear, I did. The
tears I have shed have quite washed away any wrong I did.*

155

My dear Ruth, I can never tell you what I suffered. I felt I could never look at anyone again; how I have sat in Church I don't know, it has been simply agony. Well, dear, I met him out again one evening when I was with Lily [a close friend who helped with the children] and the strangest meeting it seemed, though we never even shook hands. We just mingled together. Then he promised to come to Stroud Green to see me and to write. He did neither. It was simply brutal. Think of me there, dear, with my tormenting thoughts, my hatred of myself and yet I do love him. I knew I was determined it should never happen again. In my letter I told him there could not be passion between us. If it was to be anything it must be higher than that, [I] told him I knew it couldn't be right or I wouldn't have been so miserable about it. When I asked him if he didn't agree about the latter, he said he had come to the same conclusion. He said I was more attractive than ever and he simply dare not kiss me or he didn't know what might happen. So, dear, I do feel if it has to be anything it must be a pure and noble spiritual bond.

Ruth, you do understand, dear, all my life I was tied to the tragedy of mated loneliness if it hadn't been for Eva and Lily and my kiddies I simply couldn't have borne my life. Then to have seemed to have found your mate, and yet if I felt he was true and worthy, my life would be a great joy.

I could go on loving him and yet live and die and make no sign. I feel somehow he does lack something that Owen Aves [a member of the congregation] has got. I feel we haven't mixed enough with men to know their minds because, dear, he told me he felt like this towards Eva and wished he had given her everything. I can understand him loving you, dear, you are so pretty, but me? Somehow too I feel there is a lot in what he says in his letter. Giving Joan to Eva and Lily has made me see that in motherhood and fatherhood the bond is mostly physical and not nearly what has been written about it. You see, dear, God showers his gifts on us all and I feel we have only touched the fringe of love. It will be a hard struggle for us women; men will walk, dear, over our broken and bleeding hearts, but we must love them still in spite of everything.

The strangest thing is that I haven't felt I wronged Mrs J [James]. No, I felt, dear, what love he gave to me was mine, and never was hers, nor could be, what I felt was that we had soiled what was the pure essence from God by our lesser natures. Don't worry about me dear, I have quite regained my self-possession. If he had written and told me he felt the same and we had blundered, but to be silent and to shun one was bitterly cruel. I do hope I haven't wearied you. My heart's love dear and my life's devotion. Your own, Minna.

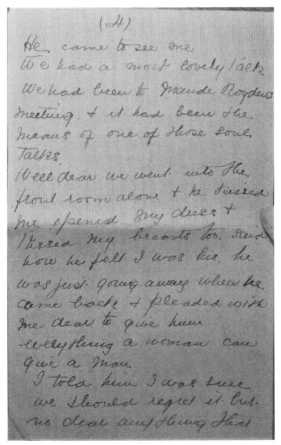

The letter in which Minna lets Ruth know of her affair.
Credit: Women's Library, London School of Economics.

Over the next few months, I read the letter over and over again because it was this stream-of-consciousness confession of Minna's that has shaped this book. Should I tell the rest of the family? If so, how much? Rightly or wrongly, I decided to divulge everything. Later, it came to light that this letter was included in *The Virago Book of Love Letters* (published 1994), sandwiched between one from Maud Gonne to the poet W. B. Yeats and another from Violet Trefusis to Vita Sackville-West.

I now needed to confront the damaging accusations in Koven's book. Was Minna the only woman Stanley had seduced while a minister? Koven writes: 'He also grotesquely abused his ministerial authority to seduce idealistic vulnerable female congregants... James preached from his pulpit the "religion of love which must unite all" while using a small private room in the church to have sex with some of them.'

The unsolved question sent me to a service at Trinity Church, Walthamstow, after which I found a storeroom which in former days had probably been the vestry – probably the 'small, private room' Koven refers to. He uses the plural – 'congregants' and 'some of them'. In the original letters and diaries, I had found no evidence that there were others. Stanley had intimate friendships with Eva and Ruth but there are no signs of anything sexual. Apart from gently hinting that there might have been other women, Thompson in *Dear Girl* offers no firm evidence, either. Yet her book was Koven's main source. It was beginning to look as if Koven had simply invented things. Had he just wanted to spice up the narrative, never thinking that Stanley's grandson would later read it?

I kept in touch with Koven and it emerged that every summer he travelled to Britain to research a new aspect of early twentieth-century social history. *The Match Girl and the Heiress* had been a part of this long-term project. In August 2018, to coincide with his visit, I arranged a tapas meal get-together in London for him, Thompson (they'd never been in contact), a cousin of mine and myself.

Immediately, almost before we'd sat down, Thompson challenged Koven about his 'embellishment' of the facts. He sheepishly admitted that it had all 'probably been a mistake'. He admitted that there was no evidence of Stanley seducing anyone else. Koven reconfirmed that his only source had been Thompson's book, not having had access, unlike myself and Thompson, to the original letters and diaries at the time of writing. Even Minna's seduction had been in the front room of her home, not at the church. Despite Koven's slapdash methods being exposed, our evening was a pleasant one and all – well, nearly all – was forgiven. He made a point of complimenting me on my research. I liked him and, besides, without his book I would never have come to know the truth – via *Dear Girl* – about my grandfather.

* * *

Exactly a week after he seduced Minna, Stanley had a pacifist poem published in the *Daily Herald,* a left-leaning national newspaper. It is called 'Sheep and Wolves' and the Biblical inscription at the top is from St Matthew, Chapter 10, Verse 16: 'I send you forth as sheep in the midst of wolves'.

Ironic Christ!
In subtle words and deep
He calls the conquerers of th'Imperial Throne
His silly sheep.
Oh wolves take care!
With stealthy footsteps creep!
This meekness cloaks a calm omnipotence
Beware such 'sheep'!
Oh little flock,
The foe may crouch – not leap.
Against the weapon of your harmlessness
Such 'wolves' are sheep.

It is hard to know whether sexual relations with Minna continued or whether they made love just the once. For all its power, Minna's writing is often idiosyncratic, and she can be unclear and ambiguous. Sometime in August, she writes to Ruth:

He [Stanley] does hurt me sometimes by his indifference and another time is so warm. He is in the city, as you know, all day and is practically very, very busy so I hope this is the reason he hasn't written. I too, like you dear, long for the love of a strong man... I try

*over and over again to know why I love him. I have met men lately
whom I know would soon love me who are much more attractive than
he is and yet my whole being is his in a most mysterious fashion. I
feel like you too that I am bound to him sexually. I have only to think
of him to find my whole being thrill and to have a child to him would
be the consummation of my existence. If I only had some money so
that I could go right away where no one would know, and it couldn't
possibly hurt her I would have one. I have such faith, my darling, in
soul union and I do feel if we are to have a regenerated world, these
children must be born. I simply crave for one and I have told him so.
My own, the things I have dared to say to thee.*

This is a fascinating letter, suggesting that Stanley's relations with
Ruth could also contain an element of sexuality – at least Minna seems
to acknowledge that Ruth has more than spiritual feelings for him. This
is echoed in some of his later letters to Ruth. But the other aspect of this
letter which is arresting is Minna's reference to wanting to have a baby with
Stanley, because 'if we are to have a regenerated world, these children must
be born'. Not for the first time, one of Stanley's female coterie sees herself
as having a mission to introduce a kind of super-Christian into the world.
Behind the bold declarations of desire between this quartet of supposed
Christians there often lies a chilling reference to the world of eugenics,
more specifically the need to create an elite race of believers. They clearly
see themselves as a bit special. These protestations left me reeling.

Soon after, Minna writes:

*I did not frame the marriage laws neither did I make Mrs J. jealous
and small. I hate deceit as much as anyone but there are God's laws
and, my dear, he is so lonely. We have got very close together, he
and I. I feel I am doing right… I do feel it is only us women who
will take these men by the hand and make them as gods. Now I feel
if I only lived with SBJ, I could do him immense good. I know his
wife is purely sex and has so encouraged that side in him, till, being
by nature passionate, his self-control is weakened. Then she cannot
talk and seems only flattered when he is making, as it were, love
to her, and this is fatal to him. I am a close observer and I know*

that type of woman. Mind, she is a brick, I know she manages all
the money, and is the man in lots of ways. Then, dear, I feel she is
responsible for letting him go. It isn't her fault. She is like us, dear.
The church is simply his living and she is such a muddle in the
house. It is revolting – dirty. I've never been in such a house. I'm
sure his lavatory was enough to create a fever and the muddle is
awful. His study is about the tidiest place. Thus to live is degrading.
I wonder what will develop.

In the family portraits taken at this time, Jess's natural good looks are
long gone: she appears thin, drawn and haggard and one can only imagine
the pressure she was under. And in the photographs taken at this time,
Stanley never appears.

Jess with her seven children in 1916. Kitty, the author's mother, is seated bottom left.

It is disturbing to read these things about my grandmother whom I knew
until the year of her death, 1963, when I was twelve. Does Minna's view
that Jess 'cannot talk' and that she is 'purely sex' come from Stanley's
own words or is it based on her observations, which may be flawed? In a
later letter to her daughter-in-law Jean, her youngest son David's wife, Jess
writes: 'To me, the most fascinating age is from birth to eighteen months.

I would always go anywhere for a tiny baby.' This certainly suggests a maternal instinct over and above a preference for the sharing of religious or philosophical ideas, not that the two are mutually exclusive, of course. Clearly, Minna knew the James family house. Maybe, with her nursing background, she helped Jess with the children. Was my mother sometimes cared for by the woman who was having an affair with her father?

Ruth must have asked Minna about contraceptive methods because she tacks on to her letter some advice:

The safest period is… as far away as possible from a period, but there are some pessarys [sic]… made of quinine which prevent anything happening. You put it as far as possible in you, dear, and let it melt. It takes about five minutes. I do hope you will be able to realise this [intercourse]. It is a wonderful experience. We simply played at it – him and I – and though I suffered so afterwards I don't feel I should again, and I do hope the day comes we may realise it.

Three weeks after seducing Minna, Stanley wrote a long letter to Ruth, who by now knew that he'd had sexual relations with her friend. But he was almost certainly unaware that Minna had told Ruth of their affair.

My dear Ruth, it was a real disappointment to me that I did not see you before you left. I had intended yesterday to go over to Tottenham to have seen you but circumstances at the last moment prevented me. This morning I learn from Lily that you have returned to York. And so, for the time being, I have missed you. But it has been a great joy to have had even the little glimpse of you that has been possible though I should like to have seen you alone. There is so much to discuss and so few opportunities! What a gracious loving thought it was of you and Minna to make me the vicarious recipient of Eva's birthday present. I feel really and truly honoured to know that you can so intimately associate her with me as this gift shows you do. And the book truly will be invaluable… And as I read it, I think my uppermost thought was to share the joy with you two dear women.

He adds that he gets 'fed up' with Christianity. 'Just at present, largely with the idea of getting away from orthodox Christian ways and thought, I am saturating myself in Nietzsche.' The German philosopher, of course, advocated the concept of the *übermensch*, or 'superman', essentially a superior individual, living outside or above the herd, who forges his own values and is prepared to put his own existence at risk for the enhancement of the human race. Stanley continues:

It came home to me what a joy it is to be able to speak freely and about all sorts of things to a woman who understands and sympathises and is not afraid. I don't think it is necessary for us to keep up any of the pretensions and false reservations that generally make intercourse between men and women difficult. I make no secret of the fact that it is in your womanhood I rejoice. Surely it is possible to face and acknowledge and take joy in the differences of sex in an honourable and wholesome way and without in any way infringing the rights of those to whom one is legally and in every other way pledged. Just in proportion as one does act without destroying, and discipline without crushing this instinct, it flowers with ever greater beauty. At least that is my experience. And I can therefore tell you without any secret blush or sense of guilt but rather with the consciousness of some divine sacrament in which the Son of Man is specially present that I love you. You will not misunderstand that declaration. It is the promise of spiritual intimacy – the assertion that the things of my soul are yours as I hope yours may be increasingly be given to me. It is so difficult to explain. We are pioneers and we have to cut out our path and create, as it were, a new medium of expression, and that takes time. But I am confident that I am understood.

He tells her that the family are going on their annual holiday to Leigh-on-Sea for a couple of weeks and wonders what lies ahead on his return. He senses that he is starting out on a new phase of his life. He says that he has been writing more in recent weeks, that the *Herald* is going to publish some of his poetry and that the *Venturer* is printing some articles. Then there was the possibility of a mission to Ireland. 'I don't know what will come of it. I want to do some good work and I know I am becoming more capable of it, but I can't see the road. Give me more and more of yourself, Yours, in affectionate comradeship, Stanley B. James.'

I asked the Nonconformist historian Clyde Binfield how he interpreted Stanley's behaviour during these months. 'He seems to be out of control, unable to curb his feelings for these women,' Professor Binfield said. 'He is also incapable of not exploring every sexual, emotional or intellectual avenue. There is an intensity about everything which proves to be his undoing. It is the beginning of the end.'

* * *

It is uncertain whether Minna knew that Stanley had been writing such heartfelt letters to Ruth. Ruth may have shielded the truth from her, possibly to spare her friend's feelings or even, perhaps, because she herself entertained the prospect of sharing something more intimate with Stanley. There again, I could have missed the whole point – that the group was, in a muted way, experimenting with the ideals of free love advocated by Whitman and Carpenter. There is a tendency in today's liberated times to assume that sexual frisson always translates into action but, in the scheme of things, this is rarely the case. Invariably, there is a highly charged atmosphere pointing to potential rather than execution.

Minna writes to Ruth:

It is his secret too, dear, and I feel the risk we run, but he is most discreet and so am I. I tremble when I think if anyone knew so burn my letters, dear one. I know Gertie [Eva's half-sister] talks because Nellie [a friend at the church] said the other evening: 'However will Minna leave SBJ?'... I will speak to Gertie. I feel she loves me enough – and him too – not to injure us in any way. But she knows nothing. It is only a guess. She is reading Eva's diary and knows all about them. She told me she thought Eva had imagined a lot around SB telling her he loved her... he might have known how it would tell on her. I think it brought her joy – I like to think it did, though she used to weep so over it... I am just going to be a loving woman expecting nothing from him. He has my love. Why I couldn't tell you, yet I feel in some indescribable way I do belong to him. But I want to be noble, Ruth, and if the time should come, when I see he prefers someone else to me, you perhaps, I want to say to myself you have fallen short of his ideal and he sees and loves in her what he thought to find in you. And I feel if we are ever to love perfectly it must be perfect freedom to love. I know he feels he is in a strange position and he struggles to have the fight to love like I have done. The price of life is always costly.

What about Jess? It may be that the marriage was on the rocks, but Minna didn't even feel the need to reference this because it was already accepted that it was like this. She goes on:

He came to me before going to Ireland and kissed me very affectionately. I do think he is absolutely cursed with passion. He said to me the worst of me is I'm so inflammable and the strange thing is that it is always when we have had the most lovely talks that he seems to lose his self-control. He is to be very busy now. He is going to the city every day to organise for the NCF [No-Conscription Fellowship]. I only hope he won't get side-tracked from the church. We haven't done anything yet in the church, but he seems happier and now the holidays are over we may get a move on. Did Eva ever tell you we used to share a husband between us and the funny part of it is, it was SBJ years ago. He was our ideal man of course in imagination and at Xmas she said to me laughingly, I couldn't share him, Minna, and I said to Eva there's no going back but that let me see... how much he was to her.

* * *

In September 1916 Stanley went to Ireland, sent by the *Christian Commonwealth* to report on the political situation there in the months after the Easter Rising. The paper believed that public opinion in England wanted to understand the Irish crisis better and people wanted to know whether there was any hope of peace or unity. Stanley was given the opportunity of talking to leading figures in Irish public life and was asked by the paper to propose solutions to the problem in a series of articles. It is highly probable that Stanley's entrée into Ireland's political scene was made possible by the influence of his anarchist friend, Captain Jack White, one of the co-founders of the Irish Citizen Army.

The Easter Uprising by sixteen hundred rebels on 24 April had not attracted the level of support from the Irish citizenry that was hoped for. But the ensuing British reprisals in May, in which fifteen leaders were executed and more than three thousand arrested, sparked widespread outrage and turned the rebels into martyrs. From that point, Irish independence – which eventually came in 1922 – was almost guaranteed. It was an Ireland seething with resentment that Stanley entered in September.

His four articles were published in successive weeks between 4 and 25 October and they are, I believe, among the finest pieces of journalism he produced. In these features he achieved a balance between the objective reporting of the opinions of the leading players, along with comments by industrial and agricultural workers, and his own views. The first one, entitled 'The Rebellion and its Political Effects', uses a description of Dublin's broken Sackville Street as a metaphor for the national confusion and lack of confidence in the Irish leaders. 'The Sinn Fein upheaval has created mental chaos,' Stanley writes. 'Those most familiar with the country do not know where they stand or what will happen next.' But the deportation without trial of the Sinn Fein prisoners, the shooting of the leaders, and the hanging of Casement in August 1916 were fatal mistakes. He was told that Casement was now regarded as a saint. 'The psychology of the Irishman is different [from that of the Englishman],' he says, before continuing:

It would almost be true to say that in Ireland nothing succeeds like failure... The effect upon the Nationalist element in the nation has been to stiffen its resolve to put up with no compromise, to allow no division... of their beloved island... One thing is obvious: English statesmanship has failed again to settle the Irish question... The anti-English feeling has never been so strong as it is today.

Even the Act of Parliament that granted a certain measure of self-government was an unhappy compromise that pleased nobody.

The second instalment, 'The Industrial Outlook', makes the point that the Irishman who is interested in social and economic reform thinks of these things in terms of a regenerated national life – Nationalist first, Labour man second. And Stanley was told in Belfast that capital was purposely fomenting the political and religious differences in order to divide the Labour camp. Nevertheless, social reform was still dependent on a solution being found to the self-government of Ireland. He writes: '[The] combination of Celtic imagination and ethical idealism with the severely practical is one of the most hopeful signs in Ireland today... The questions of political and economic independence are inextricably mingled.' He also gives us a snapshot of the desperate poverty that existed in Ireland at the time; when taken on a tour of Dublin's slums by a trade unionist, he remarks that he has never seen such destitution: six people commonly occupied one room.

The following week, in 'Settlement by Conference' he suggests that unity between Catholic and Protestant was nearer to being achieved than was usually imagined. He instances successful integrational workplaces where the two factions worked successfully side by side. Finally, in 'A Vision of Destiny', he moves towards a more poetic reading of the situation:

Poetry here is not an exotic, it is the common possession of all. For centuries this people has been tutored in pain. It has been under the dominion of men who understood little of the sensitive spirit they governed. But in spite of centuries of suffering that spirit is unconquered... a gifted race knowing the discipline of conquest yet never servilely submitting, fulfils the main conditions of future greatness... Nations do not pass through Gethsemanes for nothing... The mountains of Erin have not heaved in order to bring forth a mouse. To be a mere Celtic appendage of an Anglo-Saxon Empire is no adequate issue from this age-long crucifixion. Some greater destiny we may be sure awaits this people, though the method of its attainment may be undiscoverable at present. The first step lies with England. To this country belongs the privilege of releasing the Irish spirit to work out its own destiny and to contribute of its own special gifts to the common fund of mankind.

I sent the four newspaper extracts to Leo Keohane, author of *Captain Jack White: Imperialism, Anarchism and the Irish Citizen Army*. He thought the pieces were 'absolutely fascinating'. Stanley was an Englishman, he said, and not too many Irish people would have had the same insights. In addition, many historians would be surprised by the conclusions he came to as early as six months after the Rising.

It is not known to what extent Stanley, once back in Walthamstow, was able to share his experiences of Ireland with Jess. What we do have, however, is an amusing account by Minna, in a letter to Ruth, of how my grandfather spoke enthusiastically to her of his trip. Perhaps she hadn't been listening carefully because she has difficulty recalling the salient points. Her description is hazy and impressionistic, a kind of intuitive reflection on historical events. She writes:

Sitting waiting for zepps… listening for guns isn't the best method… he began by saying that ever since war started nothing had so moved him as the Sinn Fein rebellion. He felt that there was much more behind it than one could at first see and he was only too glad to get the chance of going over and seeing for himself… I am really no good, dear, at this job but here goes. As he rode down Sackville Street, the sight was simply appalling. It could only be described as an earthquake. The post office looked like an empty tomb. Now what the Dickens comes next? I'm hanged if I know. I want to give you my impressions of Ireland which are somewhat strong he said, and what did he say? Stanley B, come thou to me, and I will try telepathy. Of course, I told you in the beginning it resembled an earthquake. I'm quaking at the mere thought of telling you. I'll have to tell you my impressions after all. Well, dear, Ireland has wrongs, has had them since Adam and even before that, and they will never be righted till there arises one mighty atom named Minerva to lead them to liberty or death. Excuse me begging a bit of the French national anthem but are they not our Allies (all lies). Well, dear, in the first place you'll admit Ireland has wrongs, deep wrongs, that want righting (did I say this before?) I had got to the empty tomb (hark was that a bomb?) Well, he said in a most pathetic voice – you always are like that when you speak of Ireland or you ought to be – in the end he

*said all the politicians want hanging. Then he went into a teashop
where there were a lot of girls, rebels. They would sure to be nice,
rebels always are, that's why I'm one. Do be a rebel, Ruth, it makes
one feel so nice. I'm sure I'll be hung. Then it's so catching. He said
up one street where there was only one Sinn Fenian before, the next
day there were millions – nothing like hanging to make rebels. I quite
envied Roger Casement myself.*

* * *

After the holidays, most of the Trinity congregation found that Stanley's
pacifism was more than they could stomach; the axe was hanging over
his head. Against the background of such an intense local drama one can
forget that the aerial war was taking place above the streets of East London.
By 5 October 1916, nearly three months after they had sex, it seems that
Minna's request that they turn the liaison into something 'higher' had been
heeded by Stanley. One can't be sure, but it seems likely. Apparently unable
to share thoughts and ideas with Jess, Stanley now regularly confided in
Minna. 'Soul talks', as she describes them, had always been a vital part of
their connection.

About this time, a group of the more radical members of Trinity started
going to the Brotherhood Church in Hackney. This Christian Socialist,
Tolstoyan-anarchist, Congregational church in Southgate Road had its origins
as far back as 1662. In 1892 the Reverend Bruce Wallace became pastor
and instituted a programme of left-wing political activity which had only a
nodding acquaintance with conventional Christianity. In 1907 it hosted the
Fifth Congress of the Russian Social Democratic Labour Party, attended
by thirty delegates from Russia including Lenin, Trotsky and Stalin. It had
links with the ILP, the pioneer of the New Theology, the Reverend R. J.
Campbell, and the suffragettes. Annie Besant, Sylvia Pankhurst, Keir Hardie,
Bertrand Russell and George Lansbury were among those who spoke there.
Stanley, too, was a leading speaker in the pacifist cause so it is not beyond
the bounds of possibility that he addressed crowds there, too. The church
was the venue for numerous pacifist meetings during the First World War.
It was demolished in 1934 and now a Tesco store stands on the site.

The Trinity group seem to have attended the church in order to hear Captain Jack White speak on Ireland. Stanley had known the colourful, Northern Irish, self-styled anarchist who helped create the Irish Citizen Army since they'd met at the Fellowship of Reconciliation (FoR), the Quaker-based peace movement, in 1915. White, who hailed from County Antrim, was educated at Winchester College and Sandhurst, and had fought with distinction in the Boer War, was a radical aristocrat who had organised one of the first Protestant Home Rule meetings, with Roger Casement as one of the speakers. Before supporting the Republican cause, this chameleon-like figure had found time to join a free-love commune in the Cotswolds which was attempting to live according to Tolstoyan ideals.

Captain Jack White, co-founder of the Irish Citizen Army

Eventually he became disillusioned by his involvement with the Irish Citizen Army and resigned. He then gave his support to the Irish Volunteers before leaving them after a few months and returning to England. This was only an interim period and he was off again, this time to the front in France where he undertook ambulance duties as a volunteer. If he wasn't already a pacifist, the experience made him one – at least for the time being – and on coming back to England he gravitated towards the FoR where he met Stanley. When the Irish rebellion broke out, this restless man wrestled with his dual-nationality conscience about whether to join the struggle. He decided not to and instead spoke to a group of Welsh miners and urged them to come out on strike in support of James Connelly. He was arrested and charged with, among other matters, 'making a statement likely to cause disaffection to his Majesty'. He was found guilty and sentenced to three months' imprisonment in Wales. Towards the end of his confinement, he was transferred to Pentonville, by coincidence the day before Roger Casement was hanged there on 3 August 1916. On his release, he was banned from re-entry to Ireland, so he stayed in England and his friendship with my grandfather developed. White's contradictions and sense of adventure no doubt appealed to Stanley.

One Sunday Minna was among the Trinity group that went to the Brotherhood Church. There she was introduced to White and was both attracted to and repelled by him. According to ensuing letters to Ruth, my grandmother seems to have had a close relationship with White. In the first reference, Minna writes: 'I ran into Mrs James last night and she told me Captain White was feeling so ill and was on the verge of a nervous breakdown.' To have gained such knowledge, Jess must have known White quite well. Minna goes on: 'Did I ever tell you I had written to him [Captain White] several times but always burnt the letters? Well, I have written to him now. I feel absolutely that I must. I have never done such a thing before. I do feel sorry for him and interested in him.' White's popularity with women was vying with Stanley's! And now Minna seemed to be looking for another man.

* * *

Later Minna writes to Ruth:

He [Stanley] cannot see the path before him but seems inclined to leave the church. I told him I thought him a born preacher and he said he always thought so too but the deacons are such stumbling blocks he wondered if he sent in his resignation if it would decide the point and give him a free hand to follow the light. Will you write to him, dear? I will see he has the letter. He has preached some divine sermons lately.

I only wish you could have heard them. Last night he was great... if he only had the natural gift of love – somehow I feel he could move the world... I do thank God, Ruth dear, that he has given us to one another. Surely for some divine purpose. I send you his letter. Surely one could never write like this and not mean anything. I am struggling with some new thoughts conceived but unutterable at present. I think he will regret it if he gives up preaching. He is essentially a preacher I'm sure. Somehow, we women do love the weak men. I feel he needs me so.

Stanley still found time to write for publication. He had some pieces – two for children and two for adults – published in the *Venturer*. For me, they are fine articles, all the better for being concise. In 'A Strange People' a race of little people have no enemies because they are peace-loving and without property. It is a neat double-dramatisation of 'Blessed are the meek' combined with the concept of pacifism. In another story, a cyclist rests by a telegraph pole the wires of which are singing in the wind. They tell him how the pole started out as a tree in the forest and sang 'The Song of the Tall Brethren' with its fellow pines, but when the axemen came it was stripped bare of its branches and had a crosspiece nailed to it. The tree was in pain, but slowly it realised that it was helping man to communicate through telegraphy. It now sung 'The Song of Service', which included the line: 'Before we lived just for ourselves; now I am happy as I am helping others.' It had literally changed its tune.

In the pithy 'The New Legalism', Stanley attacks ossified belief systems and suggests that pacifism is the logical outcome of living with love. Morality rests not upon definite principles but on a person living as an 'artist in holiness'. And 'Through Freedom to Character' is a subtle and persuasive defence of the conscientious objector's position: 'The root objection to war is not the sacredness of life... but the sacredness of personality and its right to win moral responsibility through freedom. From this point of view the conscientious objector is cleared of the charge of indifference.'

Minna was now writing feverishly to Ruth, and we are afforded a revealing glimpse of the twists and turns of Stanley's pastorate in its dying days. Stanley announced his resignation in November and would give his last sermon just before Christmas. On 11 December Minna writes enigmatically to Ruth:

I meant to tell you that things have been getting worse [at the church]... Mrs James told me that it was Margaret Thomas's doing. I knew, of course dear, he was very friendly with them [the Thomas sisters], but she [Mrs James] told me he had almost lived there at one time, neglecting her and spending all his time with them. Many and many a time she had come home from meetings alone and he with them. [She] told me they are such backbiters and slanderers it was misery to go into their house.

Here is more evidence that Minna and my grandmother shared intimate conversations – bizarre considering the fact that Minna had been having an affair with her husband. Like much gossip, the truth is unclear, and I am unable to shed any light on who the Thomas sisters were or my grandfather's relationship with them. Minna continues:

In our search after freedom why is it women's hearts have to be so torn? My heart did go out to her, quite old, bearing those seven kiddies. She thinks he owes her absolute fidelity. I feel somewhat of a sneak when she talks to me so, but still perhaps I may be able to do her some good in her thoughts? She has never met a free woman yet. I think one of the cruellest things in life is, as in her case, she has had to be the one to have his passion that another woman has stirred, and hence all those kiddies. This ever-perplexing sex problem, so complex, so disturbing, so difficult to find anything like a true solution.

Ruth, I know I am romantic. After all, what is romance. I've wanted and longed and prayed for my soulmate all my life and I try to analyse my love for him and I cannot. But I love him with my mind, soul and body utterly. My love is so perfect and selfless that I pray that God may show him his true path even if it leads him out of my life altogether and I never see him. This would be indeed hard for me dear... I wonder what 1917 will bring us, dear. 1916 has been an awful year, hasn't it?

Minna's oldest son Horace was, meanwhile, about to be called up to fight in the war. She writes: 'If they had only let me have him till he was a man he would have been a CO [conscientious objector], what I should be so proud of a son of mine to be. I feel when I see him in khaki, my very soul will be rent.'

She brings Ruth up to date on the outcome of the last church committee meeting, following Stanley's resignation: 'He is to be asked to [re-]consider his decision... He had great talents but got hold of one idea and pursued it. He does the same with persons [sic]. I can't get away from the idea that he is a dipper... I'm sure he will go.' The word 'dipper' gave Seth Koven the opportunity to juxtapose it – out of context – with references to Stanley's seduction of Minna. Indeed, he changed it to read 'serial dipper', which was a complete fabrication. Used in this way it has sexual connotations which I do not think Minna intended five months after the event. In writing about a committee meeting and someone's point that Stanley focuses intently on one notion for a while but is unable to sustain that interest, the meaning of 'dipper' must be that he dips in and out of various thoughts and beliefs.

Radical reading is still the order of the day among the ever-smaller group of Stanley's supporters:

Gertie brought me my book – Ed Carpenter's 'Days and Dreams'. I haven't looked at it yet. Mr James wants me to lend it to him, but I do treasure it so and he makes them so dirty. By the way, he is very queer – near a nervous breakdown so Gertie said on Wednesday. I haven't seen him to speak to for months and wonder if I ever shall again, but he is so dear to me, Ruth, I have only to think of him [and] my heart overflows. What the last time he preaches will be like, God alone knows.

Will you sleep with me on Saturday night? Do you think it will spoil the evening if SBJ and she came in? I don't doubt it might at first, but I feel he has such little pleasure and he is so very hungry for affection and fellowship... We meet now on a higher plane, all passion gone. What a coward he is in some things... When you see SBJ, tell him – whatever he does – to keep the [church] together. It is one unholy and immoral thing to drive us all asunder. Tell [him] to build up a church in Walthamstow or Leyton. I feel we will all be strengthened and upheld by what we have passed through.

Stanley's last day at the church arrived – either Sunday 17 or Sunday 24 December. I have been unable to track down the minutes of Trinity Church meetings to establish the exact day. Unlike the Church of England, Nonconformist churches are under no obligation to send their records to official state archives. Sometimes, as with the Wimbledon churches, they are available. With others they do not exist or have been lost. At Trinity in 2019 I was shown an attic which was reached via a collapsible ladder and which lay beyond a mound of nursery toys. It hadn't been entered for years, apparently. 'The records might be in there,' said a Trinity member tantalisingly. 'We just don't know.' I investigated in the heat of an August afternoon, but nothing came of it.

Minna wrote a poem entitled 'Thought on Seeing the Sun Shine on Mr James Preaching for the Last Time in Trinity Church'.

Trinity thou sunlit shrine
To me thou art hallowed and holy.
Here our souls were fed with food celestial,
What memories steal over me, even as I gaze upon thy walls.
What visions called forth; what inspirations,
Here did we meet our souls' affinities
Here our dear dead have knelt and prayed.
Tears dim our eyes, and our hearts beat with the pain
To think never again can it be what it has been,
Trinity thou loved and sacred memory.

Needing more insight into the pent-up emotion swirling around these Trinity radicals, I asked Thompson what she made of my grandfather's contrasting liaisons with the three women. In her book, she had focused on the relationships between the women, whereas I had unearthed material that was directed more towards Stanley, so I asked her to take a fresh look. She said to me:

While Stanley's behaviour remains generally speaking typical of certain men, I am struck now by how lacking in appropriate boundaries he was and how his behaviour amounts to an abuse of trust – the trust placed in him as a progressive and at times inspirational church leader by Eva (before her death) and Ruth and Minna (after Eva's death). When Stanley should have been offering solace and comfort to two grieving women, devastated by the death of Eva, he was busy seducing them, more or less at the same time, when they were at their most vulnerable.

What I find particularly distasteful is the way he uses the progressive idea of a spiritual fellowship to bond with the women and gain their trust. Only a few months after Eva's death he appears to be propositioning Ruth and then seducing Minna, appealing to them both to be part of his band of enlightened followers, using religious language quite persuasively. While language for expressing sexual and emotional feelings was in short supply in the early 1900s, it is nevertheless disturbing how Stanley uses religious language as a means of seduction. He wrote to Ruth two months after Eva's death: 'I can therefore tell you without any secret blush or sense of guilt but rather with the consciousness of some divine sacrament in which the Son of Man is specially present that I love you'. He even went so far as to say that perhaps Eva had died to give them all the 'gift of fellowship'. It is not for me to decide to what extent Stanley was calculated or whether he was confused and out of control but in the context of today's feminism and the #MeToo movement there is much of resonance here about abuse of trust and manipulation of women by a powerful figure, albeit 104 years ago.

The accumulation of such serious criticisms of my grandfather throughout my research made me realise that I was engaged in far more than merely writing his life. Unwittingly, I had unearthed a tangled moral issue that was growing in complexity. It was almost as if the very lapse of time had given people of the twenty-first century the freedom to judge in a way that they seldom did when it came to contemporary examples of infidelity. Running through the issue, too, was the question of language: the rather antique turns of phrase employed by the letter writers, by their very nature, seemed to attract moral censure. Finally, the position of Stanley as a minister over a hundred years ago seemed to mean that people today expected higher standards of behaviour from him.

If pressed, I would admit to broadly sharing these retrospective views. But, in our disapproval, could we pluralist, liberal observers, comfortable in our postmodern universes and reluctant to condemn human behaviour, merely be indulging ourselves? Could we not, when considering the past, be experiencing existential glee because we feel released from the straitjacket of our own contemporary tropes? Our condemnation says as much about our own society as it does about those Edwardians.

~ 13 ~
DOWN AND OUT IN LEYTONSTONE

It is impossible to overestimate the crushing emotional and material effect that Stanley's resignation had on him and the family. The termination of his salary left a yawning financial gap and the Jameses entered a prolonged period of deprivation that would last, except for an occasional lucky hike, for more than ten years. Although the church presented him with a farewell monetary gift and he managed to secure low-paid employment at the No-Conscription Fellowship (NCF) before he ceased working at Trinity, neither sum made any appreciable difference. The church, of course, was no longer paying the rent at 118 Grove Road so the family had to look for a cheaper and smaller house.

Spiritually, the departure from Trinity unsettled Stanley and it was to be another six years before he regained some kind of equilibrium. He writes:

I found that to be unemployed as a single man was a different thing to being in the same condition when a wife and family had to be provided for. There was no lack of either sympathy or courage on the part of my wife, but all the courage in the world could not prevent our seeing secret fears in each other's eyes, and there were

*times during the interval between my resignation and the actual
cessation of my pastorate when the fiend of hopelessness seized my
heart and held it in its grip... I had come into the Congregational
ministry through the back door and appearances pointed to my
finding an exit by the same means.*

At one stage Minna says that there were plans for Jess and the family to
move to Moore Place in Stanford-le-Hope, Essex, which was a commune
in experimental living set up by Reginald Sorensen and his wife Muriel.
Heavily influenced, like Stanley, by the radical politics and liberal theology
of the Reverend R. J. Campbell, Sorensen was a Christian Socialist, a
member of the ILP and Unitarian minister of the Free Christian Church in
Walthamstow. He was also a member of the Men's League for Women's
Suffrage and a close colleague of Sylvia Pankhurst. On the outbreak of war,
he joined the NCF and declared himself a pacifist. Fenner Brockway was
his brother-in-law and in 1929 Sorensen became Labour MP for Leyton
West. Between him and Stanley there would have been a meeting of minds
and no doubt he offered the family a refuge at Moore Place – itself linked
to the Brotherhood Church – when homelessness and uncertainty stared
them in the face.

But the offer was not taken up because they found accommodation at
6 Poppleton Road, Leytonstone, and moved in. They were to be there for
about two years. To ease the financial burden, they let out the ground floor
to a family of Catholic relatives, who were probably the Chignells, relations
of Jess who had converted to Catholicism and had been cold-shouldered by
the rest of her family. Jess also went to work in central London as a clerk
to bring in more income, almost unbelievable given that she had to run a
household and was responsible – at least during the holidays – for seven
children. The oldest four were away at boarding school, Phyllis and Jessie
at Milton Mount, Bob and Eric at Caterham School. At the outbreak of war,
the girls' school had abandoned its premises in Gravesend, Kent, because of
the threat from air raids, and moved to a large building in Cirencester, now
an agricultural college. The war over, in 1920 it moved to Worth Park in
Sussex. I'm not sure how old my mother was when she first went to Milton
Mount, but she could have been as young as nine, certainly 11. Despite the
obvious financial stresses, my mother remembered those Poppleton Road

days with fondness. She used to walk out to nearby Epping Forest and sail her toy boat on the pond.

For all the acrimony he faced, it would be wrong to see Stanley's departure from Trinity solely as an ignominious exit. He had been speaking to his closest followers about setting up a more radical fellowship, just as his father had done with Christ Church, Wimbledon. The parallels with the south London church – as well as with St Paul's, Swansea – are strangely similar. In all three instances, the pastor fell out with the diaconate. There seemed to be an inability by father and son to peacefully co-exist over the long-term with the ruling body of a Congregational Church.

A few weeks into the New Year those followers located Burghley Hall, Burghley Road, Leytonstone, for possible meetings. Stanley concurred and the hall was booked for the beginning of March. At that time it was used as a social centre, holding weekly dances and regular whist drives. Today it is a block of flats, but the name has been retained in the glass above the door and on the paving of the entrance patio. On 23 February, writing from the NCF, 5 York Buildings, Adelphi (off modern-day John Adam Street), he invited Ruth to attend the church gatherings in Leytonstone. He tells her he has not been well lately and is 'going away for a few days next week to a Quaker home – friends of a friend of mine – at Redhill, Surrey. The rest will do me a world of good.' He then indulges in some wistful dreaming:

> *Oh for a long summer's day under leafy boughs or within sound of the sea-surf where we might forget cares or at least have leisure of soul and mind to rise over them. I am very hungry for the inspiration of such quiet times and the help of such fellowship as you could give. My very heartfelt good wishes for the coming year. Yours fraternally, Stanley B. James.*

* * *

It was in 1917 that the least known of my grandfather's books was published – his 32,000-word novella, *Poverty Gulch*. It may be unknown, but I think it is one of his better works and, as far as I know, it was the only piece of extended fiction he wrote. I have only ever come across one copy, and that's in the British Library. It contains some fine imagery and an intriguing narrative with a deceptively simple storyline. It is dedicated "to the woman whose love, when I would have drifted back to the scenes of this story, proved stronger than all the magic of the west". An enigmatic dedication if ever there was one.

Front cover of Stanley's pacifist novella, *Poverty Gulch*, set in the Prairies and published in 1917. Credit: The British Library

A character referred to as the Man has quit his job as a cowboy on a ranch in the prairies to buy and manage his own land. He is nicknamed the Parson by the men in Pine Creek because he has recently turned his back on his dissolute life and embraced religion. He decides to return for a brief visit to his roots in the east, but when he arrives, he finds life too fast. While walking down the street he prevents a horse from bolting and the owner thanks him, inviting him to his house. There he meets the red-haired Woman. Despite their different classes and backgrounds, they are attracted to each other. He returns to the west and they write to each other. Eventually they realise they're in love, so he comes back, they marry and he takes her to the ranch. Despite her feeling of trepidation about the isolation of her new existence, she stays and soon finds that she is pregnant.

One evening in the nearby town, a cowboy called Steve argues with another man and ends up shooting him dead. He rides away and escapes. An old timer nicknamed the Philosopher predicts that the Parson – also, confusingly, referred to at various times as the Man, the Shepherd and the Soul-hunter – will track down Steve, and rein him in. The ranching metaphors abound. The reader is left thinking that the strong arm of the law awaits Steve for the murder he's committed. But the Man's motive in searching for him is that of a shepherd hoping to recover a wayward sheep, not retribution. They meet and talk, the Man eventually convincing the young lad of the truth of Christianity, but they realise that Steve must be charged with murder. Nevertheless, his new-found faith allows him to rediscover his former cheerful self; he actually seems happier than his rescuer, whose thoughts return to his pregnant wife.

Storms have been raging as the pair ride back to their home territory and they are forced to cross a river in flood. Steve is swept away in the torrent and the Man throws him a lifeline which Steve ties round himself. But when Steve sees his companion being pulled into the flood too, in an act of self-sacrifice he cuts the rope and plunges to his death, leaving the Man free to return to his wife and new-born baby. The couple are reunited, but they acknowledge that they are only together again because of Steve's unselfish, Christian act.

To a sceptical agnostic this morality tale may well grate. It lacks a certain amount of psychological complexity or irony. But what it captures in a simple, dramatised story form – and I say this as one of those sceptical agnostics – is the sheer challenge and difficulty of being a true Christian. The Man's speeches echo my grandfather's pacifist beliefs, which were prominent between 1914 and the early 1920s. Later, the Philosopher pours scorn on conventional religion, another of Stanley's dislikes, at least in his Walthamstow days:

> *Religion is a queer thing. If you were to judge it by the people that go about spouting texts you'd say it was the foolishest nonsense a man ever listened to. Churches, and vestments, and psalm singing are poor things to judge a religion by... It's just sickening and foolish.*

Perhaps this passage when the Man reflects on how he has to stay true to his pastoral mission out west – albeit completely unofficial – rather than agreeing to his wife returning to her sociable, urbane world echoes Stanley's period as minister in Walthamstow.

> *He was providing these unshepherded sheep of his Master with a rallying point. Gradually he was acquiring the art and science of the Spiritual Shepherd and it became easier for him as time went by to understand individual idiosyncrasies. Their histories became his secrets and gave him many a clue that otherwise he would have needed. This unsought sphere of work growing up so naturally, proving itself so rich in fruit, this labour of love so sacred, so responsible, was the cause of his deepest joy in life. He seemed to be finding himself. This unofficial pastorate was becoming a divine vocation. It answered more than anything else he had done in his life, the question: 'What am I in this world for?' And the answer satisfied him to the very depths of his being. Was it not for this that he had come into his Kingdom?*

That, by any yardstick, is an immensely powerful piece of writing, as well as being a testament of faith. As a non-believer, it gives me a sense of the power of belief, divorced from doctrine. I can appreciate the effect the best of his Walthamstow sermons must have had on his congregation. I'm left wondering whether *Poverty Gulch* is not his true spiritual autobiography rather than *The Adventures of a Spiritual Tramp* or *Becoming a Man*. I think it gives an insight into the tenor of Stanley's beliefs: gentle yet uncompromising, tolerant yet stern. Not far beneath the drive and understanding lay the elements that gave rise to the controversy and unpredictability of his pastorate. Surely the passionate, preaching voice of his father can be heard in this, too?

* * *

On 25 February 1917 Minna wrote to Ruth, telling her that she had joined three others from the church, including Stanley and Jess, to hear Captain White speak about Ireland. She had kept a low profile because she didn't want to make Jess jealous… 'One has to be so careful. Isn't it hateful? O to be free and unfettered.' She reminded Ruth that the following Sunday – the first anniversary of Eva's death – would see the start of the new church at Burghley Hall.

Stanley felt that the venture was going to give him more freedom of worship than he'd ever had before. He was surrounded by his pacifist and socialist supporters, unencumbered by the more conservative elements of the Trinity congregation. He wrote that he owed no allegiance to any denominational body and that meant that he was able, in theory, to create a new religion and even found a sect of his own. And to enhance the visual impact of the meetings, he wore a cassock and placed a crucifix in a central position.

But the optimism for the new experiment was not sustained. Minna did not like Stanley's first sermon. It was all 'words, words, words'. She says he wasn't able to preach, and she had the strangest feeling that he would never do anything with his life.

Owen is fed up and believes he is going potty. Burghley Hall will fizzle out, I am sure. I had a talk with him last week and he simply doesn't know where he is. I feel so very sorry. He seems to be going back and repudiating the social ideal and laying stress only on the individual salvation of one's soul. As a challenge, last night he said you hadn't to change the social environment – it wasn't necessary. If this is so, the best thing we can do is to throw over our pamphlet stall in the street with all its social propaganda. I think, Ruth, the very hardest thing in life is to keep our faith in men and women. Faith in God seems easy [compared] to this.

A week later Minna, however, ever changeable, forgets her gloomy verdict and now appears more upbeat, saying that they have made a good start. 'On Sunday we read a piece out of the poems of R. Tagore, with the words in it "Let me carry this sorrow always, let me not forget it". [But] Gertie is much disappointed in him. He is so curt and unsociable.'

Stanley was aware that once the war was over the pacifist ideals which had drawn the group together would lose much of their relevance. As Minna noted, he was starting to emphasise the more traditional elements of religious life – and the beliefs of the Catholic Church entered more into his thoughts. Meanwhile, he himself wrote that, although he was a freelance preacher with a few pacifist followers who were together trying to mould a group of revolutionary Christians without denominational connections or precedents of any kind into a body with a distinct identity, they found themselves falling back more and more on old models created by the Catholic Church.

At that first service on 4 March had been the by now ubiquitous Captain White. This time Minna spoke to him and he sent his love to Ruth through her:

He hopes to see you when you come up. I want to be charitable and I feel I won't judge him, but Ruth he is quite repulsive to me and I feel he is a libertine. One or two friends – women – who didn't know anything of him said what a horrid man – makes you feel you want a bath. Owen Aves too spoke of him in this way – 'if that's White I don't think much of him'. Gertie says he is the only man she has ever felt she would be afraid to be left alone with. He is absolute sex. I am surprised at SBJ, but we will wait and see. I somehow feel, my own, these people are meant to come into one's life. You see, I am judging him.

Minna and other women were clearly repulsed by Captain White's physicality, but Minna found it impossible to ignore him. On 22 March she writes to Ruth:

Captain White asks me to tea – I am going. I do wish, Ruth, I was a bit good-looking. I do feel my defects. I have been trying to grapple with the sex problem. I get so much of it. You know how Eva was so interested in it. Mr James told me Captain White thinks

it is the question. I feel I should like to have some more children.
I feel so physically fit, too. I think what a splendid thing to give
some superman or woman to the world. Do pray for SBJ, as I do.
He is the strangest being. While we are doing all we can, he is still
the stiff, unsociable being he was at Trinity and you should hear
the comments. You know if there is any mud at any time thrown at
anyone, there is sure to be some of it stick and the other side are
never tired of telling us how unreliable he is, and he will let us
down.

Captain White was about to leave London. But another adventure awaited him, one that would give him a bizarre walk-on part in the annals of English literature. He had met D. H. Lawrence and his wife Frieda at their Mecklenburgh Square flat, London, in early 1917 and an invitation had been extended to him to stay with them when they moved to Zennor in Cornwall. He took up the offer, but the visit didn't go well, and the two men argued over White's political beliefs. There was also a suggestion that there was a frisson of attraction between White and Frieda, which angered Lawrence. White wrote to a friend that the novelist annoyed him and that he had punched him three times in the stomach. Ever the writer, Lawrence used the episode in his picaresque novel *Aaron's Rod* in which the character Jim Bricknell, a highly-strung impulsive man based on White, punches Rawdon Lilly, who is a self-portrait of the author.

The last known letter we have of Stanley's to Ruth runs like this:

So many thanks for your brave, frank letter. I will let you know – for
my own sake and for yours – the moment I feel that our friendship
is hindering our true life. I think one of the best tests in my case
is this – does my affection for one person lessen or increase my
affection for others? My experience has been that caring for you
as I do, or wanting to help you as I do, makes me richer and freer
altogether and enables me to give more to the one to whom I am
specially bound. That she might not so understand it at present does
not seem to alter the case. I am conscious of no disloyalty. But... if
you feel that it ought not to be so then I accept your decision. I must

not allow my liberty to be a stumbling block to another. S. I must add my deep thanks and gratitude for the confidence you repose in me – for the friendship you have given me. I hold it very precious and sacred.

One of nine intimate letters Stanley wrote to Ruth.
Credit: Women's Library, London School of Economics

Intuitively – and this is supported by Thompson – I feel he may have made overtures to Ruth and she stymied his advances, citing Stanley's married status. For all the overblown language, this has the ring of someone coming to terms with sexual rejection. And there is something in the tone that also makes it feel like a swansong. This March 1917 letter marks the end of his known correspondence with the three close friends. He may have carried on communicating with – and meeting – Minna or Ruth; we just don't know. Around this time Clara, Stanley's mother, died in Dorset where she had been quietly seeing out her days living with her daughter Daisy and husband William Sutherland.

The privilege we have had in peering into Stanley's dealings with three young, beautiful and interesting women ends abruptly. Soon the Burghley Hall meetings under his guidance would cease, too, being taken over by another pacifist and FoR member. Stanley would increase his involvement with the peace organisations that he was already working for in central London, along with attending as a layman the forward-thinking Congregational church of King's Weigh House, in central London, under the pastorate of Dr Orchard, who was about to become a massive influence on his spiritual life. The focus turns away from the recorded intimacies of the past three years and moves into the realm of social action, journalism, public speaking and debates about forms of belief. One might expect Stanley now to have more regard for his family, but this proved not to be the case. Stanley and Jess had no more children, and the family – without Stanley for the time being – were soon to leave London for good. Meanwhile, his life became ever more focused on the public arena.

THE WAR
AGAINST WAR

~ 14 ~
TAKING A STAND

When it became clear, after the initial euphoria, that the war would not be won in a matter of weeks, the two pacifists Clifford Allen and Fenner Brockway formed the No-Conscription Fellowship, an organisation which opposed the introduction of compulsory enlistment in the armed forces. Set up in November 1914, by February of the following year it had well over three hundred members, including those young enough to fight and those who were beyond military service age but who were prepared to help. Allen and Brockway, who at that time was editor of the anti-war newspaper, the *Labour Leader*, rightly foresaw that voluntarism would never win the war and that the government would be forced to introduce conscription, which it did with its Military Service Act in March 1916.

The NCF then switched its attention to providing support for the growing number of conscientious objectors (COs) or 'conchies', as they were referred to by those who derided their ideological stance. The organisation was initially run from Brockway's home in Derbyshire but, as membership grew, it opened an office in London. Its statement of faith declared it an organisation of men 'who will refuse from conscientious motives to bear arms, because they consider human life to be sacred and cannot therefore assume the responsibility of inflicting death'.

Until the end of the conflict, the NCF conducted a propaganda campaign against the authorities and supported COs when they appealed against military service and their cases were heard by specially constituted tribunals. Those tribunals were harsh towards the men whom many regarded as shirkers. Hearsay and personal opinion were admissible as evidence against them; one outspoken tribunal councillor was heard to declare that 'a man who would not help to defend his country and womankind is a coward and a cad'.

Stanley gravitated towards the NCF while he was still minister at Trinity. Indeed, simultaneously working for a number of social action and religious organisations – sometimes three at once – was the pattern of his working life between 1917 and 1923. The exact sequence is impossible to follow, interwoven and overlapping as it is. He was here, there and everywhere, so I have decided for reasons of clarity to consider his work at each organisation separately.

When, in mid-1917, he found himself without occupation or income, he landed a junior administrative job with the NCF in its offices at 5 York Buildings, south of The Strand. Two of his letters to Ruth Slate are hurriedly scribbled on the organisation's headed notepaper and in both he tells her how busy he is. The building still exists but the old front door has been removed and now serves as the entrance to a garage connected to a block of flats.

Stanley had joined the NCF about the time that Allen was imprisoned, and Bertrand Russell took over as chairman. My grandfather writes about sharing a room with Russell – occasionally deputising for him – and how he 'would draw [him] into conversation by putting some quite foolish question in philosophy which he would answer with perfect seriousness and courtesy, and at considerable length. I am afraid our routine work suffered not a little, but the intellectual stimulus was, to me, a great gain.' Russell, on the other hand, in a letter at this time to his friend Ottoline Morrell remarks that the NCF no longer interested him and the staff were 'full of petty quarrels and sordidness'. One doesn't know, of course, to whom he was referring. What neither Stanley nor Russell would have realised was that, bizarrely, they were distantly related by marriage through Jess's family and the Dukes of Bedford, the Russells.

The philosopher Bertrand Russell around the time he
worked at the No-Conscription Fellowship

The administration was meticulously organised. Stanley describes how
every official had an understudy, so that if the organisation was raided and
broken up, the whole operation could be set in motion again in a few hours.
There was in fact a secret office: a room at 8 Merton House, Salisbury
Court, just off Fleet Street. Records of every CO were kept, the grounds of
his objection, his appearance before tribunals, civil courts, courts martial,
and even which prison or Home Office settlement he was in. The NCF also
maintained contact with COs, arranging visits to camps, barracks and prisons.
Its press department drew the attention of the public to the ill-treatment
and brutality many COs were subject to. The organisation also published
leaflets and from March 1916 a newspaper called the *Tribunal*, which the
government tried to suppress by smashing the printing presses. Sometimes
the police did indeed raid the premises, carrying away stacks of papers and
following staff down the street. Stanley helped with the newspaper, writing
the occasional article. Meanwhile, the political department briefed MPs
and drafted questions to ministers. Women played a crucial part – firstly, as
mothers, sisters, wives, girlfriends and friends of the men who often had to
face hostility from family and neighbours, and secondly, as workers in the
organisation itself, particularly when the men were imprisoned.

There were many justifications for refusing to fight. The most common was that war and the act of killing were inconsistent with most religious beliefs. Many followed this conviction despite their respective churches supporting the government's position. Others posed a political argument against the war. This was the age when many left wingers thought war had no place in a truly socialist society. In the words of Keir Hardie, founder of the ILP: 'Militarism and democracy cannot be blended.' Some argued that the war had no clear moral purpose; rather it was the result of the capitalist powers manoeuvring for position. Others objected to any form of fighting, while still others opposed only the current conflict.

Overall, opposition to the fighting was a minority view, held and acted upon by less than half of one per cent of eligible men. From March 1916 until the end of the war, though, sixteen thousand men were registered as COs and were allocated alternative service 'of national importance'. Such work was primarily unarmed service in the Non-Combatant Corps or Royal Army Medical Corps, or civilian labour such as farm or factory work. Some worked as stretcher bearers, many of whom performed immense acts of bravery and suffered losses alongside their conventional comrades-in-arms. Others refused to cooperate with the authorities at all. A campaign of shaming men to enlist by presenting them with a white feather if they were not in uniform had helped create a situation in which every man had to be seen to be 'doing his bit' and nonconformity led to mockery. COs also had to withstand the pressure to conform when isolated in barracks, army camps and prisons. Some men were shipped to France in May 1916 as the government and army attempted to break their resolve; some were sentenced to death, although sentences were commuted to ten years' penal servitude.

In 1917 Stanley was given access to the personal stories of a number of COs in order to write a book recording their experiences. It was called *The Men Who Dared*, and was published the same year. I read its hundred pages in the library of the Friends House in Euston Road, London. It was with a certain amount of pride that I told the librarian, as she handed me the book plucked from the shelves, that it had been written by my grandfather. It is a moving testimony to the courage of these vilified men as they defied government edict and faced derision in the press and from the public at large. Although it contains prisoners' exact words, Stanley interpolates his own views and concludes by putting their ideological stand into a wider context. The book starts with a quotation from Stanley's friend, the pacifist Maude Royden: 'I tell you there is a mightier heroism still [than that of the brave soldier] – the heroism not of the sword but of the cross; the adventure not of war, but of peace.'

The war had been made by old men, Stanley argues, and it was ironic that just as idealistic young men were starting to shake off outmoded Victorian ways, the war intervened and halted that progress. The censorship employed in the military tribunals meant that the public learnt little of their content, a situation bolstered by the press's connivance with the military in publishing virtually nothing. But the fact that the COs were called up to make their case before a mocking tribunal paradoxically strengthened their conviction – and their faith was invariably profoundly deepened by the experience of resisting the might of the military machine. Yet more was to come in the isolation of the cell where they were encouraged 'to think the matter over'. If that failed to bring a change of heart, mental and physical bullying, abuse and even torture, were introduced.

Recruitment posters urged young men to enlist as volunteers in the First World War

The 'spiritual' headquarters of the NCF was Wormwood Scrubs where, at the time of Stanley writing *The Men Who Dared*, between seven hundred and a thousand men were imprisoned. Some relished the peace and quiet as an opportunity for reflection; others resented the pro-war message of the sermons preached to them. For people like Fenner Brockway it was a transformative experience:

> *I cannot describe to you the wonderful sense of comradeship there*
> *is among the COs in prison... I shall never forget the first day*
> *I went on exercise at Scrubs. You cannot conceive the sense of*
> *spiritual exaltation and expansion received from the sight of those*
> *200 COs marching in step around the prison yard! It gave me new*
> *hope for the future.*

There was profound learning on both sides. Nor must the COs' legacy be underestimated. The massive loss of life which resulted from the First World War encouraged much public sympathy with the pacifist cause in the 1920s and 30s. It meant that the outbreak of the Second World War would be marked by a more sympathetic system of conscription and a significantly greater awareness of the legitimacy of conscientious objection.

Stanley devotes the final chapter – 'The Fires of the Crucible' – to pondering the possibility of the appearance of a new kind of person: international man. He writes: 'There will emerge a kind of man who means with great seriousness what he says... they will carry with them a new and terrible sincerity... [there will be] a type of man in whom the religious and the social sense will be united as rarely before.' Fine words, of course, but it is the personal testimonies of the COs that one remembers.

One of the few venues which accepted bookings for NCF peace meetings was the Brotherhood Church in Hackney, which was by now a full-blown opponent of the war. It had been holding meetings since January 1916, often being attacked by pro-war factions. On 28 July 1917, 250 pacifists, including Bertrand Russell, gathered at the church for a day of action and speeches, but word got out and the hall was surrounded by a mob of eight thousand, many of them in military uniform. There was a forced entry and the pacifists were the victims of vicious attacks, the police doing nothing to protect them. Some attackers used wooden boards full of rusty nails and many received severe injuries. I have no evidence that Stanley was among the pacifists but he may well have been. Canadian soldiers played a prominent part in the raids, so it is intriguing to speculate whether his brother Norman, now over in Europe to fight with the Canadian troops, was involved. If so, I wonder what his attitude to the pacifists would have been, and what the brothers would have said to each other if they'd met.

Rioters attempt to break up a pacifist meeting at the Brotherhood Church, Hackney

The NCF left much to be desired in Stanley's eyes. While recognising that the members were united in action, he argued that their theories and motives were miles apart. In *The Adventures of a Spiritual Tramp* he writes:

> *There were representatives of weird sects who based their opposition to militarism on their interpretation of scripture; there were others who refused to fight in what they saw as a capitalist war, though they had no objection to taking up arms on behalf of a Communist revolution; some appealed to reason; not a few were just uncompromising individualists who denied the right of the state to conscript its citizens.*

He longed for an organisation that was more united in its approach and he found it in the Fellowship of Reconciliation, a Christian grouping at whose core was the principle of non-resistance. He decided to transfer his allegiance to this body. Once again, with the NCF he had lost faith in an organisation because at its heart, he argued, it lacked an incontrovertible purpose; the philosopher and theologian seeking a watertight ideological position had won out over the man of action.

*　*　*

The FoR had begun as a response to the prospect of war in 1914. On the eve of its outbreak, the former chaplain to the German Kaiser, a Lutheran called Friedrich Siegmund-Schultze and an English Quaker, Henry Hodgkin, parted at Cologne railway station with the words: 'We are one in Christ and can never be at war'. Hodgkin followed up this commitment by holding a conference in Cambridge in December 1914, attended by 130 Christians of all denominations, at which a visionary statement was drafted. The FoR saw itself as an 'international movement of people who commit themselves to active nonviolence as a way of life and as a means of personal, social, economic and political transformation'. Being at core Christian, it believed that Jesus was a 'radical peacemaker'. Its original principles were set out in what became known as the Basis.

The approach of the FoR was quiet and gentle in contrast to the more combative approach of the NCF. It also provided an antidote to the feverish passions of a war-mad world. At first Stanley thought he had discovered the heart of Christianity, encapsulated by the organisation's fervent belief in the tenets of the Sermon on the Mount. It was here that he met Muriel Lester to whose revolutionary Christian project in Bow – Kingsley Hall – he was later to lend his support; for now they worked together on the FoR's social service committee. Here, too, he met Hodgkin, and Theodora Wilson Wilson and Wilfred Wellock, both of whom were to become his colleagues in a different venture. Differences of opinion were settled in committee without recourse to vote-taking and a course of action was decided upon after prayerful silence. As a result, there was an absence of personal bitterness and intrigue. The fact that the small group was pitched against a world at war increased the sense of fellowship and deepened members' loyalty to the cause. It operated out of 17 Red Lion Square, which had been the residence of three worthies of the art world – Dante Gabriel Rossetti, William Morris and Edward Burne-Jones. Rossetti, founder of the Pre-Raphaelite Brotherhood, had rented rooms there from 1851 and then recommended the place despite its 'dampness and decrepitude' to his friends Morris and Burne-Jones, who moved there in 1856.

In a phase of cracking down on peace groups publishing anti-war propaganda, the police often raided the FoR headquarters. On one occasion they were greeted at the door by its general secretary, Leyton Richards, who told them: 'I will save you some trouble by giving you straight away the most subversive literature we have in this office.' He then handed the police officer a copy of the New Testament.

Towards the end of 1917, Stanley was appointed travelling secretary, which gave him numerous opportunities to speak on behalf of the FoR to Labour bodies around the country. Among the Durham and South Wales miners and the Lancashire cotton spinners and in the grime of the Black Country he encountered the rougher side of socialism. The visits, in which he addressed crowds on street corners and in halls, contrasted with the ultra-spiritual approach of his FoR colleagues. But he was disappointed in the way the spinners, weavers, railway men, miners and iron workers accepted the terrible conditions they worked under. He would have liked the Labour literature to be far more upbeat and optimistic, offering a real alternative to the workers' drab lives. Incidentally, Ruth Slate was at this time working at the Rowntree factory in York and Stanley made plans, on his way to a talk in Stockton-on-Tees, to stop off and see her, but events intervened.

Almost inevitably, perhaps, my grandfather eventually baulked at the very characteristics that had initially drawn him to the FoR. The habitual intellectual restlessness reappeared. This time he accused his employers of elitism and lack of humility. He criticised them for having become superior, removed from the ordinary concerns of humanity. He writes: 'I found myself longing for the appearance among us of a sweaty, mud-stained and foul-mouthed soldier from the front. It would have been such a relief to have heard somebody swear with real feeling. I did my best to supply the defect, but the inhibitions were too strong.' He thought that a body which claimed to have discovered the only true foundation of society should have had something to say about the class war and the economy, but when he raised these issues he was met with a stony Quaker silence. He objected to what he saw as the excessive kindness of everyone, when the true message of the Gospels was tough and uncompromising. He also said the people associated with the group were stodgy and lacking in humour.

Stanley's fight with the FoR had one more round to go. He now challenged it on theological grounds, asking at a committee meeting whether they were pacifists because they were Christians or Christians because they were pacifists. He was sure that there were a number of members who called themselves Christian because they seemed to find in the New Testament a type of idealism which endorsed their own. They agreed with Christianity because it agreed with them, he maintained.

Stanley had originally offered himself spontaneously to the NCF, and then to the FoR, finding a much-needed refuge at a time of turmoil after his resignation from Trinity. But in walking away from the pulpit, he discovered that social action alone would never be enough for him. Despite this realisation, he poured himself into a new area of secular activity. Another disenchanted member of the FoR provided Stanley with an opportunity to spread his revolutionary wings in another anti-war endeavour.

~ 15 ~
A CRUSADER FOR PEACE

One might expect a pacifist newspaper to physically distance itself from the hurly-burly of mainstream journalism. If its central tenet is primarily one of love and understanding one could understand why it might choose to have its offices far away in some low-key suburb. But when its message is delivered in passionate, even strident and aggressive tones, then there is a strong case for saying that it belongs exactly where hard-hitting journalism is positioned – in other words, in Fleet Street. Perhaps the name of the revolutionary Christian publication that Stanley now started writing for, the *New Crusader*, provides a strong enough clue to its character. From its inception, its editorial line was challenging and uncompromising – and it was indeed situated in Bride Lane, a stone's throw from the newspaper giants of the day.

It was a woman with the unlikely name of Theodora Wilson Wilson, a fellow escapee from the quietude of the Fellowship of Reconciliation, who threw Stanley a lifeline by asking him to write a regular weekly column. A Quaker, she was a formidable woman, a published writer of popular children's stories with a Christian message, whose 'abounding enthusiasm and courage was not modified even by that dubious quality known as discretion', according to Stanley. She had just taken over the proprietorship of the *New Crusader* after its founding editor, Wilfred Wellock, was imprisoned for declaring himself a conscientious objector. A working-class Lancastrian, Wellock had started the publication in March 1916 'for the promotion of pacifism'. On his imprisonment, the operation had moved to London.

Stanley was to write for the journal for the next four years. Over that period, until May 1923, he penned, under many different pseudonyms, at least five hundred articles. Among the bizarre bylines he used were Piers Plowman, The Tramp, The Ploughman, Peter the Hermit, Penrhys and Saggart, and on a handful of occasions his own name. The first two pen names represent his most serious opinion pieces on political and religious issues.

From this point the family seem to have drifted even further into the background, both geographically and emotionally. It may be that my grandmother had had her fill of Leytonstone and she was instrumental in the move to Rodney Stoke in Somerset. They had seen the remote cottage while on holiday and when it became available, they decided to take it. Jess felt most at home in the country and now she wanted her children to benefit from a rural existence. She may also have had enough of Stanley's zealous friendships with younger women; in any case, the family never returned to London. He, meanwhile, was only able to visit the family when the demands of work allowed, which wasn't often. 'It was a severe deprivation,' he writes. I am not sure where he lodged in London; he may have continued living at 6 Poppleton Road, but I have no evidence of that. With theological considerations coming increasingly to the fore and physical adventures receding, there's a shift of emphasis in the narrative. My grandfather, in the early years an explorer of the external world, now becomes an explorer of the heart and mind. And for that indulgence, the family paid a heavy price in material terms: their hand-to-mouth existence became the norm for many years to come.

Looking back on these days of working on the *New Crusader*, Stanley writes in *The Adventures of a Spiritual Tramp*: 'Its big headlines [and] bold display of Biblical texts broke every canon of good taste... But the opportunity of journalistic warfare was a temptation not to be resisted... There was a childish simplicity about the [journal] that was not without its delightful side in an over-sophisticated generation.' The first byline he used was 'Piers Plowman', a reflection of his love of the work for which the medieval writer William Langland is famous. While the war was still being fought, the magazine's pacifist Christian message is everything that one would expect. Christ himself was a pacifist; therefore we should not join the fight, ran the argument; we should vigorously oppose the mainstream churches' support for the call to arms and thereby hasten the end of the conflict; the enemy is not an enemy – rather, both sides are equal in the eyes of God. 'We allowed ourselves the liberty to say what we liked in the way we liked, and snapped our fingers at censorships and police,' Stanley writes. 'The latter occasionally raided our office, but somehow we managed to escape prosecution.'

Stanley now started to take his pacifism into the personal arena, forging the idea of a revolution of the soul to bring about lasting, psychological change. He continually urged people to first have a firm faith. From that sense of an external authority and permanence, believers would gravitate towards non-violence, he argued. To this would be added radical views about the way society and work were structured, the need for land reform, women's rights and so on. But these changes could not be brought about by gradual evolution. Nothing but a revolution of the soul would do. He writes:

Imagine for a moment that... Jesus emerged from our midst today and ventured with the same boldness and clearness as of yore to enunciate... the ideals of the Kingdom of God... Suppose that this Teacher secured a popular following, and that the people, tired of the game of financiers and politicians, turned to him with hope and trust, and that, in consequence, a movement that threatened militarist ambitions was initiated? Would not the authorities do all in their power to crush him? What action would those administering the Military Service Act take if he happened to be, as Jesus was, of military age? Would you... have an attempt to force this modern representation of Christ to abandon his preaching and teaching in order that he might learn how to disembowel Germans? And when he refused what would happen?

It was a hard message and one that he delivered at public meetings up and down the country, invariably to the consternation of listeners who challenged him with predictable responses. They asked what would happen if people laid down their arms and why did God allow this to happen at all. The Jesus that Stanley promoted was often the irascible one who turned over the tables of the money changers in the temple.

As the war neared its end, he – like many commentators at that time – considered the question of European reconstruction. Yet this was no normal physical rebuilding of institutions and nations. He posited the notion that what the peoples of Europe needed were 'spiritual artists', men and women who could forge a new and better world in the image of God. It was another example of his difficult and challenging ideas. He writes: 'Give us but a handful of lovers who have wandered through the glories of God's own country, and we shall soon have a wave of creative energy that shall make the wilderness that war has blasted blossom like the rose.'

With the war over on 11 November 1918, the shaken West entered into an excoriating self-examination of the type of world it wanted to reconstruct. A plethora of revolutionary social, economic and cultural movements emerged from the shadow of the conflict, and a kind of desperate optimism prevailed. Gathering Fascist and Communist forces faced each other across a new ideological divide. Miss Wilson believed the *New Crusader* needed a fresh vision that reflected revolutionary Christianity in peacetime, and resigned as editor. Wellock, now out of prison, resumed the reins at the start of 1919 and the journal changed its name to the *Crusader,* while increasing its page count. After a few issues with the enlarged format, it promptly ceased publication, then reappeared three weeks later. In desperate need of funds to guarantee publication beyond February, it launched an appeal. Donations trickled in, but these barely covered production, with contributors – Stanley included – taking what little payment that donors and readers offered. Stanley's meagre pay, compared to what he had received at Trinity, must have taxed Jess's housekeeping skills to the limit.

For my grandfather, his 'Piers Plowman' column was dropped in favour of that of 'The Tramp', which was to continue almost uninterrupted for the next three years. This new column was accompanied by artwork that said 'At Ye Signe of Ye Broken Sword', the idea being that these columns were set in a pacifist-leaning hostelry of that name. Stanley invented little scenarios in which friends hold earnest conversations with the kindly landlord looking on with an avuncular eye, adopting the role of master of ceremonies. It was reminiscent of the part played by the Philosopher in *Poverty Gulch.*

Refreshingly, the somewhat hectoring tone of some of his 'Piers Plowman' columns disappeared, to be replaced by an altogether lighter atmosphere where ideas were gently debated and made accessible to the reader. One feels oneself smiling now and again. Unfortunately, he was unable to sustain this new approach and soon reverted to the original, opinionated format.

In October the *Crusader* announced that it was undergoing more editorial changes, saying that the editor Wellock was due to move to Holland to start work on an international paper. Stanley had been scheduled to take over as editor but was 'held up' in Somerset. Miss Wilson comments ruefully: 'I hope he will turn up some time shortly.' By the following week he was in the chair. The appointment meant that he had to be in the Bride Lane office virtually every day, curtailing the number of visits he could make to Somerset.

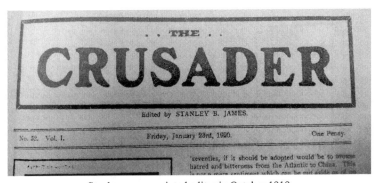

Stanley was appointed editor in October 1919

Stanley tried to justify the amount of time he lived away from Jess and the family by drawing on scripture. He writes in the *Crusader*:

It is indeed a lonely trail on which the Christian revolutionist sets forth. He must often see with sinking heart the lights of home grow dim in the distance and, in place of the cheerful babel of voices round the fireside, hear only the soughing of the wind as it sweeps through the wild places through which his path lies... If we are called to sacrifice the love of husband or wife, of father and mother, it means that the Love for which this sacrifice is made is able to take its place... Once it is realised that the relationship of the soul to God is to be at least as passionate and intimate as these human companionships, how cold and distant appear even our warmest devotions! [There are] gracious compensations which those who have made these renunciations discover.

With Wellock and Miss Wilson still contributing, as well as other prominent Christian Socialists writing weekly pieces, the *Crusader* entered a productive period of inspired and challenging journalism, even though it was still strapped for cash. The *Methodist Times* called it 'a very gallant journal' and described it as 'daring, fresh, original and thoroughly well-informed'. Stanley writes:

Controversy with other papers and between our own contributors was the very breath of life of this aggressive and militant little journal. Nor were we content with printing provocative articles. We organised means to see that those who might disagree with us should read them, for we had a band of enthusiastic helpers who patiently stood outside halls where public meetings were being held or even boldly invaded the meetings of opponents to sell the paper. We even had our banner (painted by Laura Knight) in the May Day procession. It was all great fun.

He also set up 'at home' events in which readers and supporters were invited to the journal's office to share ideas. Later these get-togethers took place at the Minerva Café, 144 High Holborn, which was the headquarters of the breakaway Women's Freedom League, a non-violent movement that took issue with the aggressive campaigning of the Women's Social and Political Union led by Emmeline and Christabel Pankhurst. The café was used by a wide range of different groups, including the Anarchist Discussion Circle and the British Socialist Party (BSP), which would go on to be an important component of the Communist Party.

* * *

With a portrait of Lenin hanging on the office wall and his feet firmly under the desk, Stanley set about turning the magazine into an organ that reflected his own socialist vision. But because he was no iconoclast, he left the door ajar to others whose views didn't concur with his own, as any good editor does. With many diverse contributors, the magazine was something of a rollcall of leading radical Christian thinkers. He himself entered the most left-wing period of his life. He saw salvation for mankind in communism with the Russian Revolution providing a template for other countries to follow. In May 1919 he writes: 'It is in local bodies and in trade unions that the new forces of government are being exercised... The most interesting example is the Soviet form of government. It seems as though [that] is what we may expect for the future.'

A portrait of Lenin hung on the wall of the *Crusader* office

Bizarrely, I found an article of his in similar mode in the pages of a Finnish language newspaper published in the US about the same time, and a former student of mine kindly agreed to translate it for me. Here is the core of it: 'The only romantic aspect of life worthy of mention is the socialist movement... It's a wonderful adventure that we all can be part of. The goal of the movement is to create a world where joy is part of normal, everyday life.' Was Stanley merely fulfilling another editor's commission when he wrote this idealistic take on socialism? In which case one might forgive him as he had mouths to feed and needs must. But if it was crafted from a deeper, more ideological part of his mind then it demands close scrutiny because it exhibits a far more utopian view of socialism than is the norm.

Others who made contributions in article or letter form were G. K. Chesterton, Bertrand Russell, Sylvia Pankhurst, Jerome K. Jerome, Fenner Brockway, Dean Inge and Bishop Vernon Herford. Writers such as George Bernard Shaw, Walt Whitman and Leo Tolstoy were quoted extensively, too. 'Marriage and the Sex Problem' was the title of a series of articles by the distinguished German philosopher and pacifist, Professor Friedrich Wilhelm Foerster. Stanley conducted an illuminating interview with Lilian Baylis, manager of the Old Vic theatre, in which they explored the common ground between theatrical performance and religious experience. 'Penrhys' was used to sign off articles about the South Wales miners, and 'Saggart' concluded Stanley's review of the biography of fellow hobo Jack London written by his wife, Charmian Kittredge.

The suffragist Sylvia Pankhurst was a frequent contributor to the paper

Stanley's old friend Captain Jack White even got in on the act by having two articles published. The message of the first – 'A Plea for Christian Communism' – is one of extreme idealism. Muriel Lester started contributing articles, in one responding to a critic who lambasted her do-gooding activities in the Bow district of London's East End with a stark portrayal of the conditions that working-class families endured. She shows that, through her access to help and funds, the lives of the desperately poor could be improved. In another article she describes her fledgling project known as Brethren of the Common Table, which one newspaper dubbed the 'voluntary poverty movement'. Its ethos was that members should pool their income after their material needs had been met. The proceeds were then distributed among the poor of Bow. Apparently, the group of four, of which Stanley himself was one, had come in for considerable criticism from various quarters of the press. Stanley, as *Crusader* editor, was giving his friend the opportunity to put her side of the story.

Muriel Lester, who mounted a stout defence of
her voluntary poverty movement

In March, in a widely circulated manifesto, the group renounced their wealth and invited the British public to join them in voluntary poverty. It received coverage in the *Daily News*, the *Star*, the *Evening Standard* and the *Christian World* in Britain and in numerous US publications. In his later writings, Stanley never once mentioned that he was a member of this group. Why was he so reticent? Was he ashamed? Of the four, he was the only man and the only one who was the chief breadwinner of a large family. Quite how much money he contributed to the cause is unknown; nor is it known for how long he continued this arrangement. What is clear, however, is the financial impact it must have had on Jess and the family. Did she even know that he was giving away money?

The manifesto affirmed their Christian obligation to share God's love through the 'sacrament of fellowship'. They sought the blessing 'derived from intimate contact with the sorrows of the oppressed'. The meetings began with silent prayer, followed by welcoming the presence of God, then 'we become severely practical, and individually declare our incomes, earnings and doles', according to Lester's article in the *Evening Standard*. 'It isn't enough to give away money,' she explains, 'we feel we have no right to possess it.'

In describing my grandfather's contribution to the cause, Lester writes: 'A great work was done by the Rev. Stanley James, editor of the *Crusader*, who served as a soldier in the Spanish American War, worked as a cowboy in the Wild West, and nearly starved time out of number.'

Members placed food, clothing and excess earnings on the table for others to take freely. Nor did they conduct any means testing, so on occasions freewheelers took the gifts without recrimination. This gave the members the chance to show God's love, it was argued.

None of the four seems to have stuck wholeheartedly to their vow of poverty, however. Lester continued to depend financially on her sister Doris (who didn't join) after their parents' death; Rosa Hobhouse had access to her husband's family trust; and Mary Hughes retained control over an inheritance which included several substantial properties in Buckinghamshire; she did, however, make these available as homes for the unemployed and 'fallen women'. One assumes that eventually Stanley's contributions petered out.

Around this time a procession of representatives from many different religious denominations and trade unions made its way down Oxford Street to the astonishment of Saturday shoppers. The theme was 'the social message of Christianity'. The participants gathered at Hyde Park Corner and listened to speeches addressing the topic of equality before God. The event achieved remarkable unity, according to the *Crusader* report. Nine months later another interdenominational procession to coincide with May Day took place and this time advance notification of the event in the form of a letter to the *Manchester Guardian* was published, with Stanley as one of twenty-one signatories. The letter urges the church to stand shoulder to shoulder with the Labour Party and to demand economic as well as political freedoms.

The journal also published a letter from the founder of the Scout Movement, Lord Baden-Powell, who expressed dissatisfaction with the negative light in which his movement had been portrayed in an article. The language is so convoluted that it is impossible to ascertain what caused the complaint, although one assumes that the offending article had wagged a finger at the movement for encouraging militarism. The hand of Stanley, perhaps?

A figure whose poems and essays appeared regularly was Vera Pragnell, who had worked for the FoR, which was probably where she'd met Stanley. She was a woman of strong socialist principles and a follower of Edward Carpenter. Having come into an inheritance, she bought fifty acres of land at Heath Common near the village of Washington in West Sussex, where she set about establishing a utopian community to put God's love into practice, providing free plots of land to all comers. By December of that year, what became known as 'The Sanctuary' had opened its doors. It lent – without any exchange of money – a half-acre plot to anyone who wanted one and the *Crusader* gave her space to publish her manifesto. The commune had no rules and was, all at once, a retreat from capitalism, a Christian shrine, a self-sufficient horticultural centre, a cooperative and a training centre where others could learn how to establish sanctuaries around the world. It also had a shop, a school and a room for theatre and dancing.

Those wanting to experiment with an alternative lifestyle started knocking on her door; among them was the Shakespearean actor Wilfrid Walter, who lived in a road mender's caravan. He described Vera as 'of magnificent stature... her great encompassing eyes gleamed gaily through a lock of chestnut hair that escaped most wilfully from a long 'kerchief, reminiscent somehow of a veil'. There was fairground lady Betty, an Indian with a white wife, a builder with a horde of children and a drunken mother, people with bizarre theories about how to achieve the good life, pagans such as the occultist, poet and publisher Victor Neuburg, and a nudist couple. An old bus with no wheels came to be occupied by the painter Dennis Earle, who for a time was Carpenter's gay lover. Earle and Pragnell formed a close relationship and married in 1927. For a while the commune thrived but, after ten years, scandals hit the headlines with stories of free love and mass nakedness. But what really crushed the idealism were the disputes between neighbours, with residents formally registering their plots as their own property.

It was probably inevitable that Stanley should call on his pacifist friend Reginald Sorensen to write for the paper. They had both been members of the NCF in the First World War and Sorensen had been Unitarian minister of the Free Church, Walthamstow, so their paths would have crossed at home, too. Sylvia Pankhurst was a close colleague of Sorensen's through his membership of the Men's League for Women's Suffrage. With his wife Muriel, Sorensen set up Moore Place, a vegetarian commune in Stanford-le-Hope, Essex, which had been suggested as a place for Jess and family after Stanley resigned from Trinity. Sorensen also ran a bookshop known as 'The Guild' from his home, 31 Palmerston Road, Walthamstow. He seems to have had an adventurous side to him because one summer he and his wife drove a caravan advertising the *Crusader* through the seaside towns of the south coast. Going by dispatches he wrote to Stanley, they seem to have had a marvellous time, although there is no indication that their venture boosted sales in any way.

* * *

In Stanley's articles one can now start to detect another element alongside the call to socialism. So subtle is it at first that one hardly notices it. In his public columns he had begun a painstaking, private exploration of the case for Catholicism, confident that none of his colleagues would realise. 'There is a certain type of person to whom Catholicism is not so much a matter of disagreement as one which lies entirely beyond them,' he writes in *The Adventures of a Spiritual Tramp*. 'That my editor was of this kind accounted for the fact that I was enabled to express my growing Catholic sympathies unchecked. My views were simply not understood.'

He was careful not to use the word 'Catholic' outright, but employed phrases that described Christian mystery and ritual. Looking back later, he writes: 'The Tramp articles are, at least, a sufficient answer to any charge of having submitted to the Catholic Church on the impulse of the moment.' Later, in a bolder move, he came out and wrote about 'Free Catholicism', the movement that Dr Orchard, minister at King's Weigh

House, was experimenting with by devising a form of service that combined elements of Catholicism and Protestantism. Stanley published transcripts of his friend's sermons from the previous Sunday.

So far, so undetected. In March 1920 the weekly journal increased the number of pages to twelve, an incredible undertaking considering the skeleton staff at its disposal. Clearly, my grandfather was working very hard. Eventually exhaustion got the better of him and in early April he was forced to take time off. Miss Wilson stepped into the breach, commenting: 'He has been working at an immense strain, and though he is keen to keep at it, we hope that he may be induced to slack off somewhat for a while. Yet even from his sick room copy arrives!' A week later she writes: 'Readers will be glad to hear that Mr James is better, but his progress is slow, and we are hoping that he will have the patience to give himself a wise resting-time.'

Stanley's team of writers had been gossiping among themselves, having detected the Catholic strain in his and Orchard's writings, and they didn't like it. Meetings grew increasingly acrimonious and it seems that Stanley had taken to bullying some members of staff. The upshot was that four leading contributors – Wellock, Miss Wilson, Will Chamberlain and J. D. Holmes – resigned from the editorial committee. They explained: 'Some of us are... finding it increasingly difficult to support the Editor [Stanley] and those who think with him in the expression of religious life known as Free Catholicism.'

To replace his writers, Stanley started wooing two men whose work he admired – the Reverend Conrad Noel, who was known as the 'Red Vicar' of Thaxted, and A. J. Penty, prominent in the Guild Socialism movement – and persuaded them to write regular columns. Conrad Noel was an acquaintance of Stanley's rather than a close friend, but their minds met and Noel seems to have willingly contributed a long series of articles entitled 'The People's Life of Jesus', which started in December 1921.

Noel had become vicar of St John the Baptist, Thaxted, in 1910, where he quickly established a reputation as an outspoken Christian Socialist, joining the ILP and becoming a founding member of the British Socialist Party in 1911. Stanley on at least one occasion had preached there during his time as a Nonconformist minister. Noel was a man of enormous energy and transformed the Essex village into a hive of political and cultural activity. He was best known for hanging the red Communist flag and the tricolour of Sinn Féin alongside the flag of St George in the church, sparking off a long-running feud known as the 'Battle of the Flags', with groups of angry Cambridge students removing the flags, only for them to be reinstated the next day. Eventually, a consistory court ruled against the display and Noel was forced to take them down. He believed that Christianity was about beauty and ritual, thereby attracting many well-known artists and musicians. For many years he collaborated with the composer Gustav Holst on musical events in the village. Later, folk traditions were added, and maypole and Morris dancing became part of the cultural scene.

ABOVE LEFT: the Reverend Conrad Noel, the 'Red Vicar' of Thaxted
ABOVE RIGHT: G.K. Chesterton, editor of *GK's Weekly*

A. J. Penty, meanwhile, wrote a series of articles under the title 'Christianity and Communism'. He was the force behind the launch of a new initiative called the Crusader League in December 1922, with support from Orchard and Stanley. The inaugural meeting, chaired by G. K. Chesterton, was held at the King's Weigh House on 24 January 1923. Its strongly idealistic manifesto sought to depart from the traditional socialist agenda based on a materialist, Marxist view of the means of production and substitute it with a system based on Christian principles. It believed in 'the primacy of spiritual values and in the imperishable worth of the individual'. At its launch, G. K. Chesterton remarked that he had no idea what the project was about or why he had been asked to promote it! The *Crusader* published a membership form which it invited readers to complete while paying a minimum subscription of five shillings per year. A handful of readers joined but within weeks the league had died without a trace.

Despite the failure of that particular scheme, Stanley had fond memories of Penty when he wrote a tribute to him in the *Catholic Herald* on his death in 1937. He had certainly had an huge influence on my grandfather:

Generally, it was at a table in an A.B.C. shop [a chain of cafes at the time] amid the clatter of plates and buzz of talk during the London rush hour that we met. We were too absorbed in the topics under discussion, however, to mind the noise... It was just after the war and the air was full of reconstruction theories. Idealists of all kinds... were trying to make themselves heard... Every school of thought imagined that its chance had come and was shouting at the top of its voice... Penty proved a real godsend. The confusion had no terrors for him. It was not perhaps a special intellectual brilliance which made his contributions welcomed by the harassed editor so much as his essential honesty. He was not a Catholic... but of all the men with whom I have discussed such subjects, he had the most Catholic outlook on social and economic questions... he had not a little to do in leading me to become one.

Stanley's Tramp column on 23 February 1923, headlined 'Labour's Dilemma', sparked another resignation, this time from a long-time and cherished pacifist writer, Will Chamberlain. In the column my grandfather drives a wedge between Labour's take on socialism and the Christian interpretation of it. A year and a half before, as we have seen, Chamberlain had resigned from the editorial committee over the overtly Free Catholic bias that the paper was displaying, but he had continued to write his column from a 'Christian Socialist Pacifist' viewpoint. Now he found it impossible to stay silent following Stanley's attack on Labour because his associates in the Labour Party were worried about his links with a publication that seemed to have less and less in common with what is generally understood to be socialism. Shortly afterwards the contributor N. E. Egerton Swann resigned.

They were falling like flies. A month later Stanley was to lose his star writer, Conrad Noel. It was a short piece by my grandfather entitled 'The Broad Issues' that caused the Red Vicar to see red and ended their professional relationship. If the article was in any way indicative of the direction of Stanley's thought, it marks a significant shift. Indeed, he seems to utterly reject the validity of any kind of secular socialism in favour of almost any initiative by any church. In it he writes:

Where it is a case of the Church versus the state... we stand every time on the side of the organisation which represents the Kingdom of God... If we have to make our choice between a state claiming to be humanitarian and progressive and a Church convicted of bigotry, greed, and reactionary sympathies, then, even in that case, we stand on the side of the church. For the worst Church is better than the best state, as the lowest type of man is a greater being than the highest type of animal. For the state, as such, is the creation of man, but the Church is the creation of God.

Where now was Lenin's portrait and where were his castigations of churches for their lack of moral fortitude? In replying, Noel doesn't hold back:

You have definitely thrown in your lot with the contemporary religious world... The assumption underlying your article that the Church of any given moment is divine, and that any form of 'secular' human society or government, be it good or bad, is 'merely' human and not divine, is to us the life-destroying heresy... Meanwhile, I fear that my 'People's Life of Jesus' is so fundamentally opposed to those things which Dr Orchard, yourself, and your readers hold dear that I am reluctantly compelled to withdraw it from your pages, Sincerely Yours, Conrad Noel.

And on 23 May, Sylvia Pankhurst, who was editing her own feminist/socialist journal *Workers'Dreadnought*, took objection to an article in praise of the Italian fascists that Stanley had somehow levered into the *Crusader*. Looking back later on these disagreements, Stanley writes:

There was a clash of divergent views on the committee, frequent
resignations after stormy scenes, all the harassing incidents
consequent upon the change of personnel of the controlling body. In
these discussions the issues dividing us became ever clearer to my
mind... I have never been able to arrive at truth by the light of the
study lamp. It has always needed some actual conflict with concrete
issues at stake. It has never been possible to think my way to a clearly
defined position in seclusion. Had I been able to do that, I might have
been spared the pain of grieving a large number of very sincere and
earnest persons and of making more enemies than is comfortable to
think of. These 'Crusader' committees gave me an arena in which,
contending with my colleagues, I fought my own doubts, indecisions
and vagueness. May they forgive me for all harsh and bitter speeches!

By the middle of May 1923, Miss Wilson, still the proprietor, had stepped in
and fired Stanley. The editorial states: 'With the next number of the *Crusader*
the present editorship will cease. On this occasion it is not necessary to do
more than state the fact.' Father John Spokes, who had long been associated
with the journal, had agreed to become editor. In his last issue Stanley writes
a farewell note to readers: 'Throughout it has been something much more
than a merely official position. The personal element has entered largely
into the relationships into which it brought me. And the severance of the
tie is consequently, in many respects, a sad one.' Stanley's departure from
the *Crusader* seems to have been particularly acrimonious.

* * *

Stanley's ructions in Ludgate Circus couldn't have been in stronger contrast
to the idyllic country life that the family were living in Somerset. My
mother used to recall their time there fondly. 'In the autumn we used to get
up early and walk through the mist to the top of the Mendips and pick the
mushrooms before the gypsies got them,' she told me. 'Some days there
were masses of them, far too many for us to eat.' So, they packed them up
and took them by bicycle to the station from where they were delivered to
London restaurants.

The James family lived out a frugal existence in their Mendip cottage, Somerset

Most of the children, in varying degrees, possessed their father's adventurous spirit, which meant that minor dramas were a common feature of their lives. Stanley was removed from the family, emotionally as well as physically, and in neither of the autobiographies do they take on any kind of importance. Because he was largely absent, these stories might seem mere additions to the main narrative, but they help to put him into context; besides, the children's escapades are fun to record.

My twelve-year-old mother Kitty spent a lot of time horse riding with her sisters Phyllis and Jessie on the hilltops above Cheddar Gorge, no doubt looking south from time to time to catch a glimpse of the Glastonbury Tor. One day, feeling that inherited family impishness a little more than usual, she chased her horse down to the bottom of a field, whereupon the frightened animal, feeling trapped, turned on her and chased her back up the slope, with who knows what dastardly acts of revenge in mind. But, luckily, her foot slipped and she fell, the kicking up of the grass and earth disturbing the horse enough to stop it in its tracks.

Stanley writes that the cottage contained a minimum of furniture and 'the conditions were as primitive as those of a Prairie shack, but no one seemed to mind'. This view was not shared by others. Auntie Jessie told a cousin of mine that they were so poor they had to live on what they could grow in the garden. There was no running water, so they had to collect what they needed from a spring in a nearby field and then carry it up the lane. The narrow house itself, rented from a landlord in the village, was built into the walls of a disused quarry, and the rough stones used in its construction were the low-quality ones left after every other house and barn on the estate had been built. The kitchen would have been a lean-to at the back of the house and the property suffered from severe damp problems.

With Stanley absent most of the time, Jess's life was one of unending drudgery and hardship. My mother said there was hardly a time when she wasn't unwell. The children, who occupied themselves with shooting rabbits and riding in the donkey cart by day, at night were forced to share beds and sleep 'top and tail'. 'The children were in their element,' Stanley writes.

One summer, no doubt cajoled into it by the mischievous Bob, the second child, the seven children cycled the fifteen miles to Weston-super-Mare to spend the day at the beach. Jess was unable to stop this bold expedition and was left waving them off down the lane with a pointless 'mind how you go'. The problem was there weren't enough bikes to go round. So, they invented a clever shuttle system in which half the party cycled ahead, with the smallest two sitting on the back, while the others walked behind. After a few miles the advance party threw the bikes into a roadside ditch and walked on. The second party reached the pick-up point and continued until they caught up with the first group – and so on to Weston-super-Mare. Even with very little traffic in those days, it was a risky endeavour. My mother told the story wondering how on earth they had managed it. In those days there was no need to travel to the Prairies to taste adventure: the highways and byways of the West Country could supply that equally well. Bob fell off his bike and cut his leg badly, but patched up the wound and soldiered on, all of them reaching the sands more or less in one piece.

On the beach Bob, who was seventeen, got up to his pranks. With the spade he'd brought with him he started digging a deep pit in the sand at the exact point where the large number of footprints indicated a well-trodden path for holidaymakers. Once he'd completed his three-foot-deep trap, he laid a crisscross pattern of flimsy sticks over the top, covered them with old newspapers, then sprinkled loose sand over the paper, making sure it covered his creation entirely. The children then sat back on the sand within sight of the structure, waiting for people to fall in. I think my mother said that one or two victims came a cropper while the children, a safe enough distance away from the scene of the crime, quietly sniggered but didn't let on. No doubt it's too fanciful to imagine that, after witnessing this act of youthful high jinks that endangered limb if not life, John, Bob's younger brother by ten years, decided to repay the James family's debt to the world by training to be an orthopaedic surgeon.

While we're on the subject of pranks, it was around this time that Phyllis – she must have been in her late teens – returning home by train after a shopping trip to Wells, pulled the communication cord at the point on the line nearest to the family home. The train came to a halt, the driver assuming that a passenger was in difficulties, whereupon Phyllis opened the carriage door, jumped out, climbed over the perimeter fence and ran home across the fields. Well, what else was one to do if your village had no station of its own? These were the tales of derring-do that my mother dropped into my childhood ears from time to time, and it was these stories that gave me my first inkling that the Jameses were a little unusual.

~ 16 ~
BILLIARDS OR BIBLE?

The unmistakeable harmonies of an Orthodox Church choir greeted me as I arrived late for Sunday service at the imposing Victorian Gothic, red-brick building in Duke Street, London. Hundreds of worshippers genuflected in response to prayers being sung by the bearded priest before the decorated altar. This was the cavernous space otherwise known as the Ukrainian Catholic Cathedral of the Holy Family in Exile. But I wasn't there to take part in the Mass but to see for myself where Stanley had first worshipped, then acted as assistant minister, from 1917 to 1923 at what was then known as King's Weigh House Congregational Church.

What was it that attracted Stanley to this beautiful building, boasting a corner tower that needled the West End sky, an elegantly gabled façade and a sweeping elliptical nave? Not so much the architecture as one man, Dr William Orchard, who was drawing huge crowds with his unique brand of socialist preaching tinged with ritualised elements, and his central desire to find a way of combining the best of Protestantism with the best of Catholicism. Orchard had been successful enough in his aims for this initiative to become officially known as 'Free Catholicism'. In aligning himself with this groundbreaking experiment, Stanley set himself on a course that would finally provide him with the spiritual contentment he'd been seeking.

Dr Orchard, whom Stanley already knew well as a fellow supporter of the New Theology and as a contributor to the *Crusader,* had introduced a service modelled on the Mass, something that Stanley had been fumbling towards in his closing years at Trinity, and at Burghley Hall with his small band of followers on Sunday evenings. For him the symbolism of the liturgy he witnessed at King's Weigh had a considerable potency. Orchard's forceful personality outstripped that of Stanley's and his massive following was testament to that. Analysing his reason for joining Orchard's experiment, Stanley makes an interesting comment:

> *I had taken up the work of a Christian minister more by accident than design... My interest in the Christian faith had at first been, to a large extent, a professional rather than a personal one. I was minister first and a Christian second... That stage, I think, had passed... My membership of the King's Weigh House symbolised to my mind my desire to remain in communion with the Christian community even though holding no other position in it than that of a layman.*

My grandfather was never one to take up an ideological position without first thoroughly examining it from every conceivable angle. So, too, with this theological experiment. 'There was a phase when the timid compromising programme of middle-class reformers, the lack of any systematic reading of history, and the sentimentality in which they often indulged, all but drove me into the ranks of the extreme left,' he writes. 'Gradually, however, the lessons of the past, the study of medieval society and, especially the story of the guilds drew my attention in another direction... One does not reach Rome by one road, but by many converging paths.' What he sought was authority... 'My mind was steadily moving towards the conception of a dogmatic and organic Faith.'

The gradual crystallisation of his thoughts was further helped by being appointed fulltime assistant to Orchard, a position he welcomed, even if the salary was minuscule. 'I needed just that framework of traditional doctrine which he was painfully recovering from the chaos into which religious liberalism had thrown non-Catholic theology,' he writes.

Dr William Orchard, a Congregational minister whose
Free Catholicism experiment sparked controversy

Soon after that, in his continuing quest for some kind of ecclesiastical authority, Stanley followed Orchard in being ordained by one Ulric Vernon Herford, who called himself 'Bishop of Mercia and Middlesex, Administrator of the Metropolitical See of Madura and Tinnevelly in India, of the Patriarchate of Babylon and the East', a title which sounds distinctly bizarre to the modern reader. Stanley claimed that this 'private adventure' gave him a kind of recognized authority. The ordination took place in private and it was preceded by the scantiest kind of instruction in the duties of the priesthood. 'In twenty-four hours, I was baptized, confirmed, ordained deacon and finally priested,' he writes.

* * *

Not that the new commitment was all plain sailing. 'It was not long before I began to detect definite and concrete flaws in the system of things in which I now lived and moved and had my being,' Stanley comments. 'In their haste to display their traditionalism, the hyphenated Catholics often exhibited a feverishness and an unbalanced zeal which were in direct opposition to the temper of a truly conservative ecclesiasticism.' He admits that he enjoyed 'dressing up', but says that it was 'the joy of the explorer rather than that of the discoverer that I experienced... Attention was fixed on ourselves to see how the new methods were answering rather than on the Church... It was necessary to keep up the appearance of being a Catholic night and day. Scarcely was it safe to go to sleep lest, during the hours of unconsciousness, one's "Catholicism" might disappear.' He still craved the unambiguous certainty of authority. A fragment of a poem he wrote at the time sums up the frustration he was feeling:

Great Jove occasion'ly will nod, they say,
One error in Creation plain to see
Proves that e'en God Himself may sometimes err,
Else would He not have thought of making me.

When prevailed upon to say Mass, he comments that it was the most painful ordeal he had ever undergone. 'I was almost incredibly stupid and slow to learn what was necessary; I made innumerable mistakes. My absent-mindedness was the jest of the parsonage. Hearing confession I dreaded with a literally unspeakable dread.'

Nor did he warm to the middle-class congregations flocking to hear Orchard, who was widely acknowledged to be one of the most powerful preachers in London. Stanley worried that his superior had little appeal for the illiterate or 'those outside the pale of social respectability'. On one occasion a woman complained that my grandfather looked like a cowboy, only to be told that he had been just that. 'Among people like this I was plainly out of place. In order to maintain my inner freedom, I think I must have adopted... the device of throwing off a smoke screen of reserve and apparent stupidity.'

Clearly, the down-to-earth aspects of Stanley's personality were craving an activity that related more to the real world. Luckily, he didn't have to leave because he was put in charge of the church's Darby Road mission in the shadow of Tower Bridge. On being appointed to this role, he was able to make use of lodgings within the Weigh House parsonage which was attached to the church in Binney Street. Although convenient and no doubt cheaper than renting his own digs, it nevertheless had the effect of cutting him off even more from the family in Somerset.

Interior of King's Weigh House. Reproduced by courtesy of the National Monuments Record

The Darby Road mission was essentially a social club offering residents of the area recreation in the form of a gymnasium, baths and billiards, and those working there were forerunners of today's social workers. The extra duties required Stanley to travel from the West End to the East End every day, a route which took him via the offices of the *Crusader*, which he was still editing. He decided to walk the five miles in each direction and relished the time this afforded him for contemplation. 'The juxtaposition of flaunted wealth and heart-breaking poverty never lost its significance,' he writes. The streets near Tower Bridge teemed with lorries going in and out of the docks and sailors from all over the world frequented the numerous pubs. Nearby a dirty, stinking Thames threaded itself along a continuous line of warehouses stretching as far as the eye could see. But he thought the people there were 'more real'. He warmed to the hard-pressed families – many were bargees from Wapping – who lived in rundown tenement blocks. No matter that they lied to philanthropists who arrived in vast numbers to help them or that they impassively endured the research groups who recorded their every move.

The building that housed the mission does not exist anymore; nor for that matter does Darby Road itself, although its name can be detected on maps of the day. The activities of the mission, designed to offset the debilitating effect of the dire poverty which the Tower Bridge community experienced, proved popular and so the premises were extended to provide even more facilities, with the overall aim of establishing a functioning settlement house – that is, a community centre offering training, education, legal advice, free meals and health services.

But Stanley's desired approach was to focus on theological matters, rather than alleviating the effects of material poverty. The established workers at the mission took a diametrically opposite view, and ideologically he found himself isolated. 'It was... the Mass that mattered. If that were once recognised as our fixed point, everything else would fall into its proper place,' he writes. 'I told myself that it might be necessary that [social activities] should die out altogether. My lack of interest in the social life was construed as due to the absence of human sympathy... I could not "come down to the level" of the folk among whom we were placed.' Besides, his fellow workers argued, Free Catholicism was the construct of cultured theorists, making it irrelevant to their clients.

Any possibility of reaching a compromise, or of using the activities as an entrée towards engaging in a more purposeful debate about the meaning of a spiritual existence, proved to be a project too far. 'I could not play billiards with zest when I was quite consciously aware that it was just such "attractions" that were... creating a false impression of our object,' he writes. Later, Stanley faced accusations that it was this stressful and unsuccessful period at the mission that had forced him away from the Congregational Church and into Catholicism. He utterly refuted that view. But one is left pondering the vehemence of his virulent opposition to such harmless social interaction, despite the fact that it may have provided welcome relief from the drudgery of those working people's everyday lives. Again, we have another instance of Stanley tackling a problem armed with a set of *a priori* ideas rather than, through organic growth, welding his ideas on to an established institution. Besides, shouldn't such alleviating measures have matched his socialist principles? Not for the first time, I am left confused – and troubled – by my grandfather's approach to change.

Phyllis, the oldest James child, leads a Christian march through
London's Bow district. Activist Muriel Lester walks behind her

Despite the opposition, he gave his remedy for East End deprivation one
last chance. He organised a series of special services to which local people
were invited. Workers visited tenement buildings handing out invitations;
there were street processions with candles and banners on the evening of
the service; and there were hymn singing and addresses at street corners.
Nothing was left to chance, but the enterprise was a complete failure. Billiards
had beaten the Bible. During a visit to the tenements, Stanley had called
on an old Irishman.

"'Who are yez?" he asked.

"'I come from the little church in Darby Street," I said.

"'There's only wan church," he hissed. "It's the Howly Catholic Church.'"

He writes that 'before this storm I bowed... I knew he was right. From
that moment, I think, my mind was made up. There was "only wan Church".'

In *The Adventures of a Spiritual Tramp*, Stanley takes Orchard to task for
being first and foremost a preacher rather than a close friend or confidant.
His sphere of operation was the public pulpit rather than the intimacy of the
drawing room. Clearly, Stanley would like to have chatted to his superior
in more depth. He says that Orchard lacked 'large simplicity' and that his
mind rarely rested. He was, Stanley maintains, more of a Cockney than a

peasant. Being essentially a Protestant, his Catholicism was of the playful kind rather than containing anything of substance. Stanley says that running through Orchard was an underlying strain of frivolity – he was, after all, known as the 'Bernard Shaw of Nonconformity'. 'His position might... be defined by saying that he is a Catholic as far as he can be without actually committing himself,' Stanley writes.

It seems no one was measuring up to my grandfather's expectations. Some of this may have been sour grapes as the two of them had stopped seeing eye to eye when Stanley told Orchard that he was considering being officially received into the Catholic Church and could no longer take Mass at King's Weigh. Orchard remonstrated that the decision would leave him in the lurch.

The comments above are based on observations in his first autobiography, which was published less than five years after these events. It was another time of uncertainty and doubt. In *Becoming a Man*, published in 1944, he had had twenty more years in which to reflect. In that time my grandfather seems to have mellowed and he takes a more considered view of those differences of opinion. For once, he mentions his family, pointing out that his indecision about the way forward needed to be resolved: 'I bore the responsibility for the maintenance of a wife and family. They had already endured enough on account of what may well have seemed and perhaps were my irresponsible eccentricities. Unless the case was absolutely imperative, I could not ask them to suffer more.'

In the later book, he also paints a kindlier and more appreciative portrait of Orchard. He acknowledges that his friend's offer to him to become his assistant at King's Weigh was tantamount to a lifeline. 'Collaboration with so stimulating a personality which he extended to me was a privilege,' he writes. 'I pay this tribute all the more gladly because, in a book I published while still anxious to burn my bridges, I did him some injustice.' Time, the great healer.

* * *

But the tensions were getting to Stanley, who was on the brink of collapse. He speaks of a time when he had been serving Mass at King's Weigh

House and was in prayer when suddenly he was convulsed by a spasm of uncontrollable sobbing. He describes how his body was shaking and he was unable to stop it. The conflicts and doubts had left him overwrought. His days at King's Weigh were drawing to a close. Despite the chance of filling a vacancy in another London Congregational church and being offered the pastorate of one in Liverpool, he pursued neither option. Intuitively, he knew it was impossible to continue in the Nonconformist ministry. He flirted with the idea of joining the Church of England but rejected it as unsatisfactory, a halfway house to nowhere. The Catholic Church was beckoning. The situation at the Darby Road mission had deteriorated beyond redemption and Orchard asked for a private meeting, perhaps to terminate Stanley's employment. Before his colleague could say anything, Stanley told him he was now fully determined to be received into the Catholic Church.

But he still held back from taking the final step, anxious to explore every corner of his being where doubt might linger. His Nonconformist roots could not be so easily abandoned; in fact, perhaps in essence they never were. To ease his passage towards the inevitable step, he took refuge in Catholic churches in different parts of London and spent hours meditating in the semi-darkness on the pros and cons of his impending decision. 'The silence was more helpful than would have been even the most eloquent and persuasive of preachers,' he writes.

He describes how he arranged to visit Father Woodcock at St Etheldreda's in Ely Place, near Holborn Circus, to talk things over:

With my hand on the bell I paused. I had not gone to ask for Instruction, yet I knew that if I rang the bell and was granted an interview, my last feeble objections would vanish, and I should find myself practically committed. At last, with the sort of jerky action you may see in a mechanical toy, I raised my hand and the peal rang out along the empty hall. I could have run away like a mischievous school-boy but something kept me rooted to the ground. There was no going back now.

In a 1949 article for the *Catholic Herald*, in a series in which converts looked back and described their 'path to Rome', Stanley comments that unless at that time in 1923 he found certainty and authority, he would have gone to pieces altogether. 'Finally... by an act of faith which was neither an experiment nor an adventure, I entrusted myself to Peter's bark,' he writes. 'In all the twenty-six years that have followed, filled though they have been with anxieties, I have never once regretted that step.'

After such a restless youth, any change in spiritual direction was bound to have a massive psychological impact on him. He devoted five pages of Chapter Ten of *Becoming a Man* to recording his feelings of disquiet prior to taking that final step. Aware that the long list of adventures he had undergone might suggest a disordered – or multiple – personality, he is keen to tie together the loose ends in order to present a picture of organic growth. 'Undoubtedly a process of disintegration can be discovered in my story. But it gives evidence, I hope, of an effort to overcome centrifugal tendencies, and, to effect an integration in which the several aspects would be found as parts of a coherent whole.' More important even than cohesion, he argues, is the question of personality. '[A man] belongs to a larger whole, a family, for instance, whose roots go back into the past, and he needs, in order to be fully man, to identify himself with those roots.'

He was fully aware that his footloose days – symbolised most redolently in his love for the poetry of Walt Whitman – constituted the abnegation of that sense of belonging, whether that be to family, denomination or country. It was too late to create that secular sense of belonging. By leaving this personal revolution until his fifties, he argues that it was impossible to make a conventional return to the fold: 'The condition resulting was like that of a foundling... by the time the Prodigal came to himself, it was too late to cultivate this type of continuity. By his own will, he had become an outcast.' All that was left was the quest for spiritual continuity:

[In Catholicism there] was a community which could trace its ancestry back to the beginning of things. It was not only the oldest aristocracy in the world but one which, apart from that, had the highest possible sanctions. It combined in itself all for which the outcast, the misfit, the ne'er-do-well clamoured... It was not Israel which was grafted into the European tradition, but Europe which was grafted into the ancient stock of Israel... What was, comparatively speaking, new was the realisation that the order imposed was... a tradition which linked us with all the generations of historic Christendom.

He had finally found a family, and the sense of belonging that this provided constituted a deeper and more nurturing relationship than anything of a more personal, cultural or domestic nature.

Two practical considerations held him back. Firstly, the man earmarked as his successor at King's Weigh was abroad and was unable to take up his duties; Stanley didn't want to leave Orchard without a successor. Secondly, he was more worried than usual about funds. The most obvious way of earning money, he realised, was to work as a freelance writer, but it would take time to establish himself.

By chance, an old friend from his early days at the FoR came on the scene. Not only were their conversations a help to Stanley, but it turned out that his friend had recently converted to Catholicism and was about to enter the Benedictine Order. He warned Stanley of the dangers of continuing to minister at an altar, the legitimacy of which he had ceased to believe. To be sure of his decision he went on a retreat at the same monastery which his friend was joining. 'I was like some shipwrecked sailor who has been thrown up by the waves on a friendly beach,' he writes.

He emphasised his sense of personal unworthiness and the need to surrender himself completely to a higher authority. No organisation or individual had ever demanded that ultimate sacrifice from him – and that is what he craved. The Catholic Church also appealed because of what he saw as its all-embracing inclusivity. He said he owed a debt to his friend G. K. Chesterton, who had opened his eyes to what he called 'the staleness of new religions' and the importance of recognising what was 'conventionally unconventional'. Psychologically, Stanley became aware that the greater freedom he enjoyed, the more he needed guidance. On his return from the monastery, he went to see Father Fabian Dix at St Dominic's Priory Church, Haverstock Hill, and it was there that he was finally received into the Catholic Church. The business-like ceremony couldn't have been less dramatic, he says. It was on 2 July 1923. But soon the positive effect of his decision made itself felt:

I experienced a new sense of liberty... It was glorious to find
life so rational and explorable... I learned from Catholic truth
how narrow and warped had been my tastes and how terribly
they misrepresented my real self. It has been and is a great joy

discovering these lost continents beneath the ocean of one's being...
Shall I be understood if I say that, standing before the vision of
Catholicism, the vocabulary of wonder breaks down and all I can
utter is some poor threadbare phrase that thousands have used
before? Of what use is speech, when that for which one was born,
for which one has starved, frozen and wandered north, east, south
and west at last breaks on one's sight? What is one to say when
the tame platitudes of youth become the flaming certainties of
experienced manhood? How is one to speak of that moment when
the ship rotting in the harbour through weary years flings out her
sails to the wind and feels the pulsing water of the open sea beneath
her? I am conscious that life is only just beginning.

He was 53.

A KIND OF PEACE

~ 17 ~
FIVE ACRES AND A COW

In embracing Catholicism, Stanley had reached the end of his open road. He claimed to have found the spiritual certainty his soul had for years been craving. I, on the other hand, almost one hundred years later, more prosaically set off down a long tarmac road in rural Hampshire, searching for the family's next residence after they left Somerset in 1923. I had googled the name of the house – Rosedale – and it appeared on a property-for-sale website, but I knew that the original bungalow was no longer standing, so I had no idea what, if anything, I would find. I had almost come to the end of the road when I spotted a newish sign saying 'Rosedale', with a modern brick house lying back from the road.

I went up to the man standing in the driveway and explained my mission. He welcomed me and started rummaging through some discarded piles of wood and netting. Suddenly, he triumphantly held aloft the actual Rosedale nameplate which had marked the house when the family lived there. I had my photo taken holding it and then he let me look round. He explained that when he bought the land the bungalow was still standing, though only just. A rope had been tied round a sturdy tree and strung across to the corner of the bungalow, all designed to prevent the unsound structure from blowing down in the wind.

A friend had made the bungalow with its five-acre plot available at a peppercorn rent. It was situated near the village of Four Marks, southwest of Alton, where a number of back-to-the-land escapees from urban life were eking out a living from small-scale farming, particularly poultry. The prospects of turning this rundown property into something habitable were bleak: the house was wooden and in need of repair, while the land was overgrown and unkempt, although beneath the undergrowth lay an ancient orchard. It hardly provided the comfort that Jess would have been looking for at that stage of her life – she was forty-four – but she brought all her skills to bear and gradually transformed it into a productive smallholding, complete with a cow, goats and chickens. Once the plot was up and running and approaching a measure of self-sufficiency, Stanley, based in London, placed adverts for selling its fruit and vegetables in the *Crusader*. Meanwhile, they were joined by Jess's fifty-two-year-old widowed sister Eleanor – otherwise known as Auntie Gane. She had married Arthur Warren in 1912 but he had been killed in the First World War. Although the land was starting to bear fruit, the family were in desperate need of cash: Eric later described it as a 'precarious livelihood'.

ABOVE LEFT: Some of the James family relaxing in the garden at Rosedale.
ABOVE RIGHT: The slogan for G.K. Chesterton's Back to the Land movement was 'Three Acres and a Cow'. Credit: the British Library

But in the early days of 1923 Stanley was working in London, renting a room with a few sticks of furniture near Tower Bridge, while trying to get writing commissions. 'Editors proved obtuse and the saints seemed to be as deaf to my invocations as the editors,' he writes. In spite of a generous parting gift from the Weigh House and help from the Converts' Aid Society, money was short: 'Though I had pulled up my belt another notch it was difficult, having consideration for the family in the country, to keep the wolf from the door.' At the same time, however, there was no going back on his decision: 'I had circled the heavens, it is true, like a carrier pigeon before commencing its flight. But once the goal had been sighted indecision and vacillation were at an end.'

He soon gave up the digs in the East End, along with any attempts to make his living on the national papers, and joined the family in Hampshire, turning the garden shed into his study and establishing a life that combined freelance journalism with working on the land. The task ahead was daunting. Before even attempting to make a living from writing on Catholic topics, he needed to immerse himself in the relevant theology and build up his list of editorial contacts. It would not be until the 1930s that his authoritative voice, eventually one of the most respected in the field, would make itself widely heard. So, in those early freelance days, he focused on secular journalism, a necessary interim phase.

The non-religious features I have been able to find through an online newspaper archive fall into two categories. There are opinion pieces of a light-hearted nature, with a marked absence of political comment, and another, second type which are best described as morality tales – fictional stories in an accessible style, sometimes set on the Canadian Prairies, where the theme is often love or death. In all, I have found ten regional newspapers that accepted his work. In those days the national papers didn't contain large feature sections and were as difficult to break into, without a specialism, as they are today. Before the advent of the Internet, it was easier to syndicate stories because the editors of local newspapers were unlikely to see articles from different regions – and this is what Stanley did. The seven features that he hikes around are: controlling the weather; how to write love letters; politics on the Prairies; living in the countryside versus the town; the relative intelligence of a rural versus an urban person; the popularity of ghost stories; and why we enjoy picnics.

The piece about controlling the weather, for example, appeared in the *Lincolnshire Chronicle*, then appeared unaltered two weeks later in the *Nottingham Journal*. It is playful and written against a background of recent, drawn-out, inclement weather. He wonders, in view of the fact that man could now prevent the spread of plagues, whether they would one day be able to induce rain. He claims that an experiment in which gunpowder was fired into the sky during a Californian drought caused rain to fall. His payoff line is neat: the downside of such an invention would be that small talk would become a thing of the past.

We can't look at everything he wrote, but how can we resist glancing at his advice on how to write love letters? He recommends:

> *First and foremost, be yourself!... Most love letters reveal a sad lack of originality... Men's love letters nearly always lack sympathy. That is to say, the writers do not sufficiently realise the individuality of the person to whom they are writing... It is not to contradict what was said concerning naturalness to add that epistles of this kind should be works of art... Love lends itself easily to beauty of language, delicate allusion and happy phrases. The stronger the passion the lighter will be the touch.*

Was he drawing on his letters to Ruth as inspiration?

In 'A Country Lane', he ponders the way the old, tree-fringed road that runs alongside his Hampshire home holds the memories of generations of courting lovers. It is heady with the scent of flowers and shrubs and pulses with more genuine life than the nearby A-road with its roar of traffic. Not a particularly startling notion, but it underlines the way that Stanley and family always had a deep love for the land.

I was able to find seven stories with a moral message. Most of these fictional works were published in 1924, although the *Falkirk Herald* carried one called 'Cupid Makes a Bad Shot' in December 1928. A reclusive art critic, jilted in love some years before, is spending Christmas alone. His world is turned upside down when he receives from an anonymous well-wisher a present of a beautiful statuette of Cupid. The package has an Italian postmark. He imagines the figure is firing arrows at him and the pangs of love return – but he doesn't associate the sensations with his previous relationship. Feeling happy, he decides to accept his friend's invitation to the family home on Christmas Day and there sees his friend's daughter Lucy in a new light. He visits the art magazine where she works with her father and their friendship deepens. Then one day he is shown an article about some recent discoveries of Cellini's sculptures, written by Clare Armitage, the woman he imagined jilted him all those years ago. He realises that it was she who sent him the Cupid. They meet and she tells him that he had mistaken her intentions and she had always liked him – and love blossoms. Don't give up on real love is the message.

'The Nugget Creek Blizzard', published in three different newspapers, is a love story set in the Rockies, with resemblances to Stanley's novella *Poverty Gulch*. As in the novel, the main character is Steve, who has robbed a bank and is on the run. In his flight he meets up with the beautiful Kathleen who is also escaping – in her case, from a cruel lover. They fall in love and have a child, who is named the Duke. The force of the law is on his trail and they push north into gold-prospecting country, where Steve strikes lucky. But the Duke falls ill and the couple argue, Kathleen wanting to move to a warmer region. Steve walks out into a blizzard, perhaps contemplating death, but he meets an old priest who is lost in the snow. Steve rescues him and they return to the hut, and when the weather abates they go back to recover the packages the priest was carrying with him on his sleigh. They contain Christmas gifts and medicines, which are administered to the child, who regains his strength. With the turn in fortunes, the couple make up. One evening Steve confesses to the priest his bank robbery and the pair invent a scheme whereby Steve, now rich with the proceeds from his gold finds, will repay the bank what he has stolen. Despite the fact that he has deposited the money, the North-West Mounted Police still pursue him. But the priest acts as a mediator and persuades the law not to pursue justice. The couple follow the priest to the Mission of the Sacred Heart and get married. Forgiveness, of course, is the theme.

The *Edinburgh Evening News* published four of his stories in 1924. 'His Wife and His Chief' is a rather interesting take on the betrayal theme. An up-and-coming, visionary politician is hero-worshipped by a young married man in his department. But the political leader is secretly in love with the man's wife and together they hatch a plan to send the young man away on an important mission which will further his career. But he returns a day early and finds his wife and boss canoodling on the sofa. Despite his wife's protestations that she only wanted to boost his career prospects, he abandons her. In a meeting with his boss the next morning, his superior's achievement on the public stage masks any wrongdoing in the private arena, and he forgives him. Only years later does he read in the politician's biography that it was at that moment that the man's career faltered, and he never became the transformative leader everyone had been predicting.

In 'Gabrielle and the Major', two Victorian maiden aunts confront the mores of the twentieth century head-on when Gabrielle, their niece, announces that she is engaged to be married. They meet the man and approve of him, but the local vicar calls round and informs them, following revelations from his son, that the Major is already married. The aunts are shocked and waste no time in telling Gabrielle. But when one of them goes to her room to give her the dreadful news, she discovers that she has run away with him. In a letter, Gabrielle writes that because the Major is already married she has had to elope – but everything is fine because they love one another.

Stanley can tell a good tale in a succinct and telling style; these light pieces are, for me, some of his best work. But at this point his journey down the lanes of secular journalism was more or less over. He would devote the remainder of his writing career to looking at issues through the prism of theology and faith: it would be a complex and challenging journey, not only for him, but for the reader, too.

Stanley speaks in *Becoming a Man* of having a wholesome life at this time and one that had a balance between thought and action. Certainly, the Jameses' existence, despite the financial challenges, seems to have become calmer. There is one photograph of him with a spade in one hand and his trusty pipe in the other. Pictures show him reading, or standing with Jess in the garden, while there are shots of the children collecting eggs from the chicken houses, tending the goats, and playing with the two dogs. He records:

As I write the primroses are blooming in our Hampshire lanes and the daffodils are showing themselves on the lawn of this bungalow that, for the time being, is our home. The skylark has commenced his serenade of the heavens, and, at a thousand points, spring breaks through into our wintry world. Fifty-four such springs have come and gone since I first drew breath but never such a one as this. For today all things are made new, not flowers and grasses, birds' songs and sunshine alone, but the inner texture of the world. Ancient stains have been erased from my mind. The creases of my

*soul have been straightened out. Something of what it means to be
'born again' comes to me on this soft April wind.*

*My wife and children, anchors binding me closely to the 'here
and now', could save me from [academic aloofness]. Small as
was our holding, it demanded some acquaintance with the land
and animals. I worked with my hands as well as my head. There
were obstacles, therefore, to my flying off into space. Conclusions
reached in meditating on abstract Catholic principles had to meet
the immediate challenge of home, field and marketplace... It kept
one alert, prevented a dull acquiescence and docile passivity and
made it positively incumbent on me to be, as far as I could, both a
good Catholic and a good citizen.*

An outward manifestation of that pledge was to be seen in the round
trip of ten miles he made to attend Mass at the Catholic church in Alton.

The family stayed in Hampshire longer than anywhere else: it was to be
their home until 1941. The children were a dynamic group of youngsters, full
of energy, constantly coming and going. The oldest children were landing
their first jobs, the younger ones helping out with the smallholding while
enduring the spartan conditions. Bicycles would have taken them wherever
they wanted to go, and one imagines Jess cycling down the lane to the
shops in Four Marks to buy groceries. They produced some of what they
needed: greens and root vegetables, apples, pears, berries, eggs, milk, cheese
and honey. There was no central heating and the flimsy house would have
been cold in winter, so logs for fuel would have been collected from their
own wood or from further afield. They were a hardy lot. Their father's and
mother's resilient natures and farming backgrounds would have much to do
with that, but the active life and the healthy diet helped – on the occasions
when there was enough to eat.

By 1923, Phyllis, who never married, would have started her first job as
a live-in matron at a preparatory school in Worthing. Always considered
the most eccentric of the siblings, she loved to laugh, was warm and could
be incredibly generous. Rosedale is where Bob established his lifelong
association with the keeping of chickens. I can imagine him managing the
smallholding with aplomb, planning the planting and the crop rotation. He

was soon to take a job on the Winchester Poultry Farm, one of the biggest in the country. The practical Jessie also turned to farm work, along with cooking, dressmaking, needlework and home decoration. She was always active, enjoying swimming and cycling whenever she could. Eric was the most intellectual of the children: his life was to be one of books, ideas and religious belief. He took his BA at Cambridge and trained to be a Congregational minister, following the route that his father had abandoned. My mother Kitty left school in 1925 and initially helped my grandmother around the house while also performing the role of supporting mother to younger brothers John and David. At some point in the 1920s she took a more challenging job at Chailey Heritage, an establishment for special needs children in Sussex. She never spoke much about her father at that stage – except to say that he was 'always in his shed, writing'.

I have a newspaper cutting from the *Catholic Times* which confirms that Jess, John and David were received into the Catholic Church in 1927, the children becoming altar boys. John, very much the scientist, resented the religious imposition and was an atheist for the rest of his life, whereas David, a quiet boy who spent time drawing, walking and thinking, remained a Catholic. Stanley wanted John to go to a Catholic school, but he refused, and a place was found for him at the local grammar school, Eggar's, in Alton. In 1928 Stanley and Jess adopted Patricia, a baby girl who was in need and lived nearby. Maybe a large, ready-made family with widely differing characters and interests made it easier for one more member to be taken in.

* * *

Stanley's best-known book, *The Adventures of a Spiritual Tramp*, was published in the second half of 1925. It is the work that put him on the map, at least in religious, especially Catholic, circles. It's a good read by almost any yardstick. But I have been able to locate only two reviews and one essay about it, whereas *Becoming a Man* attracted countless notices in 1944. At this time he wasn't well-known enough to make the same mark.

He asked the Catholic convert and priest, academic and writer of detective stories, Father Ronald Knox, to write the preface:

Who ever made a stranger course towards Rome?... Readers of
'Through the Looking-Glass' will remember that Alice can only
make her way about the garden by walking away from the object she
wants to reach... Mr James seems to have done the thing in real life;
he has reached the Catholic Church by steadily walking away from
it... I remember saying somewhere that we converts never walk into
the Church; we always stumble into it, tripping over the mat. Mr
James has gone one better; he has walked in backwards.

They are men from different worlds – Knox from the glittering halls
of academia; Stanley from his diverse adventures, both physical and
metaphysical – but the destination of their lives was the same. Even from
my own place of agnosticism, I can detect a sense of peace in their writings.

John Foster Makepeace in *Blackfriars* magazine gives the autobiography
an enthusiastic reception:

This is a book of unusual interest. It is a record of adventures such as
befall few men... It is a serious and sincere record of a real spiritual
journey... Mr James has succeeded in being just himself... All real men
love the tramp; by which we do not mean the miserable object who
shuffles from workhouse to workhouse, but the lean and bronzed lover
of the open air, whose inmost soul loathes the smug and sleek self-
satisfactions of suburban villadom... Mr James is to be congratulated
on having shown us the way in a remarkably virile book.

By cleverly juxtaposing the revelations of *Dear Girl* – particularly Stanley's
affair with Minna Simmons – and the autobiography, Professor Clyde
Binfield is able, in his 1991 work 'Collective Sovereignty? Conscience in
the Gathered Church', to extract deeper meanings. He certainly prises open
the contradictions and tensions within the pages of Stanley's autobiography.
He calls the book a 'brisk, brief masterpiece of self-centred candour'. He
goes on:

Given the tendency of younger ministers to desert objective revelation
for the psychology of religion, and given the occupational hazard of
succumbing to the brief and bright style in vogue at Brotherhoods,

*James shuddered at the secularism which yawned insistently at a
preacher's feet... James's relations with [Eva, Ruth and Minna]
shed a suggestive light on his changes in churchmanship. James was
powerfully attractive – and attracted to – women... Were some of
these 'almost undesirable' relationships almost forced upon James?...
Authority, relentlessness, demands, intimacy, romance, union, heroism,
uncompromising warfare: could there be a more suggestive, seductive
language? No wonder Stanley James was home [converted to
Catholicism] at last.*

* * *

According to the shipping lists, on 3 September 1927 Stanley set sail for
New York on the *RMS Aquitania*, arriving six days later for a fourteen-
week lecture tour, taking in a number of east coast cities. I have been unable
to glean much information about his trip, whether it was self-funded or
whether he had his expenses covered, or even which cities he visited. It
was, according to *The Universe*, a 'tour among Catholic audiences'. The
Catholic Advance records: 'After an absence of 28 years, Stanley B. James,
well-known English writer and journalist, and one-time cowboy, Socialist
and Nonconformist, who later became a convert to Catholicism, has arrived
in America and expects to make an extended tour of the country. He will
lecture in various cities.'

There seem to have been at least six different talks. The titles were: 'Human
Milestones on a Pilgrim's Way', which covered the 'various strange types
of character encountered in the course of his journey', 'From Communism
to Catholicism', 'The Religion of the Hobo', 'The Apostolate of the Pen',
'The Catholic Novel' and 'The New Race'. A flyer states that he was based
at 50 Morningside Drive, New York City, where people wanting to hear
him speak should contact him. The 1925 publication of *The Adventures of
a Spiritual Tramp* proved to be just as popular in the US as it did in Britain.

Through a family connection the transcript of one of the lectures came
my way. Although delivered from a Catholic perspective and delivered to
a Catholic audience, it is largely secular in nature as Stanley revisits the
people and places his agnostic self knew in North America in the 1890s –

events I have recorded here. It is the only surviving example we have of one of his talks. Of course, he delivered hundreds of sermons, and addressed countless political and pacifist meetings in halls and on street corners but – apart from one or two reported extracts of his sermons in Eva's diary and in her letters to Ruth – none of these remain.

His editor at the *Catholic Herald*, Michael de la Bédoyère, wrote in his obituary that Stanley was a better speaker than he was a writer. And, despite the difficulties he encountered with his congregations for espousing radical causes, it seems he was usually an inspiring preacher. The New York address shows a different side to him, one in which the style is more humorous and accessible. He introduces his talk by stating: 'It has been said that there are three kinds of personal memoirs – biographies, autobiographies and ought-not-to-be-ographies. I hope that what I have to say will not fall into the last of these three categories.'

There is nothing like present contentment for enabling one to look back at past failures with searing honesty. He seems liberated when he maps out for his audience the route to his enlightenment: 'The pathway was found through a series of mishaps, of butting into this wall and falling into that ditch; and, finally, the path was at last found that led to peace.' Over and over again, he takes people back to life in the Rockies, either as a source of entertainment or because the memories allow him to draw some kind of moral:

The Rocky Mountains seemed to act as a kind of breakwater, along the bases of which were strewn the flotsam and jetsam of our civilisation... When our newspapers report that a gentleman has disappeared, having been last seen setting out for his office and then heard of no more, I think that some of them pop up again out there.

He then recaptures the sense of poetry that natural scenery can engender:

As one lay looking up at those unheeding stars, feeling the cutting of the wind going deeper into one, there grew an indescribable sense of peace and strength. One had looked the worst in the face. One's soul had been bared to the ultimate reality of things, and somehow... there grew the sense of a spirit of strength and utter peace.

While he was in New York he went to the cinema to see Cecil B. DeMille's new film *The King of Kings*, a silent epic which depicts Jesus's last weeks. With the opening scene and the resurrection in Technicolor, it is the second in the director's Biblical trilogy. Stanley reviewed it for the *Catholic Times* and, unlike the critic in *The Universe* who considered it to have very little religious merit, he adjudges it to be 'entirely Catholic'. While acknowledging there was 'considerable freedom in the interpretation of Mary Magdalene's character and an altogether untraditional account of her relations with her lover, Judas Iscariot... those were not allowed to mar the main movement of the story, which adhered for the most part to scriptural lines'.

He also wrote a 'little play' about a Polish American who had succeeded in his adopted country but who abandoned everything to return to his native land, which had remained special to him because of all he had endured there in his early years. I know no more than this, neither where it was performed or whether he acted in it. He arrived back in Southampton on 14 December 1927.

In early 1929 he produced a promotional leaflet advertising the fact that he was planning another US lecture tour later that year, and in it he includes reviews by five Catholics who had heard his talks during the first tour. The themes of the lectures, for which the charge was $50 per person (£650 in 2020), had changed slightly: 'The American Adventure', 'St Francis of Assisi and Our Age' and 'G. K. Chesterton and the Catholic Revival in England' had been added to the list. He planned to be in Chicago for six weeks from the middle of September, in St Louis in November and in New York until the end of the year. In the event, he never made the trip because Jess fell ill and he was forced to stay at home, another reminder for him of the dangers of following one's own path without thinking sufficiently carefully about the impact such a course of action might have on others.

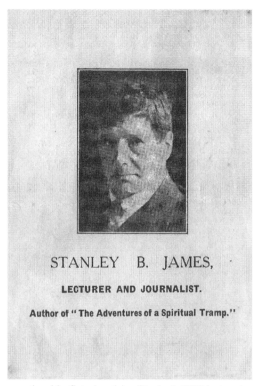

A promotional leaflet advertising Stanley's 1929 lecture tour of
the US, which was cancelled because of Jess's ill health

~ 18 ~
SPREADING THE WORD

Next to the perimeter fence in the garden at Rosedale there is a scruffy, largely unused shack, its grimy windows looking out over the house and the adjacent plot of land. It was here almost a hundred years ago, in – one hopes – slightly cleaner surroundings, that my grandfather turned himself into a serious freelance writer. That shed became an engine room of literary endeavour that would see a little-known journalist become one of the world's leading Catholic commentators. Driven by the twin impulses of giving voice to his new-found faith and the need to provide for his family, Stanley worked tirelessly on his books and articles. The long hours spent at his manual typewriter while puffing on his pipe were lightened – at least intellectually – by working on the land. He also used his time to read voraciously. Of that period of growing contentment he writes: 'I was gradually losing the restlessness of earlier days.'

The articles, which amount to several hundred, form a teeming kaleidoscope of ideas, considering questions thrown up by his new Catholic vision, as well as reflections on contemporary life. He covered issues concerned

246

with authority, the polarities of communism and fascism, tradition versus revolution, Distributism and land reform, mysticism and contemporary literature – all of these being allied to his staggering knowledge of the Bible. The three main strengths he possessed – the dynamism of the social reformer, the scholar's deep understanding of the Scriptures, and an overriding sense of the mystical and supernatural – gave his writing power and insight, provided he checked a tendency towards the didactic. He may have found some measure of personal inner peace, but that didn't mean that his writing lost its bite. Supported by his freshly-acquired Catholicism, he looked sternly on the world and commented on what he saw as its shortcomings.

From his ivory tower of certitude, he puts institutions under the Catholic microscope, along with secular, cultural and political ideas and various individuals and, invariably, they are all found wanting. He is drawn towards the grand statement and an apocalyptic voice is never far away. His relentless pursuit of what might be called the supranatural *zeitgeist* turns him into a kind of meta-historian of spirituality. Some of his projections into the future – predictions even – are just downright strange. Yet he still seeks to pose theological arguments which are watertight, and he is intent on finding neat, organic structures and synergies of meaning. It is a complex picture.

And it is as if the very thoroughness and unforgiving nature of his personal search leads him to an equally uncompromising point of stasis. The struggle towards meaning has been so heartfelt and drawn-out that he no longer has it in him to entertain a tolerant, liberal attitude towards issues of faith or contemporary affairs. He seems to be saying: I have suffered to reach this position, so the last thing I am going to do is make this easy for you. More charitably, one may say that he genuinely believes that living according to the Catholic faith – particularly for a convert – is hard and to suggest otherwise is to mislead people.

But I was left wanting more gentleness; seldom does his writing focus on the intimacies and comforts of faith. Nor is the individual soul examined, or any sense of contentment or quiet truth articulated. True, in the tales he invents for the *Franciscan Fables* series and the essays about the relevance of St Francis's life to modern-day society there is a genuine sweetness which conveys the spirituality of belief. People spoke of his compassion and kindness, but these qualities appear rarely in his works. Was he afraid of appearing sentimental? That's tantamount to a sin for a journalist, after all.

As a freelance journalist myself, I know that only occasionally do one's written words match one's innermost convictions. Most of the time one is fulfilling a commissioning editor's brief or at least echoing the likely sentiments of that publication's reader profile. To that end, one manufactures a voice that fits the circumstances. Sometimes that voice is authoritative, but that, too, is artifice. What's more, my pieces never involved issues of spirituality, unlike Stanley's, for whom faith provided the raw material for almost all of them. Nor was I a columnist, which he almost exclusively was, so we operated in different spheres. A columnist is paid to be thought-provoking, entertaining and challenging, aspects of journalism that my grandfather had little difficulty in producing.

This fact has left me wondering to what extent his voice was authentic. Often, he writes with seeming conviction, with a passionate voice, arguing the case for belief over non-belief. At other times, I can detect less engagement, as if the need to make money was paramount. Of course, he may also have been using these articles – once he was established and valued by editors – as a sounding board for his beliefs, just as he did in his Piers Plowman and Tramp columns for the *Crusader*.

While turning out his secular journalism, he was making himself known to editors of Catholic publications. He endeavoured to secure commissions – or even better, permanent contracts – throughout the English-speaking world. He was extremely successful in this and by the end of the decade had become widely known and respected. I have identified twenty-two religious journals, almost all Catholic, that he wrote for. Twelve are British, five Irish and five American. The majority of his articles appeared in four British publications – *Blackfriars*, *The Month,* the *Clergy Review* and the *Catholic Herald* – and three Irish ones – *Assisi, The Cross* and the *Irish Monthly.* There was likely to have been a certain amount of syndication. His average annual income eventually grew to about £400 (£25,000 in 2020).

So, what were his main themes? One is the question of authority. Stanley's early revolts were an indication that he had issues with recognising authority when he was expected to accede to it. At Whitgift School he scorned the conventional curriculum in favour of his own reading; those prophets of revolt and individual freedom – Walt Whitman, Ralph Waldo Emerson and Edward Carpenter – became his heroes; after formal education he quit numerous training courses; he was hardly on speaking terms with his father;

he enjoyed freewheeling days as a cowboy and hobo and then reported for the *Calgary Herald* unafraid of treading on toes; his affair with Minna Simmons and close relationships with other women pointed to the rebellion encroaching on matters of the heart, too; at the NCF, the FoR and as editor of the *Crusader*, he fell out with colleagues.

Only on being received into the Catholic Church did this rebelliousness lose its edge. Now he was able to claim that he had found what he had been looking for over the previous decades; the pilgrim had reached his destination. And this time, the authority – that of God and Jesus Christ in the Church of Rome – was one that he was able to accept. The relief he experienced in this discovery turned in his writings almost immediately into a rigid conservatism.

In 'The Catholic as Citizen', published in the *Catholic Herald,* he writes: 'The Catholic lives under authority. He belongs to an ordered society to whose discipline, though it is enforced by no other than spiritual means, he is expected to be sincerely loyal. And that discipline involves the acceptance of principles which underly all properly constituted societies.' But, he argues, that authority paradoxically provides personal freedom. It is only by acceding to the demands of God that the individual can be truly free, because he has been released to function in accord with the law of his being.

Stanley's revitalised sense of spiritual authority translated into a largely uncritical theological view. He wanted to become the 'classical type of Catholic', while remaining a layman. And he quickly realised that it was in the Liturgy of the Mass that the heart of Catholicism was to be found. For the true Catholic, all cultural, humanitarian and political movements were subordinated to worship. *The Cross*, a monthly magazine published by the Passionist Fathers in Dublin, took many of the articles he wrote in this orthodox vein. They were what modern journalistic parlance calls 'think pieces'. A twelve-part series from 1935, entitled 'The Divine Tragedy', is introduced with these words: 'The Gospel is a Tragedy in the classical sense of the word. Its hero is 'The Man of Sorrows' and the scene is set for suffering in its extreme form... The Cross is the climax of the Gospel story.'

When he turned his attention to temporal matters, we see a seismic change of view compared with just a few years before. The new vision made it impossible to adhere to former political beliefs, and the atheism of the communist system was one of these. Likewise, his attitude to the concept of the supreme leader experienced a shift, too. Two 1933 articles devote themselves to a consideration of Mussolini. In 'Some Mussolini Paradoxes', he suggests that the Italian fascist leader was a misunderstood figure. Rather than being a simple autocrat, he was a complex, creative, flexible and intuitive force. He had plumbed the depths of the Italian soul and had given it strong leadership, utilising the intense nationalism that had emerged in the country at the end of the First World War. He also had humility and had 'stooped to conquer'. What's more, he was curbing capitalism, not just communism, and was opposing a world 'deeply tainted with the philosophy of socialism... The Duce actually managed to infuse with enthusiasm a movement which stood for the traditional institutions of Christendom... fascism has been a stimulant.'

Several readers wrote in to say these views were hogwash. One letter says: 'The article by Stanley James has caused me alarm... The conclusions that Christian civilisation may only be achieved when the anti-Christians have been "answered" (?), simplify the problems very ineptly... In other words, set up Mussolinis, stifle all criticism of the state, and the millennium has been glimpsed!'

Commenting on another article by Stanley which extolled the virtues of fascism, a reader writes:

> *[So] Hitler and Mussolini embody in themselves the real spirit of the nations they govern? Is the official neo-paganism of Hitler's Nazidom a manifestation of the true German spirit? From the Catholic press alone, there is ample evidence of priest-torture and murder, and pitiless persecution of Catholic societies and confraternities in the early years of [Mussolini's] rule. Not an action or speech of his suggests the slightest acquaintance with Catholic moral theology.*

Stanley's writings on this topic were also noticed by Jay P. Corrin, who in *Catholic Intellectuals and the Challenge of Democracy*, states that 'the authoritarian bias can be seen in the political realm in the writings of the Catholic convert journalist Stanley B. James'. Corrin writes: 'It was necessary, wrote James, that Catholics adjust to the demands of dictatorship. Their religious background, he asserted, would make this transition easier than for other people. Democracies were losing out, claimed James, because they bred factiousness and were inefficient.' My grandfather had clearly travelled a long ideological road since the 'red' days of 1910-22.

Fascism was not just a political phenomenon either, Stanley argues; it also related to the behaviour of the individual. It prevented blasphemy, regulated family life and prohibited houses of ill-fame. In a paean of praise to the system, he says that the far-right movement respected the basic needs of human nature everywhere, and that it claimed to have rediscovered, 'under the distortions effected by false types of government, the real man – God-fearing, property-holding, domesticated'.

In 'The New Race' he explores the idea that the Catholic Church was producing a never-before-seen group of believers. He writes; 'While eugenists [sic] are busy contriving methods for improving the breed and picturing the day when they will be able to produce the superman, the Church has already achieved this end – has not only produced the superman, but laid the foundations for the super-race.'

Once or twice I had heard the family refer to their father's 'disappointing' conversion, but I hadn't heard them express anything about how his views changed so dramatically as a result of his conversion. I was shocked by these writings. The exclusivity of the Catholic position expressed above points to a kind of spiritual hierarchy. Why, my agnostic self asks, should an individual belonging to one sect – in this case Catholicism – supersede that of another? My mind harked back to those earnest discussions he'd had with Eva, Ruth and Minna about giving birth to a race of super-Christians.

The need for authority was paramount. So, it follows that its absence can produce a negative outcome. He claims in 'Modern Civilisation and the Transformation of Man' that the Russian Soviet Republic was deliberately turning men into 'godless robots indifferent to individual rights, as tyrannically governed by the mass-mind as a hive of bees or a nest of ants, and addicted to a promiscuity which outrages what until now have been considered the decencies of human society'.

But Western civilisation was in danger, too: 'Biological changes are taking place which, in a few generations, may make the normal man, as we now know him, with healthy human instincts and unperverted [sic] tastes, a rare specimen, where Christian forces fail to operate.' Everywhere people fall short, particularly in England. He talks of the 'spiritual paralysis' gripping the modern mind, especially the English one. Its people are wanting in vitality and their psychological machinery has run down. The English soul is 'devitalised, exhausted, spent'.

* * *

Stanley's first book that focused exclusively on the Catholic issue was *The Evangelical Approach to Rome*, published in 1933. It is about 25,000 words long and in seven chapters. I have my mother's copy and it's inscribed 'From Daddy, Christmas 1933'. In the preface Stanley acknowledges a huge debt to Orchard and his autobiography *From Faith to Faith*, which describes his friend's conversion to Catholicism some ten years after his own. He quotes large passages and says his book is merely its footnotes.

But Stanley does have his own rather erudite theme: that evangelicalism had its roots in Catholicism and that it was misguided to see it as an exclusively Protestant phenomenon. Wesley's Methodists preached in the simple language of the friars that went before them, he says, and the straightforward language of the Bible supplanted the flowery Johnsonian prose that was prevalent in the pulpits of the time.

In the chapter entitled 'Crisis' he comes back to his theme that much modern worship was anodyne. In fact, a kind of inertia and excessive urbaneness was affecting mankind and preaching was impressive rather than regenerative. Religion had become a matter of temperament. He suggests that only the Catholic Church could preach the Gospel properly, not saying that this was the God the worshipper wanted, but that this was the God who wanted the worshipper.

The nineteenth-century belief that the voice of the people was the voice of God had been found wanting, he says. Democracy was in the melting pot, and dictatorships – although he holds off using that word – were the only logical outcome of such a mood of paralysis. All this inadequacy pointed to a revival, with Rome at its centre. What was needed was Catholic family life with its ideals of marriage, wholesome pleasures and cooperative labour un-harassed by commercialism.

By now, Stanley had established his reputation as a respected Catholic commentator

It would be wrong to think that Stanley became a conservative in all things. He transferred some of his former radicalism to two Catholic movements which aimed to improve the lot of the poor: Catholic Action and Distributism. The first aimed to address the issue of industrialised poverty by advocating a return to the land. The initiative would constitute more than just a switch to a simple agricultural existence; it was an endeavour with spiritual dimensions, too. To this end, in 'The Soul and the Soil', Stanley advocates the establishment of Catholic centres in the countryside, where people would have the freedom to worship God without being answerable to a boss or to market forces. 'The soil and the soul are intimately related,' he writes.

I have a postcard of the Cote d'Azur sent by Stanley to Jess from Monaco on 24 September 1937. He writes: 'All OK. Leave today for Rome, arriving 8.15am on Saturday. Will write as soon as I can. Love to all, Stan.' Through the columns of the *Catholic Herald*, he had come into contact with a young priest and philosophy professor who was involved in the Young Christian Workers (YCW) movement, an offshoot of Catholic Action. Stanley invited him to Rosedale and their long meeting in his garden shed kickstarted a new venture which put an end to my grandfather's growing sense of inertia. Father Bernard Goode told him how the YCW had been founded in Belgium under the guidance of Father Joseph Cardijn, before spreading to France and the rest of Europe. Its aim was for lay people to evangelise from within the academic, commercial and industrial spheres in order to influence public life and to spread the word. The spearhead of this movement were the Jocists, working-class youths who 'were filled with an apostolic spirit and seemed capable of carrying all before it'. The trip to mainland Europe would enable him to speak to the people who headed the movement.

In Rome he visited the catacombs and he also 'saw' Mussolini, but on what basis, I'm not sure. He then travelled by train to Brussels where he inspected the impressive offices where the activities of 250,000 young Christian workers were coordinated by Father Cardijn, with whom he had a private audience. Then, armed with the necessary material for his new book, *Christ and the Workers*, he returned to England. He wrote it quickly and it appeared early the following year.

Distributism, an economic ideology which had many influential followers at the time, including G. K. Chesterton and Hilaire Belloc, acted as a foil to a widespread sense of unease about modern working practices. The philosophy goes back to the late nineteenth century and is based on the principles of Catholic teaching, especially the pronouncements of popes Leo XIII and Pius XI. According to its tenets, both capitalism and socialism were equally exploitative. The proponents of Distributism believed that the world's productive assets should be shared by as many people as possible. More accurately, they opposed monopolies rather than capitalism *per se* – they wanted vast swathes of people to benefit from the fruits of capitalism and believed in local solutions rather than centralisation. Distributism constituted a middle way, had much in common with E. F. Schumacher's 1970s 'Small is Beautiful' movement, and was linked to the Guild Socialism ideas of A. J. Penty. At its core, it held four principles: respect for property, respect for family, respect for human life and respect for government.

In 'The Reign of the Peasant', Stanley attacks the mania for machinery and how it was destroying the dignity of work, hoping that the tendency towards mass mechanisation would fail and the peasant would become the dominant power in society, the peasant, being 'pacific in disposition' was seen as the normal man, who believes in having a small property, working hard and living frugally.

'Three Acres and a Cow' had been the slogan of the land reformers of the late nineteenth century. It was taken up by G. K. Chesterton in his book, *What's Wrong with the World*, in order to sum up the aims of Distributism. By chance or design, the Jameses' outdoor life in Hampshire followed the ideal almost to the letter, except they had been lucky enough to have five acres rather than Chesterton's three! And this love for the land was a far more enduring influence on the family than Catholicism ever was. Virtually every one of my uncles and aunts devoted a part of their lives to farming, horticulture or a love of gardening. It is also worth mentioning that the political ideas of Stanley's brother Norman, who in 1935 was elected as the Acadia representative of the Social Credit Party to the Alberta Legislature, encompassed those of Distributism. His party believed that workers should get a bigger slice of the public cake. The party had had a landslide victory, as hard-pressed farmers in the wake of the Depression sought an answer to their desperate predicament. As the brothers were not in touch, I doubt they knew that their thinking overlapped.

* * *

Through his own father, Daniel, and his wife's uncle, the Reverend John Pulsford, Stanley had inherited a strong mystical strain. In his Nonconformist days at Trinity, he had introduced an element of mysticism into the services but then it had been to offset what he saw as an over-secularisation within the church. In those days it had seemed an awkward fit. Now it was central to his faith and he thought it provided the key to the transformation of personality.

'It is,' he writes, 'in proportion to my immediate contact with the Divine Reality that the essential "me" comes alive. What biology is on the lower levels of existence, the laws governing the mystical life are in the realm of personality... Rightly understood, mysticism gives us the secret of personality, the source of spiritual dynamism.' Of the many mystics he wrote about, three in particular stand out: William Langland, St Francis of Assisi and Richard Rolle.

Stanley believed that the ills of modern society could be alleviated by people rediscovering the sense of mysticism that prevailed in medieval times, not least through the inspiration provided by William Langland in his poem *The Vision of Piers Plowman.* His essay 'Piers the Plowman', published in the *Irish Monthly* in 1932, laid the ground for his 1935 book, *Back to Langland,* which gives a fuller treatment to the allegorical poem. This medieval masterpiece was a favourite work of his; he had used 'Piers Plowman' as a byline for his first articles for the *New Crusader.* Enthusiasts for William Langland's poem, which is both mystical and satirical, liken it to Dante, while Stanley calls him 'the last Catholic poet to have the ears of the Commons of England... not only do the terrible alternatives of salvation and damnation face each individual, but society as a whole will receive either the blessing or the chastisement of God... a sense of coming doom suffuses the work.' To modern readers the poem's pathos and its apocalyptic nature may be off-putting; in its scorn for the concept of the power of money and corrupt practice it certainly comes across as sombre.

William Langland
Piers Plowman

Above Left: Francis of Assisi, the gentle saint **Above Right**: The medieval poem doubles as Christian vision and satire of the times

St Francis was my grandfather's favourite saint and something of a mystical hero. *Il Poverello*'s gentleness, humanism and love for humanity and God chimed with the more settled life that Stanley was now living and over the course of nearly thirty years he wrote scores of essays about – and stories based on – the thirteenth-century Umbrian friar. In 1931, in the journal *Assisi,* Stanley wrote a series of twelve articles entitled 'St Francis and Our Age', arguing that there were innumerable reasons why the saint was relevant to the modern world. He claims that, rather than being seen as an inspirational, otherworldly man of God, removed from the realities of everyday life, *Il Poverello* spoke to the present-day 'pagan man'.

In Stanley's view, precisely because he was more concerned with eternity, not time, and with heaven, not earth, the saint provided the panacea that society craved. His love of nature – more accurately his love of animals and flowers rather than the abstract idea – was a healing balm to the stressed, over-industrialised world. Stanley writes: 'He is the leader of all who resent the tyranny of the mechanical age, and of an interpretation of democracy which forbids the rightful claims of the individual. He delivers us from the newspaper mentality, and from the effects of mass-production.' In a society that was intent on avoiding future conflict, the Italian mystic's natural pacifism showed the way forward and we could learn from his belief that war has its roots in greed. Stanley is a better writer when constrained by a theme. When he abandons his didacticism and lets his playful, light touch have sway, the effect can be wonderful.

In 1933 he started a series of five charming, fictional, morality tales based on the saint's life, which were published in various journals, starting with *Assisi*. This series is introduced with the words: 'Stanley B. James, a Franciscan scholar of high repute, begins a short series of stories descriptive of interesting scenes from the life of the *Poverello*. The incidents mentioned have no historical foundation but represent what may well have taken place.' These were trial runs for a more extensive series published in the *Catholic Fireside* in Britain and in *St Francis Home Journal* in the US, fourteen of which in turn provided the material for his 1937 book, *Franciscan Fables*. In a preliminary note to that book he writes: 'The author claims no historical value for them; he will be satisfied if they are found to be in some slight measure reminiscent of the *Fioretti* whose spirit he has attempted to recapture.' *I Fioretti di San Francesco*, or *The Little Flowers of St Francis*, was a fourteenth-century Italian collection of stories about the life of St Francis.

Stanley's collection of stories captures the spirit of Assisi's self-deprecating saint by positing whimsical back stories to the lives of St Francis and his followers. A critic, writing in the *Catholic Standard* in October 1937, states:

> *These stories, so delightfully illustrative of Franciscan simplicity and spirituality, show a deep insight into the life and times of the little poor man of Assisi. They… illustrate most amply the life and teaching of St Francis and his brethren. They are decidedly humorous and at times delightfully witty, with an underlying note of kindly mockery at the poses, pomp and false attitudes towards things eternal of many worldly people. The stories not only show the inventive genius of Mr James, but they make clear how very thoroughly he has assimilated the meaning of the life and thought of St Francis.*

In each story there is a psychological turning point, from which the characters – and the reader – are offered the opportunity to learn. In that sense, each one contains within it a moral lesson. One of the threads that runs through the pieces is the quality of quiet attentiveness, a trait of St Francis, as a character either listens or watches hard and is then instructed. In some stories the character sees the error of their ways and in a dramatic turnaround receives God into their life, while the psychological weakness that these vignettes of human life display is telling and perceptive. Above all, though, there is the transformation of personality trait or situation into something divine, and over and over again weakness of character is transformed into strength of character.

There is one beautiful insight into the personal sacrifice that St Francis himself made in his life. In 'The Bambino' he walks for hours to fetch the husband of a woman who is pregnant with the couple's first child, but who has been taken ill. They reach home in time and a boy is born. St Francis seems as pleased as the parents but when he is handed the boy (named Francis) to hold, a strange change comes over him. 'On the Saint's face were the signs of an acute struggle. A look of pain came over his eyes. It was as though he had received some sudden wound.'

He marches off. Later that evening he explains to his followers: 'All the joys of fatherhood... took possession of me. Then did it seem that nothing would content me but that I must wed that I might have that great privilege. I regretted the vow I had taken to abandon the world.' His soul is tortured, but recompense is at hand. It being the Christmas season, he says: 'I wish to present in lifelike and visible manner the birth of the Infant of Bethlehem.' In a remarkable creative act, he arranges for a manger to be filled with hay, and an ox and an ass to be put inside and in that way the famous Crib of Greccio came about.

Stanley also champions Richard Rolle, the fourteenth-century Yorkshire mystic, writer, hermit, wanderer and spiritual tramp. The rebelliousness of the 'Hermit of Hampole' was clearly a point of attraction for him; at Oxford University Rolle 'got into a scrape' and left of his own accord. 'He appears,' Stanley writes, 'to have been one of those that "have a way with women".' He had 'got religion' but was not going to spend his time quibbling with other believers and commenced his life as a nomad, wanting to free himself entirely from every encumbrance that would prevent him from giving himself entirely to God. Significantly, my grandfather says:

You might say that his outlook as he started out on this strange quest was a medieval version of Whitman's emancipation from convention... Youth of his type have often run away to sea. Those who have run away from home and theological colleges to live with and for God are a smaller number... Between Rolle's circumstances and mine were great differences which suggested that we must part company at an early stage of our journeying. Like Francis of Assisi, whom in so much he resembled, he had freed himself from earthly ties whilst I bore the responsibility for the maintenance of a wife and family.

Despite appearances on occasions suggesting otherwise, Stanley's body of work is not a treatise on the relationship between Catholicism and modern-day life. The wireless played an increasingly prominent role in his and Jess's lives and on the back of that, he wrote a piece in praise of the BBC's output. Giving it a religious twist, he says it's good that believers listen to other denominations.

By this time, feminist issues were no longer playing the role in his thinking that they once did but, in passing, it is instructive to look at two instances when women do walk on to his pages. In 'Virgin and Mother', in the context of talking about chivalric conventions, he writes: 'The lover had his wife... but in addition he had a paramour who was released from these prosaic duties. The division of labour which made the wife responsible for fulfilling the practical requirements of life while the paramour satisfied the demand for romance was particularly congenial to the medieval mind.'

And in another piece, he writes: 'Life is seen from the woman's viewpoint. That does not mean that it is dull and monotonous.' In 'The Feast of All Mothers', in a feature which otherwise pays homage to motherhood and the Virgin Mary, Stanley writes: 'Women have distinguished themselves in literature, art, science, politics, and even in war. But in none of these do they appear in their distinctive role as women.' Did Ruth, Minna or Eva come before his eyes as he wrote that, eighteen years on? Did Jess ever read it, or for that matter any of the articles he penned between 1923 and 1951? Did she ever bring him a cup of tea in the hut, lean over his shoulder and read his words?

My grandfather continued to read voraciously both modern and ancient religious and non-religious works, as well as journalism, and wrote frequent book reviews for his editors as well as think pieces on various authors. Secular writers don't escape having the slide rule of taste run over them. Among those who received the stamp of approval for their wide human and empathetic vision are Shakespeare, Dickens and Walter Scott.

Towards the end of the nineteenth century it was possible to detect, Stanley claims, 'the growth of a movement the end of which can be nothing less than the Catholic Renaissance for which we plead'. In G. K. Chesterton, he says, we see the beginnings of that movement, so much so that his 'laughter is itself a presage of victory'. To bring about that victory, he calls on Catholic readers to engage more. 'Every time we choose our reading matter from the shelves of shop or library, and every time that opportunity presents itself for recommending the good things we have read we either shirk or accept that responsibility.'

But the wide sympathy of the Catholic spirit is largely absent among contemporary secular writers, he claims. 'It is not too much to say that our present literary output is either too colourless to deserve any sort of cultural designation or is frankly pagan. To make unfashionable the sensual, morbid, restless and cynical tone now prevalent will demand prolonged and heroic effort… Everywhere is confusion and indecision.'

The absence of the concept of evil and any moral element from the thinking of modern man made his literature a paltry thing, says Stanley in 'The Human Tragedy'. Modern works were largely 'insipid and the strong flavour we detect comes not from the food itself but from the condiments thrown in, to disguise what would otherwise be the tastelessness of the dish. It is precisely because the cooks are conscious of something seriously lacking in their menu that they adorn the dishes they serve with so much artistry… Modern realism is the product of men who have refused to face the fundamental facts concerning themselves and their fellows. They will not admit the idea of sin.' In another piece, Stanley suggests that good literature must always be aware of its traditions, but the problem is that the contemporary writer is navel-gazing without submitting 'to the wisdom of the ages'.

I have in front of me Stanley's 1932 first edition of *Selected Essays* by T. S. Eliot, which he drew on for an article entitled 'Tradition and Inspiration in Literature'. I can see his scribbled notes and markings in the margins he used to identify quotations, which concur exactly with those in the article. Stuffed between the pages are notes for other pieces, and he has used the back of discarded medical case notes – the paper now yellowed and faded – of his son John. Inside there's an abandoned cutting from *The Times* of 12 May 1936, reporting on a speech given by Dr Goebbels in Munich, in which the German 'minister for national enlightenment and propaganda' announces Nazi funding to turn the theatre into 'a moral institution'. There's another faded sheet which is Stanley's copy of an article headed 'The English Dante' – his beloved William Langland, of course. Finally, to my embarrassment, there are some student scribblings of my own in the *Selected Essays*, the very book Stanley used which came into my hands in the 1970s. I must have been particularly exasperated by Eliot's sententiousness because I've scrawled in the margin: 'Ugh!' and 'Dear, dear' – in biro – in reaction to two of the poet's more pompous statements. Unforgiveable! The book has travelled a long way since it stood on Stanley's shelves in his Rosedale writing shed over eighty years ago.

DO NOT GO GENTLY

~ 19 ~
FLYING THE NEST

Stanley's older children were far too independent-minded to accede to their father's wish that they convert to Catholicism. They resisted long enough that by the time they had reached their teens and left school they had landed their first jobs, and either lived away from home or spent most of the day at work. Jess, out of perceived duty rather than conviction, in 1927 nominally accepted the change without ever understanding what it meant. It was the younger ones – my mother Kitty, John, David and later Patricia – who found themselves under the most pressure to convert.

Stanley's religious quest had always made an impression on his oldest child Phyllis and she, in turn, experimented with different forms of Christian belief. Around this time, she declared herself a member of a spiritualist church, the only member of the family to do so. Her father's sense of adventure had also made an impression: one summer in the early 1930s, aged about thirty, she persuaded my mother Kitty to join her on a trip to Reykjavik, Iceland, booking berths on a cargo ship departing from Wick in Scotland. I have on my bedroom wall two framed photos of rugged volcanic scenes which my mother brought back with her. Once she ruefully commented that the people there played a lot of chess and had 'lax morals'.

In 1936 Bob became manager of the poultry farm where he was working. He was engaged to Beryl, a local girl, but sadly she fell ill with TB and died: he was heartbroken. His asthma was causing him problems, and that spurred him towards moving to the warmer climate of South Africa. He was planning the move when he met a young girl called Betty, who used to cycle over to the farm to buy eggs. He asked her out, they went ice-skating together and they fell in love. His health remained a priority, however, and he set out on a planned two-week voyage to Cape Town at the end of 1938, vowing to return to Betty, who had just turned sixteen. But the war intervened and prevented either of them making the trip. They wrote every week, their letters arriving in batches of six, but they were not to see each other again for another eight years.

In 1934 Jessie married Bernard Frowd, a civil engineer. After their two children Christine and Tim were born, they moved to Bournemouth. When the war came Bernard went to work abroad, overseeing the rebuilding of roads and bridges in Asia, while Jessie fostered a boy called Alan, receiving a thank-you letter from the Queen Mother for her act of generosity. Ever the practical one, she fashioned petticoats out of used parachutes for herself and her neighbours.

Religion was the driving force in Eric's life, and he often said how he had been inspired by his father's theology. His brand of faith was Congregationalism. By now he was established as a pastor in Buckinghamshire and he was involved, like Stanley, in the peace movement, meeting Mahatma Gandhi in 1931 – there is a photo of him standing next to the famous man in Jill Wallis's book, *Valiant for Peace*. He married Joyce Shepheard, a Quaker, and they had two children, Martin and Frances.

Stanley's attempts to cajole the four youngest children into accepting Catholicism was successful with just one boy – David, who remained in the faith for his whole life. In the end, two – John and Patricia – became convinced atheists, while my mother Kitty gravitated towards the Church of England. When she left to become a matron at Stowe School in Buckinghamshire, it must have been a wrench for Jess, who overnight lost her trusty support around the house. In the mid-1930s my mother left Stowe and joined the nursing staff at another public school, Haileybury College. There she met my father, Alec Nurden, a teacher. They fell in love, and a protracted romance followed. Unfortunately, she didn't take to the new school and returned to Stowe, which meant that my father used to travel to see her on Sundays so they could steal a few hours together.

I have seen a letter from Stanley to Norman in Canada, written on New Year's Day 1936, one of eleven from him to his younger brother that I found in the archives of Calgary's Glenbow Museum. Norman donated three boxes of his personal papers to the museum following the thirteen years he had been a representative of the Social Credit Party. In the letter Stanley tells Norman about the family, but there is one glaring omission: my mother. Strangely, she is not mentioned at all. The true running order goes Phyllis, Bob, Jessie, Eric, Kitty, John, David and Patricia. But in his letter, he jumps straight from Eric to John with the words: 'Eric took his BA at Cambridge and is settled as a Congregational minister in Buckinghamshire. He has two children. Then comes John...' Why did he omit my mother? Did they fall out over her refusal to convert? Wasn't she worth mentioning? All the more surprising because my mother told me that her father had always had a soft spot for her. Had the fact that she had left home and taken a job away disrupted the domestic dynamics? Was the appearance of my father on the scene a bone of contention for Stanley?

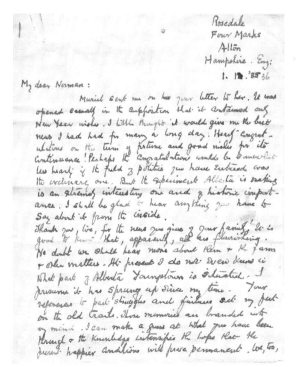

The 1936 letter from Stanley to Norman that broke years of silence between the brothers

Kitty, the author's mother, at Rosedale

Jess in her late fifties

Whatever the reason, my grandfather was upset at her marrying my father, a Protestant. Stanley's level of opposition to the relationship can perhaps best be understood by reading an extract from an article – one of many expressing similar sentiments – that he produced for the *Catholic Herald* around this time. In 'The New Chivalry', he writes:

We [Catholics] are different. We constitute a new, superior Race...
Living and working in a non-Catholic community, we are in danger

of losing our identity. The more we mix with others… the more must the fact that we are a Chosen People be stressed… The more we are called to be in the world, the less must we be of it.

The elitist fervour could hardly be more fulsome. Perhaps my father, a well-intentioned, honourable man if ever there was one, never stood a chance of overcoming Stanley's disapproval.

Yet in none of Stanley's late letters is Kitty named whereas everyone else at least gets a mention. It's possible that in the 1936 letter, the notoriously absentminded Stanley had just forgotten to refer to her. Her career would hardly have appeared stellar in his eyes. Other reasons come to mind. Auntie Gane, Jess's older sister, being childless herself up until 1910, had apparently asked Jess if she might 'adopt' my mother, ostensibly to ease Jess's parenting burden. Jess refused. Why was my mother chosen? The omission of her from the list is so glaring that the mind wanders yet further into wondering what other reasons there might be. I shall probably never know. As my cousin Rosemary says, the whole episode is ironic as my mother was the one child whom everybody loved.

John excelled at Eggar's School in Alton, gaining a scholarship to University College Hospital, London, after which he worked at different hospitals, qualifying in 1938. Despite his professional dedication, he managed to squeeze in a distinctly Stanley-type adventure. While in Cairo in 1939, he heard that the woman he loved, who had initially spurned him, had changed her mind and wanted to be with him after all. The problem was she was now living in Mombasa, Kenya. So, John bought a motorbike and rode the 3,500 miles to see her. But any hope that they would renew their love and live happily ever after came to nought. One story said that the woman had changed her mind – again; another version had it that he realised she wasn't for him. He said goodbye and headed south, meeting up with his brother Bob in South Africa, before selling his bike to pay for the voyage home by tramp steamer.

David preferred the outdoor life and was studying horticulture at agricultural college when at the age of nineteen he developed polio, forcing him to give up his studies: he was never expected to walk again. After spending several weeks in Inwood Cottage Hospital, Alton, where Stanley visited him frequently, he recovered sufficiently to take up work on nearby farms, while developing his lifelong passion for beekeeping. He met and married Jean Trapaud and soon became a tenant farmer, building up a pedigree herd of Jersey cows.

* * *

Stanley was moved to write that letter to Norman on New Year's Day 1936, their sister Muriel having forwarded their brother's letter. I haven't seen Norman's original letter, nor do I know if he had kept in touch with Muriel in the intervening years, but it is clear that much had happened in his life. He had married Ettie in 1899 and his first child – also named Muriel – was born in Alberta in 1900. We know they were in England in 1907 because his second child, Harold, was born there. He went back to Canada, then returned to Europe to fight in the First World War, before returning to Canada in 1919. Then a short time later he came back yet again to look for somewhere to farm in Devon, having despaired of making a decent living on his homestead on the unforgiving Prairie soil.

The brothers probably met then, but they seem to have drifted apart for about the next fifteen years. There may have been other reasons – clash of personalities perhaps – but nothing is documented. Nothing came of the Devon venture and Norman returned to Canada. Incidentally, a bizarre thing happened during this trip. Ettie got 'fed up' waiting for him and thought she'd spring a surprise by taking the boat across to England to see him. Simultaneously, Norman gave up on his enterprise and caught a boat back to Canada without telling her: their paths crossed mid-Atlantic. He waited for her to return and they met up again in Montreal, penniless. So, they pawned some possessions before he took a job as a foreman on a building site in North Ontario, never having had any previous experience in the construction industry.

In his 1936 letter Norman had obviously related how hard life had been for him and his family. Elsewhere he explains how in the wilds of Canada, long after Stanley had returned to England, he had become a kind of unofficial pastor to the Prairie farmers. The community of Youngstown chose him to conduct their funerals and preside at weddings and christenings, despite him being a reluctant participant. As he points out, he had no faith of any kind, let alone a calling for the ministry.

Likewise, when he became a member of the legislature in 1935, it was under duress, his constituency having voted for him despite him saying he didn't want to do it. He describes how at the hustings, twelve candidates had four minutes in which to present their manifesto. Norman made sure he was the last to be called but after the eleventh man had spoken, he had disappeared. It transpired that he was hiding behind a grand piano. He was persuaded to make his speech and congratulated the others on their performances, saying how any one of them would do an admirable job. The result? The voters opted overwhelmingly for him. He was dumbfounded by his landslide victory, but went on to be their local politician for a little over four years. In 1940, boundary redistribution saw Acadia merge with another district and Norman decided to run for re-election in Edmonton, where he won the third seat out of five. In the 1944 elections, he scraped in by the narrowest of margins.

One of the most important pieces of news for Stanley to impart was his conversion to Catholicism. He also says that it had been tough for Jess and him, too. 'It was a heart-breaking time for a while,' Stanley writes. 'We have five acres and a good deal of it is under cultivation so that we did not starve, but it sometimes came near that.' Then things began to mend a bit: his first autobiography sold quite well, and more articles were getting accepted. There were two more books, which didn't sell well. 'I work daily in the garden shack... and turn out a good deal of stuff.' He says that Jess had had 'some bad times with various ailments... She is white-haired but as cheery and almost as active as ever.' He talks over the course of the four-page letter of the loneliness he is suffering as a result of the remote location. 'The district is a poultry farming one and we have not many congenial friends in the near neighbourhood.'

Kitty and Alec Nurden, my mother and father, married at St Mary's parish church, Stowe School, Buckinghamshire, on 20 August 1940, the same day that Sir Winston Churchill delivered his 'Never has so much been owed by so many to so few' speech. Only six other people attended the distinctly low-key occasion. William and Jane Nurden, my father's parents, found it impossible to make the journey from Kent, probably because of the difficulty in travelling across London during the war. Because my father was a Protestant, Stanley prevented any of the Jameses, even Jess, from going to the wedding, but John ignored his strictures and gave my mother away. My mother referred to the episode only once; otherwise the issue sank quietly into that unspoken territory where so many family secrets lie buried. After all, they could always blame the war, which they did.

By mid-1941, Stanley and Jess were seventy-one and sixty-one respectively and, finding it hard to maintain Rosedale's five-acre plot, were looking around for a home that was easier to run. John managed to find them a property to rent near Hemel Hempstead, in Hertfordshire, but there was a snag: the house wasn't yet available and Jess and Patricia were forced to live temporarily in a ramshackle caravan in one corner of the Rosedale property until they received the go-ahead. By a happy coincidence, about this time, as many of the children as were able to gathered for a summer party, a family get-together that even Stanley mentions. It was also about now that he was offered the job of assistant editor of the *Catholic Herald*, which at his age was no mean achievement. He 'accepted with alacrity' but, as this required him to be in London from Monday to Friday, he needed to find lodgings during the week.

Eventually the family made the move to Hertfordshire, but any idea that Stanley, Jess and Patricia – the only one of the children still living permanently with them – might now at last enjoy some level of home comfort proved to be far from the case. Long Dene Cottage, Bunkers Lane, pretty with an old-world, flinted, Chiltern charm on the outside – there were even roses round the door – inside was as primitive as can be imagined for the 1940s. It was small with just two bedrooms and because it stood more than a mile up a remote lane and away from the national grid, it had no mains water, electricity or gas. Water had to be drawn from a well in the garden and then heated on a wood-burning stove, while the toilet was outside. Heating came from either logs on the fire or oil-burning stoves. So, the spartan conditions that Jess had experienced in Somerset and Hampshire continued with their move to Hertfordshire.

She tried to replicate the self-sufficiency that she had partially achieved at Rosedale but with her advancing years found it hard. Nevertheless, she grew a wide range of vegetables and kept chickens, the garden being attractive enough in the summer for passers-by to stop and admire. The car they had was frequently out of order and presumably they didn't have enough money to have it repaired, so Jess must have either cycled or walked to the shops. In later years, there were plans for John to either buy Long Dene Cottage and install proper facilities or for them to move to a more manageable property in Abbots Langley, but both plans fell through.

Long Dene Cottage, which had no electricity, gas or running water.

With Stanley away during the week, it was Jess who felt the full impact of these challenging conditions. At least Stanley acknowledged this, writing to Norman that the house was 'difficult to keep clean'. He also complained of the cold English winters and when one January Eric landed a temporary post as chaplain to a group of religious tourists in north Italy, he was envious. He frequently wished he could travel again, appearing quite nostalgic for his former days as a tramp, although he retained his fitness, chopping logs to fuel the open fire. In the evenings, not having electricity, Stanley and Jess listened to their battery-operated wireless, read books or sewed by the light of oil lamps, which Stanley said he preferred. Or they listened on their wind-up gramophone to 78 rpm records. I remember my mother saying that her father's favourite piece of music was Beethoven's *Seventh Symphony*. He reread Shakespeare, which he enjoyed 'more than ever' and he started to paint. The 'gorgeous display of colour' one autumn, which reminded him of the fall in North America, inspired him to take up his brush. 'Churchill in his old age exhibits pictures at the Royal Academy so why shouldn't

I, though older than he, turn out a few daubs now and again?' he writes. His study – another outdoor shed, as at Rosedale – had a neatly displayed rack of pipes fixed to the wall, and when he was in attendance was always full of tobacco smoke, a cousin recalls. If it was a Sunday, he may have been on his four-and-a-half-mile journey on foot and by bus to the church of St Mary and St Joseph in Boxmoor to attend Mass in the morning and Benediction in the evening.

Throughout his life Stanley had spurned the pursuit of wealth or comfort and had been content to live frugally, even giving away some of the little money they possessed to the voluntary poverty movement. Beautiful as the location of their Hertfordshire home was, it must have been extremely demanding for both of them – but particularly for Jess – to tolerate such conditions after a lifetime of hard work.

~ 20 ~
BACK TO FLEET STREET

A number of factors made the war years particularly challenging for Stanley's literary output. In 1939 he was sixty-nine years old and his energy levels and creativity were starting to wane. In addition, the closure of many merchant shipping routes meant that his overseas markets virtually dried up. Consequently, yet again money became extremely tight. He was forced to resign himself to being an impoverished freelancer for the rest of his working life.

Imagine his joy then, when, out of the blue, in 1941 he was offered the assistant editorship of the *Catholic Herald,* the journal he'd been writing for on and off for a number of years. It was more than he could have hoped for and marked a powerful return to weekly journalism. Now, after twenty years away, he was back in Fleet Street, at number 67, just a few yards up from Bride Lane, where the *Crusader* office had been. Now, for the first time as a writer, he had job security and for the next six years or so he had a salary coming in, even though it was at the lower end of the pay scale. One can only wonder how different their lives might have been if a publication had offered him a staff post twenty years earlier.

He relished being back in the bustle of journalism, particularly at the paper itself, which was establishing a reputation under the capable editorship of Michael de la Bédoyère for tackling progressive ideas while focusing on the laity, even drawing in non-believers. 'In the interest [the *Catholic Herald*] showed in every phase of contemporary life, it marked a departure from the tradition that had governed Catholic newspapers,' Stanley writes. 'Though not agreeing with everything it said, I was alive to the advantage of being associated with a going concern of this character.'

In a later article, De la Bédoyère highlights some of my grandfather's strongest points as a journalist:

> *What attracted me to James's writing was its astonishing vitality and optimism... He writes as though he were determined to lead a long-term movement of Catholic rejuvenation in which he intends himself to play an increasingly important part... The same remarkable elasticity and vigour of mind are reflected in his adaptability. Launched a few years ago into a staff of men and women whose average age was half his or less, he was still ready to learn and to redirect, as it were, his unchanging convictions along the channels of the day... when all is said and done, he's a journalist – one who loves to write and argue about events and their significance, who looks outward to the making and moulding of the things he loves, who instinctively detects pretence whether in himself or others.*

In my research to find a photograph of de la Bédoyère for this book, I hunted down the modern-day offices of the *Catholic Herald*, which occupy pleasingly disorganised rooms in a building attached to the Roman Catholic Church of St Joseph in Lamb's Passage, London. The décor – or rather the lack of it – reminded me of the offices of my first local newspaper, the *East Grinstead Observer*, in the 1970s. The editor kindly let me rummage through their non-digitalised picture library and there I found the photograph I was looking for. For one enjoyable hour I had been privileged to share the genteel world of Catholic journalism with my grandfather.

Michael de la Bédoyère, editor of the *Catholic Herald*.
Courtesy of the *Catholic Herald*

Stanley found lodgings in the House of Hospitality at 173b Haverstock Hill, a hostel for the homeless a stone's throw from the Dominican Priory, the very place where he had been taken into the Catholic Church eighteen years previously. Whenever he needed to be in London, which in the first years in the post was five days a week, he stayed there living cheek-by-jowl with down-and-outs. He points out that it was a way of life he knew well, having slept in doss houses many times in the past. Even if he didn't return to the actual life of a tramp, he was reminded vividly of his vagabond days.

The editor asked Stanley to write full-length columns under the banner Week by Week, which continued for about two years. In 'The Challenge' there is a rare example of Stanley marking out a modern-day event and celebrating it; it is almost unheard of in his writing. He praises the bravery of the warrior Englishman, making particular reference to the heroism of the Battle of Britain fighter pilots, but he goes on to give the phenomenon a spiritual element, speaking of the 'renaissance' of the Englishman. I'm not really sure what he means by that; why must religious writers – and Stanley is far from being alone in this – so often give a one-off event spurious universal significance? Suffice to say, if it needs to be said at all, he was no longer a pacifist.

CATHOLIC HERALD

"To Give Reliable Information" — To Set Forth Sound Christian Principles Of Life"
(The Aim For Which Pius XI Founded the Catholic Herald)

No. 3019   (Registered at the G.P.O. as a Newspaper)   **FRIDAY, JANUARY 7, 1944**   PRICE 2d.

HE RUSSIANS REACH POLAND

ster Answers Vital Questions in
view with "The Catholic Herald"

The Russians have reached the Polish frontier. This event
cessarily brings into the realm of practical politics the
ole question of Polish-Soviet relations and Soviet inten-
ns as regards the eastern half of Poland.
The Polish Cabinet has met and reported to the Polish
sident. The official attitude of the Polish Government

Mgr. Griffin says Goodbye to Coleshi

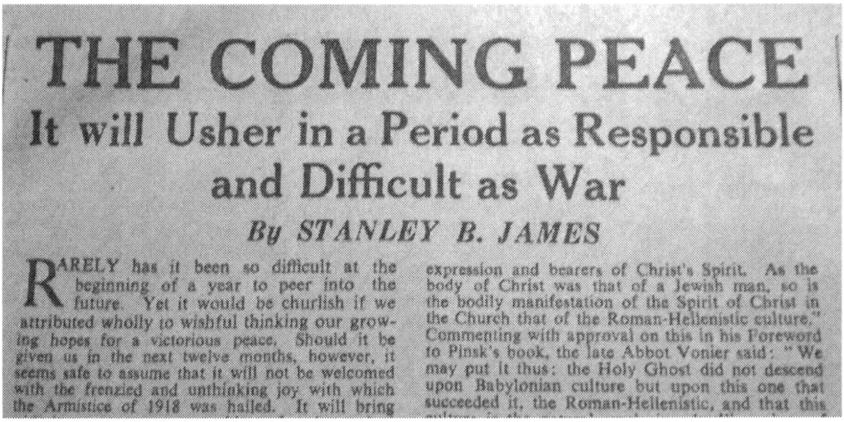

[column of faint text]

THE COMING PEACE
It will Usher in a Period as Responsible
and Difficult as War
By STANLEY B. JAMES

RARELY has it been so difficult at the
beginning of a year to peer into the
future. Yet it would be churlish if we
attributed wholly to wishful thinking our growing hopes for a victorious peace. Should it be
given us in the next twelve months, however, it
seems safe to assume that it will not be welcomed
with the frenzied and unthinking joy with which
the Armistice of 1918 was hailed. It will bring

expression and bearers of Christ's Spirit. As the
body of Christ was that of a Jewish man, so is
the bodily manifestation of the Spirit of Christ in
the Church that of the Roman-Hellenistic culture."
Commenting with approval on this in his Foreword
to Pinsk's book, the late Abbot Vonier said: "We
may put it thus: the Holy Ghost did not descend
upon Babylonian culture but upon this one that
succeeded it, the Roman-Hellenistic, and that this

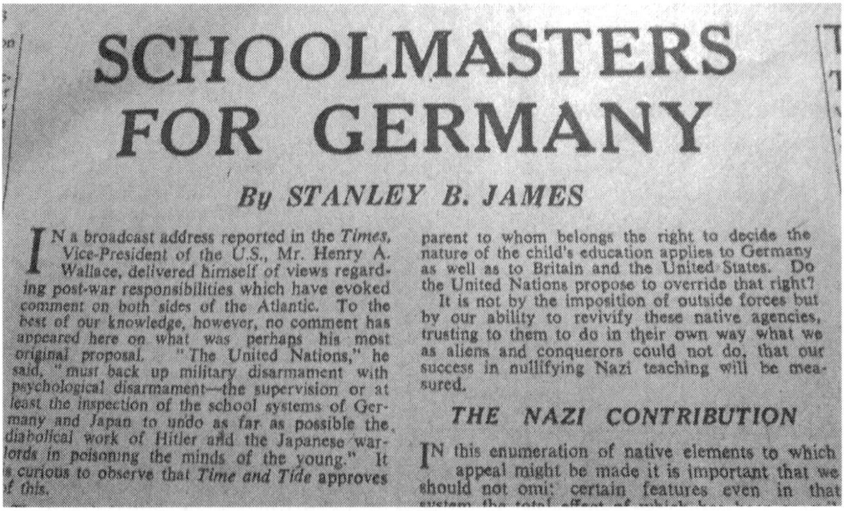

SCHOOLMASTERS
FOR GERMANY
By STANLEY B. JAMES

IN a broadcast address reported in the *Times*,
Vice-President of the U.S., Mr. Henry A.
Wallace, delivered himself of views regard-
ing post-war responsibilities which have evoked
comment on both sides of the Atlantic. To the
best of our knowledge, however, no comment has
appeared here on what was perhaps his most
original proposal. "The United Nations," he
said, "must back up military disarmament with
psychological disarmament—the supervision or at
least the inspection of the school systems of Germany and Japan to undo as far as possible the
diabolical work of Hitler and the Japanese war-
lords in poisoning the minds of the young." It
is curious to observe that *Time and Tide* approves
of this.

parent to whom belongs the right to decide the
nature of the child's education applies to Germany
as well as to Britain and the United States. Do
the United Nations propose to override that right?
It is not by the imposition of outside forces but
by our ability to revivify these native agencies,
trusting to them to do in their own way what we
as aliens and conquerors could not do, that our
success in nullifying Nazi teaching will be measured.

THE NAZI CONTRIBUTION

IN this enumeration of native elements to which
appeal might be made it is important that we
should not omit certain features even in that

A selection of Stanley's articles written in the 1940s

NO MORE CHARITY?
And Yet Love Can Find a Place in a Beveridgised Community
By STANLEY B. JAMES

AN interesting article by Lady Sinclair in a recent issue of the *Star* posed a problem in connection with such schemes as Sir William Beveridge's which deserves consideration. "Assuming," she says, "that our ideas of the obligations of the State towards individuals are far higher than we have hitherto been willing to accept, and that it will be

And in this way it lessens the temptation to that very servility which it is supposed to foster. The patronage which so often accompanies private "charity" is bad both for the giver and the recipient, encouraging spiritual pride in the former and undermining the self-respect of the latter. When the community as a whole gives through legal channels and those who receive do so as citizens

POLITICS ARE DYING
Real Reform Demands Life, Experience and Thought
By STANLEY B. JAMES

SIR Stafford Cripps remarked recently that the peace will not be an artificial order imposed on the community from outside but an organic thing growing up during the war and owing its main features to the exigencies of war. Much of the legislation passed "for the duration" and many of the relationships, national and international, inspired by comradeship in the common struggle we may well believe will be found to have permanent value. The work of reconstruction, on this hypothesis, will not begin on the bare ground; the foundations are being even at present laid on which the future will build

which have overtaken our interpretation of democracy concluded by putting party politics in their place as subordinate to a National Government. The need for sacrificing sectional interests to the whole is especially apposite, says the writer, in time of war. "But it will remain valid in the period after the war, when the maintenance of some form of National Government will be almost equally imperative if the problems of demobilisation are to be met without disaster; and it will remain valid even in those remoter days of an eventual resumption of party politics."

MISSION TO THE JEWS
Is it a Condition of the Success of the Apostolate of the Modern World?
By STANLEY B. JAMES

THE apostolate for the Christianisation of the modern world is a phrase which may sound magnificent, but, without further definition, is apt to lose itself in vagueness. In spiritual as well as in military warfare something in the nature of strategy is essential. One must try to seize key positions. Before battle is joined decisively there is a period when the contending forces manoeuvre for position. Divinely guided, the apostolate of the first century had a goal. St. Peter and St. Paul converged on Rome, the centre of the world. If Rome was won, the rest of the Empire in due course would follow.

(through the same circumstances as those just mentioned) is commercial, so is that of the people whom Napoleon called a nation of shop-keepers and their Transatlantic allies. So obvious is it that there is scarcely need to mention the rootlessness which is common to both and which distinguishes them so strikingly from the peoples of an older time. Those who are exiles under century-old compulsion and those whom the Industrial Revolution deprived of their rural birthright and in whom easy modes of transport have accentuated the desire to travel are now kindred nomads. These are but a few points of contact, but they might be multiplied

On 7 November 1941, with the twenty-third anniversary of Armistice Day approaching, he wrote a piece headlined 'The Unfinished War'. I found this moving and thought-provoking, a fine piece of journalism. He is at his best when he revives the spirit of the Nonconformist pulpit, in particular his own and his father's inspiring sermons. He argues that the partial and superficial treatment of evil leads to unending conflict. 'It is our whole world which is diseased and though the symptoms are as varied as the nations suffering from them, they have a common spiritual root. It is at the root that we must strike.' Moving on to consider Hitler, he writes:

The outstanding figure of the tragedy possesses obviously an unbalanced mentality. The racial egotism... has been carried to lengths which can only be described as insane. In that respect, he is the product of his age... Modern man has experienced the breaking up or disintegration of his personality... It is that state of things in the modern world which accounts for the fact that it has thrown up a Hitler... The world, poisoned by partisan propaganda, looks like going mad with hate.

He regularly wrote about how the war impinged on the realm of the spirit – and vice versa. Christians, he says, should take advantage of the current chaos to impart the Gospel message to the discombobulated mob. He devoted some articles to considering what form reconstruction should take after the war – and who should lead it. In 'A New Rome in Eire', he suggests that the Vatican should move from Rome to Dublin, for a number of reasons: the world was becoming increasingly English-speaking, Ireland was a centrally positioned Catholic country, and it was culturally nearer to America than Italy was.

In October 1943 these columns ceased to appear on a regular basis. His editor now asked him to write a weekly piece entitled Sunday Readings, in which he commented on the texts of the forthcoming Sunday's epistle and gospel. This was a chance for him to display his deep knowledge of the Bible and it earned him greater respect with the readership, continuing for exactly a year before being superseded by a new venture called The Liturgy Week by Week, another twelve-month series.

In addition to enjoying working side by side with journalists, Stanley clearly relished the buzz of living in a city at war. He volunteered to be a fire-watcher, which required him to work nights.

'War-time London with its blitzed buildings, varied uniforms, babel-like mingling of continental tongues and the personal contacts for which the *Catholic Herald* office provided opportunity had a stimulating effect,' he writes. 'The burden of my seventy-odd years grew lighter. Talking with American soldiers, I could almost fancy that I was again one of themselves. History was being made at an unprecedented pace and, floating on the swiftly-flowing stream of events, one became nervous. Whither were we moving? Towards some cataract?'

Bomb damage at Ludgate Circus, London, during the Second World War

In 1944 Stanley repeated the format of *Franciscan Fables* by writing *In the Light of Day*, a series of twenty-five short stories based on characters that appear in the New Testament, the starting point for twenty-two of them being passages from the Bible. They focus on imaginary situations leading up to those passages, or imaginary events that occur afterwards. As he himself says, they are 'modern apocrypha' which he hopes 'will serve to make fresh and humanly interesting the somewhat faded background of the Gospel narrative'. The preface is penned by the Catholic priest and author Ronald Knox, who writes:

There is… a tantalising quality about the New Testament record.
It is so superbly economical; characters rush on to the stage, say
their lines, and then exeunt, before you have time to cross-examine
them… 'What happened then?' we are continually wanting to ask, and
revelation is silent… At the end of every paragraph almost you find

*loose threads like these... [Mr James] provides imaginary answers...
And I, for one, feel that the familiar story of our Lord's life glows with
softer colours when the secondary characters in it are made, thus
putatively, into men and women of flesh and blood.*

Stanley employs a light touch and, although there is less humour than in
Franciscan Fables, the tales are accessible and often illuminating. Some of the
passages are fragments about little-known characters, which he embellishes
to create meaningful episodes. Then there are the familiar stories of the
shepherds in the fields around Bethlehem being visited by the angel; the
rich young man who asked what he should do to inherit eternal life; the
widow's son who was raised from the dead; Pilate in judgement over Jesus;
and the experience of the Apostles at Pentecost. For me, there were two
unexpected results of reading Stanley's little stories. Firstly, I began to get
a sense of the impact that conversion has on ordinary people and on their
relationships with others. Secondly, I started to understand the tenor of my
grandfather's evangelical mind. Could he have been so steeped in these
Biblical stories, even from a very young age, that in some paradoxical way
they were more 'real' to him than his everyday experiences?

* * *

Not many people write an autobiography, or have lives that merit it, but
Stanley managed two. Not that he felt the psychological need to trumpet
his own life. De la Bédoyère urged him to write a second because he
thought that *The Adventures of a Spiritual Tramp* did not adequately describe
his path to conversion. At the time of its publication in 1925, the *Times
Literary Supplement* says: 'Mr James does not explain very lucidly...
the connection between his temporal and spiritual vagabondage.' Stanley
somewhat reluctantly agreed and in the 1944 preface to *Becoming a Man*,
he hopes that the defect has been remedied.

He was obviously aware that he had produced something which was
different from his customary output. For me, it succeeds but only up to a
point. He does spend more time in explaining his state of mind in Alberta
– he introduces an imagined dialogue between his young and old selves

which works well – but I was left little clearer about those steps towards conversion, even though another twenty years had passed since he entered the Catholic church. Having said that, it has other merits. The main difference is in the gusto and lucidity of the prose and the way action itself is celebrated as much as the thought behind the action. The prose is zippier and less circuitous, particularly when recording the years in North America.

I have two copies of *Becoming a Man* in my possession, one of which is the 'author's copy'. Tucked inside the flyleaf is a scrap of paper with the editor's proof marks on it, maybe the hand of de la Bédoyère. These eight errata have been meticulously transferred by Stanley to the pages of the book for correction. Sadly, for whatever reason, the corrections have not been incorporated into the published version so that every book contains the same errors. It is dedicated to 'my wife, children and grandchildren', so I feel able to own a little bit of it. Despite the book's greater immediacy, it is still essentially an autobiography in which the soul plays the central role and other people and events are subplots. By 1944 his Catholicism had matured, and this confidence is captured in his description of a vision he had during Mass at the local Catholic Church:

> *With head buried in my hands, I kneel while the Priest makes his offering. But when I lift my eyes the scene is transformed. The little church has become a vast temple, the altar rises from the midst of the earth, and on it have been flung all the prizes of this world – health, wealth, honours, the love of women, the joys of the artist, the triumphs of the solitary thinker. It is as though the Priest was an incendiary. The words he utters kindle a spark. The piled-up treasures smoulder and an acrid smoke rises and fills the place.*

Because he was well known by this time, *Becoming a Man* received many more reviews than his first autobiography. I have located eleven in all, every one complimentary. Ten of the eleven reviews are in the religious press; the sole secular one was a short article in the *Times Literary Supplement*. De la Bédoyère remarks that the price of the 126-page book – 8s 6d – is steep but then goes on to guarantee the quality of the contents. He says the book is charmingly written and full of adventure, while at the same time offering important reflections on the spiritual life.

The Tablet review focuses on the language. It quotes two passages, the first in which Stanley considers the meaning of self-realisation: 'Not in the narrow individualistic sense: that's mere egocentrism. To be a person, and therefore in fellowship with all other persons, actual or potential, and to refuse enslavement, by things or in any other way, is the real object of existence.' Then: 'The world is like the landscape which is freshest and loveliest after drenching flowers. Its beauty is seen only through tears.' The reviewer goes on: 'Were these words found in an accepted master they would be acclaimed as literature of high quality. Mr James has not received his due as a writer.'

The Month believes that the book 'is one of the best spiritual Aeneids we have read… Mr James's intelligence, integrity, and detachment enabled him to live richly and dangerously without ever resting in the second-rate or the substitute.' For the *Catholic Fireside*, 'it is the spiritual odyssey of a man who has travelled the long and narrow path of bitter experience, of frustration, sometimes almost to despair, but with his eyes always on the far horizon and his mind questing for the holy Grail of the full Truth'. The *Baptist Times*, the only Protestant journal on the list, takes him to task for not making it clearer why his quest for the church ended in Rome: 'Certainly, it will appear to many readers that he took much of his Puritan heritage with him – such as his profound love of the Bible and the doctrine of the priesthood of all believers.'

Finally, the *Irish Monthly* dwells on the psychology of the man, pointing to how typical he is of his age – 'unrooted, sceptical, inquiring… Mr James must be one of those happy spirits that never grow old, because his heart is generous and his intellect lit by the never-ageing faith. This book is a tonic to the soul.'

In his articles, Stanley continued to address key moral issues of the day, and one of those contemporary preoccupations was 'The Jewish Question', to borrow from Karl Marx's well-known essay. Before considering my grandfather's thoughts on the matter, it is important to remember that they were formulated before the tragedy of the Nazi Holocaust and even Pope Paul VI's 1965 *Nostra Aetate* transformed the way in which Jewish matters have been considered.

Up until these events, widespread anti-Semitism in differing guises was common currency. The attitudes rolled out with sickening and unashamed regularity seem a long way from prevailing attitudes in the twenty-first century, despite a worrying rise in anti-Jewish feeling in recent years. Such issues are now handled with greater sensitivity and caution than was ever the case before the onset of the conflagration. Stanley's contemporaries G. K. Chesterton and Hilaire Belloc were arguing in *GK's Weekly* that two of the pressing issues facing Western society – the Bolshevik threat and usury – emanated from the Jewish people. Many other intellectuals, as well as journalists in the secular and Christian press, voiced similar views in varying degrees. But, apart from one article about unemployment, Stanley didn't write for this journal; his thoughts on the issue were better suited to the more overtly religious environment of the *Catholic Herald, The Month*, the *Clergy Review* and *Blackfriars*. It has to be said that he was writing for an exclusively Catholic readership where his ideas were less likely to be challenged. Just how his expressed views would have been received by a more general audience – let alone by Jews themselves – is open to question.

In a range of articles and pamphlets written up to the late 1940s, he covers the Jewish issue from religious, racial, historical and economic points of view. These are often subsumed into the same article and conflated, making it hard to decipher what his true beliefs were. Different emphases at different times add to the problem of deciphering his meaning so that, yet again, we are left wondering how much the notions he puts forward are those of a freelance writer wanting to appear readable and challenging, and how much they emanate from deeply held beliefs. Before launching into the content of the more important essays, it might be enlightening to record something my mother said to me. Her father told her how much affection he had for the Jewish people and how he admired the way spirituality informed their daily lives. In his various spells in London's East End, he enjoyed their company and claimed his Celtic temperament had more in common with their Hebrew one than it did with, say, the Anglo-Saxon mindset.

His columns examining the issue from the religious perspective invariably took the then traditional Catholic line that the Jews had committed deicide in murdering Jesus. Linked to that was the – again traditional – view that Catholics should attempt to convert Jews to Christianity. He writes: 'The Christian apostolate… is called, as the last and most exacting of all its tasks, to bring about by God's help the reconciliation of the Jews with their Messiah.' So far, so conventional, however much such sentiments may grate with twenty-first-century thinking. But he takes the argument further. He suggests that Christianity had been damaged by not paying enough heed to its Hebraic traditions, an error that a rereading of the Old Testament would rectify. He argued that Christianity had been greatly enriched by Greek and Roman contributions, but this enrichment had been at the cost of obscuring that Hebrew element which was its foundation. Salvation lay in recovering this Hebraic character.

The overwhelming note is one of respect for Judaism, which is seen as the foundation of Christianity. He writes that the Hebraic people possessed the truth which was to be the foundation of the greatest civilisation the world had yet seen. There was a sense in which the Jew was not a particular kind of man, but every man was potentially a particular kind of Jew. In the story of this exclusive tribe lay a broad catholicity. Jesus's presence in Palestine was seen by early Christians as a continuation of the Hebrew tradition, not as a departure from it. And because the Jews rejected the Messiah they missed the gift of the Holy Spirit, the consequence being that Judaism ossified into a legal system.

Stanley also tackles the race issue. He feels there are stark truths to be spelled out, sentiments which appear crude today. In his 1942 piece, 'World Citizenship – Nationalism and Racialism Have Failed', he writes:

Nazi Germany is the modern version of the segregated and fanatical Jewish racialism with which the primitive Church had to contend. There is again poetic justice in the fact that its most cruelly treated victims should be the descendants of those Jews who had, in the first century, adopted a like attitude towards the outside world.

In 'Christian and Jew' (September 1942), Stanley suggests that other races could be absorbed but that Jews resisted assimilation. In any population, the Jew remained an alien and subject to the suspicion of having loyalties that ran counter to complete citizenship. The case was made worse by his aggressiveness and by the superior abilities which allowed him to push his way to the front in every profession or business that he entered. Where Jews were found in large numbers and were tolerated, he continues, this aggressiveness was revealed in a provocative manner which invited suppression. The problem was not a religious one but an ethnic and social one. Given the intellectual abilities, tenacity of purpose and physical resilience which distinguished the Jewish people, their eventual domination of the world seemed inevitable. Wasn't the inferiority complex that this engendered what lay behind Hitler's hatred of the Jews? he asks. I swallowed hard when I read that.

Stanley is mentioned in *Church, Nation and Race: Catholics and antisemitism in Germany and England, 1918-45* by Ulrike Ehret. She writes:

Only a few authors reiterated [Hilaire] Belloc's argument in Catholic publications [that Jews living in Britain should be segregated]. Yet it was consistently the desire to protect the British nation that led authors to see the Jews as racial adversaries. An interesting example is that of the Distributist Stanley B. James. Contrary to the widespread assumption that history and religious customs shape a people's character, James proclaimed that the Jews' race determined their faith. 'Judaism for instance starts with certain racial characteristics and builds on them a religion calculated to meet their needs and to exult their importance. It makes God, as was said, the servant instead of the Lord of a certain people. Catholicism, on the other hand, draws its recruits from all quarters and out of this raw material supplied by the ethnological varieties to be found in the world, fashions without obliterating the natural differences therein expressed, a new type'.

But, in his accustomed spirit of trying to reach an understanding, Stanley goes on to invoke the healing balm of Catholicism, quoting Pope Pius XI: 'Anti-Semitism is unacceptable. Spiritually, we are [all] Semites.' He says that the very catholicity of the Church means it is opposed to racialism of any kind. The argument becomes complex. He seems to be saying that the Catholic Church has the power to reproduce the very spiritual qualities that distinguish the Jew. The type of civilisation created by this super-naturalised Israel would be of such a character that the bad Jew would be unable to flourish in it, he suggests. The bad Jew was a parasite who battened on to the weaknesses of society and, if those weaknesses didn't exist, he would cease to be. The only fundamental cure for the evil which anti-Semitism attacked but which it was unable to overcome was such a complete Christianisation of society that the essence of a degenerate Semitism would be unable to find a place and would eventually die off. In 'The New Race' he puts forward some challenging notions, to say the least. He concludes: 'It may be that, at some far-off date, the final clash of warring elements in this world will come between... Catholic and Jew [who] may yet prove to be the final, surviving protagonists in the struggle for the mastery of the world.'

As the Second World War progressed, and the full horror of Nazi Germany became known, Stanley's views changed. In his 1943 article, 'Mission to the Jews', he writes: 'Hitler's cold-blooded efforts to exterminate... the whole Jewish Community... has cast a lurid light on his sinister figure... [we now have] a profound hatred of anti-Semitism... It is something other than humanitarianism that makes us the Jew's champion.'

De la Bédoyère persuaded him to publish in pamphlet form two articles on the Jewish issue. In the 1944 piece, 'A Catholic Angle on the Jewish Problem', he suggests that post-war planning will suit the Jewish talent for reconstruction. But then he returns to some familiar tropes. The problem, he says, was found in the fact that the increasing influence likely to be exercised in the future by the Jew was of a character that we must regard as essentially non-Christian. It was the influence of a people whose antagonism to the Church was in their very blood and had its roots in history. He argues that the 'menace of the Jew' was greater because it was more subtle than that of the Muslims.

The second pamphlet, 'Jews – A New Catholic Approach', was published in 1948, one of the last works he wrote. After describing the Zionist project to establish a homeland for the displaced Jewish people as an unsatisfactory palliative, he then sounds a more optimistic note. Against a background of an alleged growing number of Jews discovering Jesus and a consequent spiritual reinterpretation of Judaism, he sets about envisaging a Christianity that assimilates the two spiritualities, Judaism and Catholicism.

Less contentious articles constituted the staple diet of Stanley's output, which is not to say that they lacked critical edge. Modern literature, especially poetry, came in for admonishment. With exasperation in the final chapter of *Becoming a Man*, he addresses the contemporary writer: 'Do but catch a glimpse of the Glory that is above and around you, and you will find yourselves restored to sanity and in possession of a peace and joy which nobody and nothing can take from you.' He even finds time to take a pot shot at Walt Whitman. 'Those who, a few decades ago, discovered in the cosmic sentimentality of Whitman evidences of the supreme prophet of democracy are manifestly less certain of their creed.' When he aims a jibe like that at his old mentor, one knows that the revolution of the soul is complete. One can see, in that quiet sentence, the utter transformation that has taken place.

Generally, he is surprisingly generous in his appreciation of the other side of the theological divide but in 'The Church Apostolic', while underlining the importance of missions, he makes comments that are distinctly prejudiced and difficult to read today:

The missionary laboured... in remote countries and among 'inferior' races... The native who once found relaxation in cannibalistic orgies now sits to watch a Hollywood film or listens in to cabaret singers and... we have borrowed from him not only his barbaric 'music' but also practices even more indicative of barbarism... It is one thing to plant a mission among the devotees of Mumbo-Jumbo and another thing to establish it where commerce and a Wellsian conception of civilisation have corrupted the native.

Stanley's editor also ran a series entitled Why I Became a Catholic, with an accompanying talk at Foyles art gallery and, naturally, my grandfather was commissioned. In an otherwise conventional article, Stanley confesses that one of the very earliest motivations for conversion had been that he wanted 'to be Everyman... Slowly, the idea of the Catholic Church began to fill the landscape – and I did not like it,' he recalls. 'It seems to me I came into the Church for negative reasons – there was simply no other alternative.' This is an astonishing admission, but I think it can be best understood in the context of the convert's struggle to free himself from the chains of familiar theological habits to reach out for something new – and better. He is describing the start of a long, drawn-out process in which the convert fiercely resists the forces that are trying to change him. As St Augustine had it: 'Lord, make me pure, but not yet.'

And in 1945 de la Bédoyère asked him to write a weekly series under the banner A Layman's Pulpit. These five hundred-word pieces were conventional meditations on the life of Christ and the shorter format, I would argue, suited

Stanley's style better and prevented him from speculating too wildly, although he continued to write occasional longer features, columns and book reviews. When De la Bédoyère determined in 1947 to make the *Catholic Herald* more populist, Stanley's output suffered as a result. The editor hired others to write less scholarly and more light-hearted pieces, and my grandfather's services were dispensed with, although he remained on a small retainer.

~ 21 ~

TWILIGHT AT LONG DENE

Any more writing that Stanley did from 1947 onwards was performed in the garden shed at Long Dene, now that he no longer worked at the *Catholic Herald*. As money yet again became a problem, his, Jess's and Patricia's horizons were limited to this corner of leafy Hertfordshire. Here he chopped firewood to provide fuel for the fire, Jess tended the garden to provide vegetables and Patricia helped her mother around the house. As far as I can ascertain, Stanley didn't reconnect with the publications he'd been writing for before the war. A few months into this new self-imposed isolation, he swallowed his pride and wrote to Bob in South Africa to ask for financial help. His son responded with a generous gift, as did his other sons. Stanley was especially grateful to Bob as the donated funds had the effect of delaying his son's move into his new home.

In letters to Bob, Stanley says that he and Jess were suffering more and more from the harsh English winters. 'Fortunately, we have plenty of fuel from the adjoining wood,' he writes. 'I have been busy chopping up timber which fell in recent gales, which were exceptionally heavy.' Amusingly, he speculates that the increased use of civil aviation might mean that 'some day you may be able to drop into tea, returning to South Africa for breakfast next day. We promise you a good spread.'

In the hot summer of 1947, Jess fell seriously ill and, according to the doctor, her life was in danger. It is not clear what her medical condition was, but exhaustion likely had much to do with it. She went to live with Jessie in Wendover, Buckinghamshire, and her daughter nursed her back to health, while Stanley was grateful to Patricia for her help in coping with the 'domestic crisis'. By January 1948 Jess had recovered and was back at home. In a letter to Bob soon afterwards, Stanley is ruminative about the current state of Britain:

We lack the clear knowledge of what we want. Leadership is lacking. There is a general feeling of frustration owing to uncertainty as to the future and to the confusion that rapid changes in the political and social sphere are causing. There are times when I am almost thankful that I shall not live probably to see the evil harvest of present sowing. But then, again, I regain confidence in the ultimate good that must, in God's mercy, result from all the suffering now endured.

These sentiments sound remarkably similar to those expressed in some of the last features he wrote. He continues: 'We go on much as usual. Of course, age is slowing down my powers of production. I still write a good deal, but there is not the same elasticity of mind I once enjoyed, nor the ability for sustained effort. But that was to be expected. We have much for which to be thankful – this quiet corner of old England, our health (now that mother is better) and Pat's help. Her youthfulness and liveliness help us to keep young. I don't know what we would do without her – perhaps go into some institution for old people! It is also rejuvenating to be able to live in the lives, plans and ambitions of our children. We share your hopes for the new home you are building and the new business you are creating. Blessings be on you both and on the newcomer (Bob's first daughter, Anne).'

Later that year, he writes: 'Mother, Pat and I live very quiet lives (barring complications in our large cat-family and the effect of frosts etc on garden produce). I forgot the car which, like other cars, is temperamental. The variation in its moods makes me think that it must be a she.' However much he may have neglected his children in earlier days, in these letters he shows genuine concern for them and their families.

In 1948 Stanley entered a period of regular correspondence with Norman, as if making up for lost time. He tells him how much he enjoyed *The Autobiography of a Nobody*, which his brother had published the previous year. In this 18 November letter Stanley writes:

[Daisy – their cousin] has passed it [the autobiography] round to other members of the family who have, all, enjoyed it. She herself speaks of failing health. I was down that way when I went to see the last of poor Muriel [his older sister] but, though I could see Newport across the water, I had no time for a visit.

Muriel died in Wells, aged seventy-seven, in September 1948. It was also that year that Norman, at the age of seventy-six, finally retired from provincial politics because of his disillusionment with the direction the Social Credit Party was taking. But the writing of his autobiography seems to have inspired him to write more and he says he is working on a second book. He had already been writing a weekly column called Main Street for the party newspaper and had gathered a considerable following.

Stanley speaks warmly of his brother's ability to write light verse, referring particularly to an amusing poem about gophers which Norman had sent him. He also congratulates him on having his book translated into French and then draws parallels between their lives: 'I think we are both so made that we must have some cause for which to fight, something bigger than our private concerns. Fortunately, in my case, I am still able to do something – though it is not much – in the Good Cause.' In April 1950 Norman and Ettie celebrated their golden wedding anniversary and sent Stanley a cutting with their photograph from an Edmonton paper. But when Norman hints that his autobiography had not been a commercial success, Stanley remarks that his wife saw this as evidence that books never pay.

In the batch of ten letters written between 1948 and 1951 Stanley updates Norman on the family, though he only focuses on the two offspring he sees as having slightly unusual and successful stories to tell, his sons Bob and John. He hardly mentions the others. Bob wrote frequently to his father and mother, often sending books about South Africa, where he by now owned his own poultry farm near Paarl. He had real ability at water divining and had purchased a rocky tract of land for his farm after detecting water deposits beneath the ground. He had been confident that he could create enough wells – and therefore procure adequate water for his poultry – to make a deal for the land worth his while, all of which proved to be the case. Was the natural spirituality of Daniel and Stanley revealing itself through an unconventional channel?

In 1944 Bob had written to Betty and asked her to marry him, a proposal which she accepted, whereupon he posted her an engagement ring. She was working as a nurse in a hospital called Clearsprings in Bagshot, Surrey, but when the war came to an end she was free to travel out to South Africa to be with him. The problem was that most flights were full as they were taking soldiers back to the colonies. But all was not lost. One day in a Dorset hotel, Phyllis overheard a pilot at the next table talking about his charter flight to Johannesburg which still had some available seats. Phyllis went over to him and told him she knew someone who would take one of the spare places. The upshot was that Betty joined the passenger list, paying £225 for the trip. On the flight were Lord and Lady Delamere, en route to their estate in Kenya, where they were a part of the notorious, hedonistic Happy Valley set of English expatriates (depicted in the 1987 film *White Mischief* starring Charles Dance and Greta Scacchi). The ten-seater biplane, with nine passengers on board, took off from Gatwick on 17 February 1947 and took fifteen days to reach South Africa. It made twenty refuelling stops on its six thousand-mile flight, and everyone survived a forced landing in the jungle. Bob flew up to Johannesburg from Cape Town to meet Betty and within three days they were married.

Bob tried to persuade Stanley and Jess to up sticks and come to South Africa – and Stanley was tempted. He writes:

Book-writing could also go on in the Karoo, and perhaps would be all the better done for the distance from this crowded and noisy land – though, of course, we have not much of which to complain in this corner of ours. But I do sometimes think that I should like to get away from it all and look at the scene from some remote perch. One thing in our favour, both mother and I have learned to do with quite a little and we are used to comparative solitude.

They didn't make the trip out there, so they never saw Bob's highly successful poultry business (named Clearsprings) which was going from strength to strength. Stanley's letters continue to paint a picture of post-war Britain. 'You would see much changed,' he writes. 'There are parts of London so blitzed that they are scarcely recognisable. Looking from Cannon Street, for instance, towards St Paul's you see the cathedral stand out like the pyramids in the desert, only instead of sand you have the debris of destroyed buildings and large open spaces that have been cleared of rubble.'

Jessie, meanwhile, moved in May 1951 with her family to East Africa where her husband Bernard Frowd had been contracted to work on building projects in Tanganyika and Uganda. It was to be the happiest time of her life, establishing her garden with the help of her Maasai neighbours. Eric was continuing his ministries in various Congregational churches around the country. By 1946, my mother Kitty was with my father Alec, Richard (born 1942) and Jane (born 1944) at Haileybury. The family, without my father, often travelled the twenty miles to Long Dene, the journey involving three bus journeys. They appear lined up rather formally in a number of photographs taken in front of the cottage with other members of the family. My father probably couldn't join them because of work commitments, but I suspect that he and Stanley never saw eye to eye: one, a shy, classics scholar with a highly developed sense of service, the other a bold advocate of personal fulfilment and the pursuit of truth at all costs.

John had had an unconventional war. One evening we had a long chat and he told me he had been a member of the Royal Army Medical Corps. At the end of 1943, at the age of thirty, he joined the Special Operations Executive, which worked with resistance groups. In a hush-hush mission he and five other doctors travelled by convoy to Gibraltar, where they were met by Argentine-born British waiting to infiltrate Spain if Franco came in on the side of the Germans. They then went by plane to Algiers, before eventually being flown to Cairo, where John followed his briefing instructions and tried to contact a secret agent without success. But the doctors contacted their unit and were taught elementary sabotage and learnt parachute jumping in the desert. After two unsuccessful attempts, John was finally dropped into the mountains of Montenegro at night, landing in a tree. This was his introduction to the months he spent supporting Tito's Partisans fighting the Nazis. They were engaged in a fierce guerrilla war and John travelled with them as their doctor in freezing temperatures over the snow-capped mountains of the Balkans. He treated and operated on the injured by candlelight in caves, huts or the goats' quarters of peasant houses. The fighters often contracted a deadly kind of typhus and wounds sometimes developed gangrene, which required amputation. His services were recognised after the war by being awarded the Order of the Yugoslav Star. In Athens he was put in charge of a surgical division, with the rank of lieutenant colonel. Back in England, he continued to make strides as a doctor, being appointed deputy director of the orthopaedic unit attached to University College Hospital, London, at the age of thirty-five. Stanley says in a letter that he will 'do well for himself'. John visited his father and mother frequently and helped out financially.

David continued to farm in Hampshire for many years until, following a series of wet seasons and consequent financial losses, the family decided to up sticks and move abroad, although it would take a while before they decided on the actual location. Patricia went to a boarding school in Abbots Langley, where she was the only day girl, returning to Long Dene every evening. After leaving school and having considerable artistic ability and a love for wildlife, she enrolled on a course in botanical painting.

Stanley explains to Norman that he had resources to draw on: his state pension, his retainer from the *Catholic Herald*, generous contributions from his sons, and the vegetables they grew. He says he could always reactivate his agreements with a number of magazines if needs must. 'Somehow we scrape along,' he writes. When Norman sent a large piece of ham from Canada every Christmas, Stanley thanked him and said how much it was appreciated; on one occasion it was distributed among other members of the family. One year, Norman offered to help out financially, but Stanley refused any assistance. Another time, my grandfather apologised for not being able to reciprocate with a present for Norman and Ettie. He regularly bemoaned the current state of British politics, particularly the ineffective Labour Party whose lacklustre performance left the way open for a strong Conservative Party. But Churchill's best days were over, he believed, and the Tories were made up of 'such little and such shallow men'. In a wider context, he says 'the world situation appears to be deteriorating. I can see no end to present trends except a crash in which the whole façade of our civilisation will come down. The only thing an individual can do is to dig himself in, spiritually.' He seemed to want to make a stronger connection with Norman. He continues:

As one grows older, family ties come to mean more. I suppose that we are better able, as we near the end, to get down to the physical roots of our being; the more superficial kind of relationships mean less while those based on kinship reassert themselves. But there is a still stronger tie. Your mention of our Lord warmed my heart towards you as even the physical tie could not. In spite of all our differences, this is ground of unity... It is very, very good to have this token of continuing affection. As Daisy recognises my existence only at Christmas, you are the only member of the inner family circle left me, the only living link with early days. It means a lot to me, therefore, to have these remembrances.

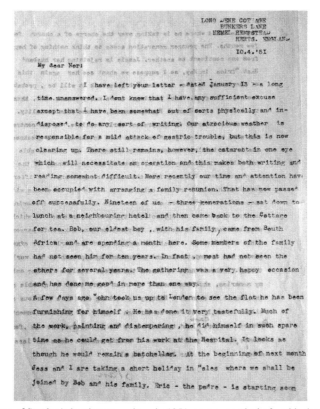

One of Stanley's last letters, written in 1951, seven months before his death

The family gathered in Hertfordshire in April 1951 to
celebrate the couple's fiftieth wedding anniversary

Clearly, he is lonely:

*The great drawback of this place is the absence of congenial
company... Even though I can and do get about there are very
few here with whom I can have intimate relations. There is an old,
retired priest some miles away whom I visit periodically, one of the
best-read and most travelled men I have ever known. It is always
refreshing to spend an afternoon with him. But the exception proves
the rule, and this exception makes the dearth of real friends more
apparent. I have correspondents all over the world, some of whom I
have never met in the flesh. But that is not the same thing as having
friends with whom one can talk face to face.*

His sense of separation from what is going on around him deepens:

*Outliving one's contemporaries is not altogether a pleasant process.
Quite naturally, the younger generation has its own interests and
friendships, and this makes the older folk feel a bit lonely. So,
every token of fraternity is a gleam of winter sunshine. But if being
forgotten is painful, it is salutary. Old age brings a detachment
that purifies one's vision. We who belong to the past can overlook*

the world as from a mountain peak which transcends the scene. As external activities become less, the powers of contemplation, the consciousness of things invisible, become greater.

He mentions his current reading: *Elected Silence* and *The Waters of Silence* by Thomas Merton, formerly a loose-living bohemian who 'sought refuge from a rotten world in a Trappist monastery in Kentucky'. He tells Norman he would like to fly over to see both him and Alberta again.

On 17 March 1949 it was Patricia's twenty-first birthday but any notion that her day might be marked with a celebration, however small, proved wide of the mark. Finding herself confined to the house, she turned on the BBC Light Programme in order to fill Long Dene with the sound of music. Stanley strode into the room and told her to 'turn off that rubbish'. 'I didn't like him,' she once confided to me. 'He could be a cruel man. His Catholicism and his attempts to make everyone follow him tore the family apart.'

This negative image was echoed by my cousin Tim whose mother Jessie used to take him over to Long Dene when he was a young boy. He remembers Stanley as a severe man, closed off in his own thoughts and wrapped up in his own world with his pipe for company. Jess, on the other hand, was a loving person, always ready with a smile and a cuddle.

By now Stanley was attending Mass at St Saviour's, Abbots Langley, making the journey on foot and by bus, as he had previously to Boxmoor. Incidentally, the village is the birthplace of the only English pope, Adrian IV (Nicholas Breakspeare). In August, aged seventy-nine, Stanley was about to start work on a book about the life of St Paul. This was inspired by an enthusiastic response he had received from a Californian lawyer who, after reading an article of his about the saint in *Columba,* a US magazine, thought such a book could form the basis of a film. Stanley appears never to have finished it. Even earlier, he had personally approached the film magnate J. Arthur Rank to suggest making a film based on the life of the saint, but the film magnate merely 'shook his head'. The financial imperative took precedence over any artistic considerations. Stanley comments: '[It's] a difficult subject but a fascinating one. What a film his life with its Mediterranean background would make!... It will be done some day, I am sure.' But generally he was winding down from writing and often apologised to Norman for being indolent in replying to his letters.

And so, to the last letter of Stanley's to Norman that I have, written – on 10 April 1951 – seven months before he died and three weeks after I was born. It is worth reproducing it in full:

I have left your letter... a long time unanswered. I don't know that
I have any sufficient excuse except that I have been somewhat
out of sorts physically and indisposed to do any sort of writing.
Our atrocious weather is responsible for a mild attack of gastric
trouble, but this is now clearing up. There still remains, however,
the cataract in one eye which will necessitate an operation and this
makes both writing and reading somewhat difficult. More recently
our time and attention have been occupied with arranging a family
reunion. That has now passed off successfully. Nineteen of us –
three generations – sat down to lunch at a neighbouring hotel and
then came back to the cottage for tea. Bob, our eldest boy, with his
family, came from South Africa and are spending a month here.
Some members of the family had not seen him for ten years. In fact,
most had not seen the others for several years. The gathering was a
very happy occasion and has done me good in more than one way.

That 1951 reunion, which doubled up as an early fiftieth golden wedding anniversary, may have been a joyous occasion for him, but no Nurdens were present, even though they lived nearer to Stanley and Jess than any other family members. The reason was that I had just been born – on 19 March – and my mother was looking after me. But in his letter to Norman Stanley makes no mention of the fact that one of his daughters, at the age of forty-two, had given birth to a boy called Robert or that it was a shame that she and her family couldn't have been there, let alone that they were missed. I am told, however, that I was taken to Long Dene that summer and that he blessed me.

The last letter continues:

A few days ago, John took us up to London to see the flat he has
been furnishing himself. He has done it very tastefully. Much of the
work, painting and distempering, he did himself in such spare time

as he could get from his work at the hospital. It looks as though he would remain a bachelor. At the beginning of next month Jess and I are taking a short holiday in Wales where we shall be joined by Bob and his family. Eric – the padre – is starting soon for the USA where he is taking over the charge of a church for a few months. The younger generation seems to think nothing of hopping from one continent to another. Jessie is re-joining her husband in East Africa in May, so I suppose we shan't see her again this side of the Great Divide. And when Bob goes back it will be, probably, good-bye for good. These partings are a nasty wrench. But, thank God, the Eternal Family remains, immune from mortality. Not that one's interest in the present world declines. On the contrary, one sees more clearly and realises more intensely the greatness of the issues involved in our earthly struggles. And one is able to renew life vicariously in the fortunes and experiences of the younger generations. The very fact that they are scattered in different parts of the world and are cultivating different interests widens one's outlook and anchors one to the here and now. In following their careers, one is led to appreciate types of experience to which otherwise one would lack the key. There is nothing like this personal link with diverse vocations and parts of the world for giving one a sympathetic and understanding approach to the world of today. I should hate to become the morose recluse living only in my memories, shutting oneself up in an ivory tower to grumble at the course of events. History is working out to a glorious climax even if it does so through tragedy and disillusionment. Adverse factors can lend themselves to the Divine purpose as, for instance, when the possibilities of atomic warfare make war less probable. Our love to you all, Stan.

In May he went into St Mary's Hospital, Paddington, for an operation on his stomach. It was there that, while in conversation with his nurse, he discovered that her father had also fought in the Spanish American War of 1898, one of only seven men remaining in Britain who had done so. All of them were drawing a US army pension of $90 a month (£770 in 2020). Stanley, by not being unduly concerned with money at any point of his life, had therefore missed out on many years of an army pension. His nurse advised him of the appropriate channels through which to make an application, which he duly did. His appeal was granted and for the last few months of his life he received the money, but unfortunately the Americans did not backdate it. It is painful to speculate just how different Stanley and Jess's life would have been if he had received the pension much earlier.

After being discharged from hospital, he never regained good health: by now it was clear that he had stomach cancer. He stopped writing and spent his time reading or just sleeping. Perhaps he had looked upon that April gathering as a symbolic event, realising that it was the last time he'd see many of the family. In October his condition became so serious that he went back into St Mary's Hospital. Jess said later that 'he became very depressed and ready to go at the end'. Thanks to his son John's generosity, a bed was secured for him in a private wing. My mother, Richard and Jane went to visit him there, as did many others, including Jess, Patricia and his *Catholic Herald* colleague Andrew Boyle. By coincidence, Sir Winston Churchill was being nursed back to health down the corridor of that same private ward. Stanley died on 1 November (All Saints Day) 1951 and was buried in the Catholic cemetery at St Lawrence Church, Abbots Langley, five days later, following a short, graveside ceremony.

A time for reflection at Long Dene Cottage

Stanley is buried in the churchyard of St Lawrence, Abbots Langley

As was noted in the introduction, his headstone has the unexpected inscription 'Strong and content I travel the open road', a quotation from Walt Whitman, which seems strange for a man who held his Catholic beliefs so strongly. Stanley left Jess effects to the value of £209 8s 6d (£6,500 in 2020), though the probate mentions no money, so she wouldn't have had the funds to pay for the funeral and burial. As with so much else in the final years, John may well have covered the costs. In December 1951 Daisy Greener, cousin of Stanley and Norman, wrote her usual Christmas card to the Jameses, not knowing that Stanley had died. Jess wrote to her, giving her the news. In her letter of 23 January 1952 to Norman, Daisy explains that she had no idea where Stanley was buried or if he had been cremated. And she adds: 'I could never understand why he turned Roman Catholic. He told me some time ago he was writing his last book. I doubt if he ever finished it. Of course, I never heard.'

I have found two obituaries, one in *The Times,* the other in the *Catholic Herald.* There were also some death notices in US publications but no full-blown dedication that I have been able to find; but there were probably others, particularly in Ireland where his writing was well known. *The Times* says:

While studying himself for the ministry he entered a period of
intellectual disturbance caused largely by his interest in Walt

*Whitman, whose work turned his mind to problems affecting
the nature of man and human personality. Whitman's influence,
overlooked today, had a profound effect on many of his readers at
that time; it was felt particularly by G. K. Chesterton, for whom
James was later to feel the affection of a friend as well as that of a
follower... He aged gently, making as many new friends in younger
generations as he retained in his own, finding more time for the
contemplation he had always desired without losing the active zeal
that had been kindled in him by his life in the world.*

Andrew Boyle penned a lovely portrait of him in the *Catholic Herald*.
He calls Stanley 'the straightest, youngest and serenest practical mystic of
the old guard of Britain's Catholic journalists...' and writes:

*Mr James, as he was always called out of the profound respect he
inevitably inspired, was a character of many sides and virtues. His
career was a quiet epic, and the quiet was largely due to his wise
humility... Outside the cloud-cuckoo land of Hollywood, he was
the only man in my limited experience who included among the
many parts he played, those of cowboy, hobo, soldier-adventurer,
Congregational minister, author and journalist... He could combine
contemplation with an untroubled grasp of the shifting kaleidoscopic
modern scene. But his social ideal was bound up with an England
of guilds and craftsmen: England that was merry, the England
of the Canterbury Tales and The Vision of Piers Plowman... His
experience of life and books – apart from his staggering knowledge
of the Bible – was evident to all. But his learning was worn lightly,
always. And his humility and natural deference often led him to
suppose we were 'with him' in some of his deeper intellectual
excursions. It was impossible not to love Stanley James.*

After Stanley died, Jess received half his pension for the rest of her life.
She and Patricia made frequent visits to us at Haileybury, and we to them,
this time with me in tow. A strange thing has happened as I have been writing
this book: a previously indistinct memory of Long Dene has sharpened
and come to the front of my mind. I can now clearly remember looking, in

bright sunlight, up at the cottage's distinctive windows and flinted façade, quite possibly in the summer of 1953. After Stanley's death, our families established a closer connection.

Jess and Patricia eventually moved to 12 Lynford Avenue, Winchester, and my mother and I used to go and stay with them. The semi-detached house had been bought by Bob as security in the event of him being forced to return from South Africa. I remember Jess, then in her late seventies, stooping awkwardly over the kitchen stove, wearing a long, billowing, black dress. She came across as quiet, a bit stern, caught up in her own thoughts and memories. Once I shut her black and white cat in the front room 'just for fun'. When she found out what I'd done, she scolded me rather more severely than I thought the occasion merited and from then on I was a little frightened of her. But still I loved those trips from Hertfordshire to Hampshire. We arrived by steam train from Waterloo, Patricia meeting us in her spanking new Austin A30. In the grate of the dining room there were the largest fir cones I'd ever seen; Patricia had collected them while walking in the New Forest. Out in the garden the chickens clucked and pecked and I always had a deep-yellow boiled egg for breakfast. At night, as I drifted off to sleep, I traced the patterns of the 1950s wallpaper in the half light, as the boat trains hurtled and whistled their way down to Southampton.

Of Stanley's remaining siblings, Daisy Sutherland, his younger sister and by now a widow, died in unusual circumstances at the age of eighty-one on 1 August 1956 in the Ulsterville Private Hotel, Boscombe, Dorset. The coroner recorded a verdict of death by misadventure from asphyxia due to coal-gas poisoning. Norman continued to write occasional articles for the Canadian paper and lived another twelve years with Ettie in Edmonton, before dying on 12 December 1963, aged ninety-one, just months before his wife passed away.

Stanley's oldest child, Phyllis, a good while after his death went to live with Bob in South Africa, before becoming a school matron there. On her return to England, she joined a religious sect called the Infinite Way, while acting as a live-in companion to an older woman. Later she herself had a residential carer, Margaret. One of the tasks Phyllis undertook was to write a chapter covering Stanley's years at Trinity, Walthamstow, for inclusion in a booklet on the church's history. She died in a nursing home in north London in 1992.

Bob's poultry business in South Africa continued to thrive, and he became a respected and leading voice in the business community there. His skill at divining for water never left him and he changed the lives of farmers all over the country by finding water on their land, but never took any payment. He also detected an area of oil under the seabed, which an oil company later excavated and brought to the surface. He and Betty had four children – Anne, Rosemary, Margaret and Wendy – and after retirement he visited England from time to time. He died in 1987.

The Frowds returned to England in 1954, settling in Southampton. Some time after this, Bernard asked for a divorce, from which Jessie never fully recovered. She became manager of a sports shop which was used by footballers from Southampton F.C., buying her own house in Netley, near Southampton. Every day, come rain or shine, she went swimming in the Solent, dismissing all comments as to her courage. Towards the end of her life she went to live with her daughter Christine in Cornwall. She died in 1993.

Eric spent his life with Joyce working as a Congregational minister in different districts, mostly in the south of England. Having retired as a minister, he ran an ecumenical prayer centre called Benifold, in Hampshire. When the organisation he worked for put the large country house up for sale, members of the band Fleetwood Mac came to view it, eventually buying it. Eric's job was to show them round and, by all accounts, both parties hit it off splendidly. When they played at my college, I went backstage and introduced myself as Eric's nephew and they confirmed the story. Eric died in 1988.

My mother, Kitty, worked as tirelessly as her mother had, running not only her own family household but also being on call for duties as a housemaster's wife at Haileybury. In 1965 my father retired, and we moved to Pembury in Kent, at which point he was taken on as classics teacher at a nearby prep school, which meant that my mother had to drive him to work every weekday. Tragically, soon after making the move, my brother Richard died suddenly at twenty-three from an illness. My mother died in 2001.

In 1958 John was appointed professor and chair of orthopaedic surgery at the University of Edinburgh, training doctors from around the world. Nicknamed 'Jip', he pioneered groundbreaking surgery into scoliosis and hand reconstruction. He was extremely proud of his appointment as Fellow of the British Orthopaedic Association, an exceptional accolade even for a past president. On one occasion he had to call at Sir Winston Churchill's London flat to remove the stitches from Lady Clementine's hand after she'd had a minor operation. Apparently, Churchill commented: 'I hope you're not going to hurt her.' He also worked as director of orthopaedic services in Kuwait and Saudi Arabia. He married Margaret, a GP, in 1968, finally retiring to Slad in Gloucestershire. They had two children, Jonathan and Tamsin. My favourite uncle died in 2001.

In 1952 David had written to Norman asking him about agricultural prospects in Canada. In the end he and Jean decided to join his brother Bob in South Africa, where David became involved in various agricultural enterprises ranging from fruit to poultry. They eventually retired to Robertson in the Worcester region of the Cape. They had five children, Susan, Tony, Linda, Barry and Robin. David died in 1998.

Patricia trained and worked as a florist for many years, one of her jobs being at Moyses Stevens, the upmarket floral business in London's Belgravia. She then took the decision to train as a landscape architect and worked for the Greater London Council, the Thames Flood Barrier being one of the prestigious projects she worked on. She created a wonderful garden in her house in Winchester and remained close to my family. She died in April 2015.

Finally, Jess herself. I remember my mother receiving the phone call telling her that her mother had died, and crying. Jess left all her furniture and household items to Patricia, her shares to Phyllis and the remaining cash split equally between her four daughters. Eric, in his guidelines for the minister officiating at Jess's funeral, writes of his mother:

Being of Irish-English stock, she was a mixture of romantic rashness and steadfast loyalty. She needed to be to marry my father... My mother carried out the burden of hard years of strain and poverty with great courage and loyalty. Brought up a Congregationalist in comfortable circumstances in a farming and professional family, she never really changed her outlook. Although she was received into the Roman Catholic Church, she never followed it up in practice and, in later years when she could, attended Winchester Cathedral. She loved country things and was a devoted gardener. The demands of family life meant that, with indifferent health, she could do no more than care for her children

*and the family affairs. She did the business and took the heavy end
of responsibility. She has been the link holding the family together
and keeping in touch. The bold integrity of my father in defence of
his principles often meant sacrifice at home. My mother remained
loyal, often without full understanding, and spent herself for her
family. To the end she could get thrilled with things she loved and
with the news of her children scattered about the world... It is fitting
to quote Proverbs, chapter 31, verses 25-28: 'Strength and honour
are her clothing; and she shall rejoice in time to come. She openeth
her mouth with wisdom; and in her tongue is the law of kindness.
She looketh well to the ways of her household; and eateth not the
bread of idleness. Her children arise up, and call her blessed; her
husband also, and he praiseth her.'*

Jess died in 1963. I may have missed it, but not once do I remember
her mentioning to anyone the happiness of her life with Stanley. What I
do remember is the way his children – my mother and uncles and aunts –
maintained an almost universal silence about him. Were there still more
secrets that they vowed should never come out?

EPILOGUE

I looked through the gate of Long Dene Cottage as the September sun spread its warmth across the dewy lawn and the raised bank of grass where my grandfather's study had been. The rooks in the nearby copse had flown since I made my first visit. That time I'd knocked on the door; now I stayed in the road. Down in the churchyard at St Lawrence, Abbots Langley, the damp grass clung to the sides of his grave. I read: 'Strong and content I travel the open road'. I, too, had been travelling an open road and I asked myself, now that I had reached its conclusion: what had I discovered? Had I found the real Stanley? Did I now know what had driven this restless man?

In a turbulent life, one thing stands out: the energy he expended in what he called the search for truth. As a disaffected student, he soaked up the ideas of radical thinkers Emerson, Whitman and Carpenter. As a thoughtful cowboy, he ruminated on the meaning of life while herding cattle on the ranch. As a Congregational minister, he mined the depths of the New Theology, suffragism, socialism and pacifism before preaching their tenets to his congregation. And as a freelance journalist, he examined aspects of culture, politics and history from his new-found Catholic perspective. Nor must we forget his pacifist novella *Poverty Gulch,* his poetry, his plays and his talks. His output was prolific. From time to time, a few determined souls do commit to such an unrelenting quest for meaning; my grandfather just happened to be one of them – and I'm proud of him for that.

Of course, having an adventurous spirit helped. So did his bravery: he needed courage to express his controversial views at Trinity, at the peace organisations he worked for, at the *Crusader*, at King's Weigh House and the Darby Road mission, and to risk the love of Jess in this unerring pursuit. With this went passion, and when he converted to Catholicism, that idealism focused on the Church's radical movements. Those who knew and worked with him spoke of his youthfulness and the interest he showed in contemporary issues to his dying day. Adopting the role of a revolutionary Christian came easily to him and this made it impossible for him to live a comfortable, suburban existence.

Many writers manage to separate their work from their lives and relationships; their creation exists in a different realm. When the writer is with friends and family, he or she can usually shelve the book and revert to a 'normal' existence. But with my grandfather, this was not the case; because he was a religious writer, his beliefs were connected directly to his life. And because that metaphysical search was all-embracing, it touched all those he was close to. It seems he was unable to put his faith to one side when he was with the family. He couldn't shake off the religiosity and found it hard to enter their worlds. The impish sense of humour and comic acting were aspects of a previous life.

I don't know how much Jess or other members of the family knew of his womanising. Certainly in 1916 he and Minna managed to keep their affair secret, although there were hints that others in the congregation had their suspicions. Once Jess told Minna that in the early days Stanley had spent considerable time at Margaret Thomas's house and was even contemplating moving in. Jess told Minna about the gossip she was subject to – again, no further details. Then there was the woman he was previously engaged to, as Eva recorded in her diary. In writing his life, I stumbled across the revealing letters and diaries of Minna, Eva and Ruth, but it is not unreasonable to assume that he had relations with other women of whom we know nothing. As Clyde Binfield says: 'James was powerfully attractive – and attracted – to women.' For the record, neither my mother nor any uncles or aunts alluded to anything untoward – to me at least.

Stanley acknowledged the problems he caused Jess and the family: 'They had already endured enough on account of what may well have seemed and perhaps were my irresponsible eccentricities… I could not ask them to suffer more.' And when discussing the English mystic Richard Rolle, he writes: 'He had freed himself from earthly ties whilst I bore the responsibility for the maintenance of a wife and family.' To what extent would Stanley, a married man in his fifties, even then have preferred to live the life of a tramp in devotion to God? *Poverty Gulch* is dedicated 'to the woman whose love, when I would have drifted back to the scenes of this story, proved stronger than all the magic of the west'. Even if Jess did know of his transgressions, there was little she could have done; divorce was out of the question, if only for financial reasons.

As pastor of two Congregational churches, as assistant editor of the *Catholic Herald* and at odd times as a freelance writer, Stanley's income levels were reasonable but at others they were derisory. He saw the money-making process as an intrusion into his spiritual life, to be circumvented whenever possible. Add to that his membership of the voluntary poverty movement and one senses the extent of his financial irresponsibility. Minna commented: 'Jess is the man of the family.' Despite the passion and genuineness with which he espoused revolutionary causes, he failed to see – or mitigate – the impact it had on his family. Thanks to his forebears and his own temperament, he was locked in a theological prison.

It is easy to portray Jess as the defenceless victim – and there is no question that she was exactly that. He did stray but, in mitigation, perhaps Jess was unable to understand his thoughts and doubts to such an extent that he needed to engage with others. She herself admitted that first and foremost she was a mother. Was she merely uninterested in the life of the mind and soul? Minna did attest to that – and Stanley's consequent loneliness – as early as 1916. His letters to Ruth also bear that out. He certainly cuts an isolated figure and the family seem a peripheral concern. Once the tramp, always the tramp. He even pointed up a Biblical text which extols the superiority of the 'supernatural family' over that of blood relatives. He wrote to Norman almost pleading for connection. The apparent ease with which he would have upped sticks to be with his son Bob in South Africa shows that he had few, if any, close friends in England that he would miss. It suggests that the hours he spent alone in his study were not just down to meeting tight deadlines; it could also be because he preferred his own company, or felt trapped. Catholics thousands of miles away were more familiar with his views than his own family were. I have sometimes wondered if the very energy he expended on such professional connections, ideas and ideological positions masked an inability to relate to people – including his own family – on simpler, more emotional terms. Those terms, fundamentally, were those of an attentive and loving Christian.

In following him through these choppy ideological waters I often wondered at the sincerity of his beliefs. As far as his religious writing is concerned – and by that, I mean Catholic – it is hard to know which views are his own and which are those of a jobbing journalist. As a rough rule of thumb, I think the ideas expressed in his books closely match his own; the articles less so. Having said that, he was writing for a niche Catholic audience – in journalistic terms, a backwater – and felt no compunction to dilute his views for a general readership. Nevertheless, he was regarded as one of the leading Catholic writers of his generation. He combined the enthusiasm of the social reformer with a natural mysticism and deep knowledge of the Scriptures. Some of his best works, however, are those with a more general audience in mind; his supreme achievement, in my view, is the set of charming and accessible *Franciscan Fables*.

He undoubtedly inspired love – and I don't just mean the love of women. So, I find it strange that he wrote so little about it. In his articles he seldom talked about the private intimacies of faith or the comforts and sense of peace it is supposed to bring. Issues around personal morality or how we should treat our fellow human beings are hardly mentioned. His father Daniel at Castle Green Church, Bristol, spoke intimately and endearingly of his congregation, but Stanley, in the Trinity pulpit, continually sought out fresh theological thrills rather than working with his congregation. For all his egocentricity, paradoxically he was happier commenting on the public rather than the private arena. Maybe the private held terrors into which he dared not stray.

He had a tendency to be didactic and to indulge in speculative guesswork, a weakness which, I would argue, prevented him from being in the top echelon of religious writers. That original 'strictly second division' appellation still applies even though I now know him better. An apocalyptic vision is never far away, one of the final expressions of which is in his last letter to Norman: 'History is working out to a glorious climax even if it does so through tragedy and disillusionment.' I have wondered if these strange predictions come from his reading of obscure academic, religious and mystical texts rather than from close observation of society. That could account for his arcane views on 'the Jewish problem'.

I would also maintain that there is an even deeper thread which characterises his writing, as well as his life. It is the perennial need to be different and to pursue a sense of otherness. In Catholic terms it takes the form of a trajectory towards saintliness: 'Oppressed by the increasing evils fostered by a materialistic civilisation, the faithful may escape from mediocrity and essay the way of the Saints,' he writes. Throughout his life there was seldom a time when he was not occupying a self-conscious, solipsistic position, whether it be shunning the school curriculum, quitting training courses, making a hero out of Walt Whitman, playing the part of the loner-cowboy round the campfire, testing out his pacifism on the frontline in Puerto Rico, preaching socialism to the middle classes of Walthamstow, falling out with his contributors at the *Crusader*, trying to establish a Catholic form of service among East End dockers, or extolling the hitherto unrecognised virtues of Mussolini. Did he find it difficult to get on with people? Was he a misfit? Whatever the answer, there is a kind of dogged heroism in this which is unusual, maybe even admirable in its way.

So, I return to 'the search', the driving force of his life. What was this truth that he was after? Was it truth at all? As an agnostic, I would argue that truth is unobtainable, forever elusive. Yet, he claimed to have found it. Wasn't it, rather, certainty that he sought, which is a very different thing? In conflating the search for certainty with the search for truth, was he deluding himself? The wide horizons he embraced in that quest didn't translate into a wide acceptance or tolerance once that supposed sense of peace had been achieved. It morphed into an inflexible faith, criticism of others' beliefs, an odd predilection for the notion of a superior human being, and even a respect for fascism. The liberal outlook of the early years hardened into a conservative vision. He turned off the open road and locked himself up in a citadel of certainty. He claimed to have found the peace he'd been looking for. If so, I would argue, it seems a distinctly uneasy peace. There is even a loneliness, or a kind of awkward emptiness, there.

Mysteries remain. How much did guilt over his relationship with Minna play a part in his lurch towards Catholicism? Did the confessional process absolve him from taking responsibility for past and present sins? I would like to ask him whether he really was an inveterate womaniser and, if so, what were Dorothy Minto and Margaret Thomas to him? And why, over and over again, did he leave my mother out of the roll call of children in the letters to Norman? Did he repair relations with Daniel before the latter died in 1900? What was the real reason that his brother Norman and sister Daisy chose not to stay in touch with him for so long? What did they know?

Then there is the continuing mystery of the grave inscription: 'Strong and content I travel the open road'. Surely, a conventional Christian inscription rather than the mantra of a freewheeling wanderer would have been more appropriate? Who chose those words? We will never know. It is the height of irony that Whitman's pagan sentiments are fixed to the headstone of a Catholic convert. Yet it is also strangely fitting: the words encapsulate his deep contradictions.

What is clear is that, at best, Stanley was inspirational, visionary and challenging. At worst, he was confused, combative and highly egotistical. His dogged pursuit of certainty brought its rewards for him in the shape of the Catholic Church, however misguided that quest may have been. It also impacted positively on those who in the early days heard his sermons and those who later read his articles. Indeed, his conversion to Catholicism may be seen as a deeply conservative act, a natural continuation of his father's adherence to spirituality and formalised worship. But something is left seriously wanting when such a dogged pursuit is conducted in blinkers, at the expense of family harmony. Such a single-tracked search reaps little if loved ones are not at its heart. Stanley remained a divided man, caught between Heaven and Earth.

TIMELINE

1869: Born 9 December to Clara in Bristol where his father, Reverend Daniel Bloomfield James, is pastor of Castle Green Congregational Church.

1871-78: Daniel appointed pastor of East Hill Congregational Church, Wandsworth. Family moves to London. Muriel, Norman and Daisy born.

1878-83: Daniel becomes pastor of Walter Road Congregational Church, Swansea. A dispute with deacons brings about his resignation.

1883-87: Family moves again when his father becomes pastor at Christ Church, Addiscombe. Attends Whitgift School, winning literature prizes. Hero-worships Scottish writer George MacDonald, friend of Daniel's.

1887-93: A period of turmoil during which family moves to Wimbledon when Daniel becomes pastor of Worple Road Congregational Church in 1889. Leaves Whitgift and attends Amersham House, Caversham, then Aberystwyth University, leaving early, then taking two separate courses to become Congregational minister but abandons both. Also gives up training to become Unitarian minister. Fails to become professional actor. Teaches at private schools in London, meeting Engels and the Chartist George Julian Harney at Richmond lodgings. Daniel resigns from Worple Road after congregation splits and sets up Christ Church, Alwyne Road, Wimbledon. Adopts Walt Whitman and Ralph Waldo Emerson as his literary mentors. Ideological differences with father.

1893-6: Emigrates to Canada with brother Norman. Works as cowboy, shepherd, wood-cutter and farmhand in Jumping Pound district, Alberta. Writes poetry, stories and farces which are performed by local community. Becomes local correspondent for *Calgary Herald*.

1897: Appointed deputy editor of *Calgary Herald*, moves to Calgary and is fired under mysterious circumstances. Wanders south to High River, Fort Macleod and Lethbridge and carries out series of short-term jobs: hay-maker, shop-keeper, navvy, bridge-builder. Becomes a hobo and jumps trains to Toronto with friend.

1898: Joins US army in Fort Porter, Buffalo, sent to Puerto Rico to fight in Spanish American War. Falls seriously ill and invalided out, convalescing in New York military hospital. Reads voraciously, finding inspiration in the Bible.

1899: Returns to England to find father in poor health at Christ Church, Wimbledon. Despite having no qualifications, assumes responsibility for church services. Meets Jess.

1900: Daniel dies on 28 June. Stanley takes over as pastor of Christ Church for several months. Becomes engaged to Jess.

1901-6: With the help of his mother Clara's Devon connections, appointed minister of Teignmouth Congregational Church. Marries Jess in Wing, Buckinghamshire on 1 October. Children Phyllis, Bob, Jessie and Eric are born.

1906: Moves to Walthamstow to become pastor at Trinity Congregational Church.

1908: Adopts revolutionary Christian stance, introducing New Theology and socialism into services, dividing church, losing traditional worshippers and gaining younger radicals. Kitty is born.

1910: Joins International Labour Party, supports suffragism and speaks at street corners during controversial Walthamstow by-election. Befriends Ruth Slate and Eva Slawson.

1913: John is born.

1914: Outbreak of war in August. Preaches pacifism, further alienating worshippers and deacons while receiving increased support from progressives. Befriends Minna Simmons.

1915: David is born.

1916: Has affair with Minna. Church in turmoil and Stanley is forced to resign. Family moves to Leytonstone, where he establishes Burghley Hall, introducing strongly socialist/pacifist style of worship. Works part-time at No-Conscription Fellowship, alongside Bertrand Russell. Visits Ireland, writing series of political articles for the *Christian Commonwealth.*

1917: Quits No-Conscription Fellowship and joins Quaker-based Fellowship of Reconciliation. As travelling secretary gives pacifist talks around the country. Befriends Captain Jack White, founder of Irish Citizen Army. Attends services at Dr Orchard's King's Weigh House experiment, which seeks to combine Protestantism and Catholicism. Publication of *Poverty Gulch* and pacifist book, *The Men Who Dared.* Clara dies.

1918: Starts writing for pacifist journal the *New Crusader* under bylines Piers Plowman and The Tramp. Appointed deputy to Dr Orchard and takes charge of Darby Road mission, Tower Bridge. Family moves to Rodney Stoke, Somerset.

1919-22: Becomes editor of the *Crusader,* instigating meet-the-reader gatherings at Minerva Café while commissioning Reverend Conrad Noel and other pacifists. Leaves King's Weigh House after attempts to introduce Catholic form of worship in East End mission fails. Joins voluntary poverty movement.

1923: Received into Catholic Church at St Dominic's Priory, Haverstock Hill. Family moves to Four Marks, Hampshire, where under straitened circumstances Jess tries to make five-acre smallholding self-sufficient. Stanley stays in London to work as secular freelance writer with national papers, but fails to secure enough commissions. Joins family in Hampshire and freelances for twenty-two Catholic publications worldwide. Children start to travel and take jobs.

1925: Publication of *The Adventures of a Spiritual Tramp.*

1927: Jess nominally joins Catholic church but children, with one exception, refuse. Stanley conducts fourteen-week lecture tour to Catholic audiences in the US.

1928: Family adopts Patricia. Stanley befriends G. K. Chesterton.

1929: Plans second lecture tour in US, but abandons project when Jess falls seriously ill.

1933: Writes series of articles on Mussolini, Guild Socialism and Distributism. *The Evangelical Approach to Rome* is published. Embraces and writes about Catholic Action.

1935: *Back to Langland* published.

1936: Writes to Norman in Canada after years of silence to congratulate him on being appointed Social Credit Party representative. Brings brother up to date on himself and the family.

1937: Travels to Rome and Belgium to research book about Jocist movement. Publication of *Christ and the Workers* and *Franciscan Fables.*

1941: Takes post of assistant editor of the *Catholic Herald.* Family moves to Hemel Hempstead, Hertfordshire. Stanley stays in lodgings in London during week. Becomes fire-watcher. Writes series of articles and pamphlets on 'the Jewish problem'.

1944: *In the Light of Day* and *Becoming a Man* published.

1947: *Catholic Herald* no longer requires Stanley's features as paper switches to more popular content. Despite being kept on retainer, period of hardship ensues and sons come to parents' financial aid. Norman sends large joint of ham at Christmas. Jess falls ill and her life is in danger. Son Bob tries to persuade parents to emigrate to South Africa. Norman publishes *The Autobiography of a Nobody.*

1948: Stanley writes to Norman every few weeks. Muriel dies in Wells, Somerset.

1951: Family reunion at Long Dene to mark fiftieth wedding anniversary. Stanley falls ill and goes into St Mary's Hospital, Paddington, for stomach operation. Nurse tells him he is eligible for US army pension, which he successfully obtains. Leaves hospital for few weeks but returns with diagnosed stomach cancer. Dies 1 November, All Saints Day. Buried in Catholic cemetery, St Lawrence Church, Abbots Langley, with Whitman inscription 'Strong and content I travel the open road' on headstone. Leaves Jess effects to value of £209 8s 6d. *The Times* publishes his obituary.

THE FAMILY

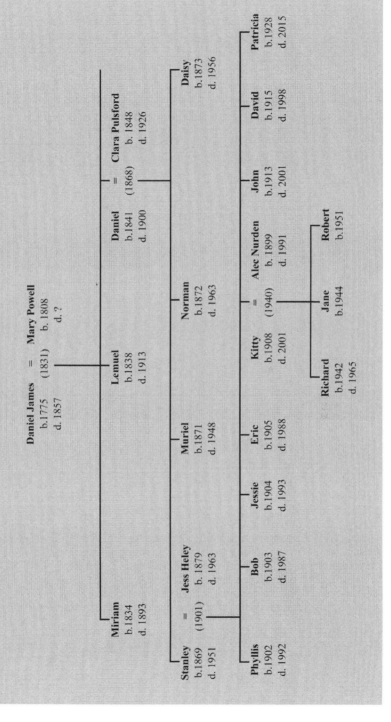

Daniel James = Mary Powell
b.1775   (1831)   b. 1808
d. 1857   d. ?

Miriam
b.1834
d. 1893

Lemuel
b.1838
d. 1913

Daniel = Clara Pulsford
b.1841   (1868)   b. 1848
d. 1900   d. 1926

Stanley = Jess Heley
b.1869   (1901)   b. 1879
d. 1951   d. 1963

Muriel
b.1871
d. 1948

Norman
b.1872
d. 1963

Daisy
b.1873
d. 1956

Phyllis
b.1902
d. 1992

Bob
b.1903
d. 1987

Jessie
b.1904
d. 1993

Eric
b.1905
d. 1988

Kitty = Alec Nurden
b.1908   (1940)   b. 1899
d. 2001   d. 1991

John
b.1913
d. 2001

David
b.1915
d. 1998

Patricia
b.1928
d. 2015

Richard
b.1942
d. 1965

Jane
b.1944

Robert
b.1951

SELECT
BIBLIOGRAPHY

Archives

British Library (News Media)
The Women's Library (London School of
    Economics and Political Science)
Gwent Archives
West Glamorgan Archive Service
Surrey History Centre
Croydon Museum and Archive Service
Bristol Archives
Teign Heritage Centre
Vestry Museum, Walthamstow
Essex Record Office
London Metropolitan Archives
Dr Williams Library
Society of Genealogists
Library of the Society of Friends
Peace Pledge Union
Glenbow Museum, Calgary, Canada
Galt Museum and Archives, Lethbridge

Books and Pamphlets by Stanley James:

'Shelley Compared with Keats' (1886)
Poverty Gulch (1917)
The Men Who Dared (1917)
The Adventures of a Spiritual Tramp (1925)
The Evangelical Approach to Rome (1933)
Back to Langland (1935)
Franciscan Fables (1937)
Christ and the Workers (1938)
Becoming a Man (1944)
A Catholic Angle on the Jewish Problem (1944)
In the Light of Day (1946)
Jews – A New Catholic Approach (1948)

Books and Pamphlets by Others:

Binfield, Clyde. *So Down to Prayers – Studies
    in English Nonconformity 1780-1920* (1977)
Binfield, Clyde. 'Collective Sovereignty?
    Conscience in the Gathered Church c. 1875-
    1918' (1991)
Brockway, Fenner. *Towards Tomorrow* (1977)
Buckley, Evelyn. *Chaps and Chinooks – a
    History West of Calgary 2 Volumes*
Burton, Derek. *The First 100 Years at East Hill*
    (1960)
Canning and Clyde Road Residents Association
    and Friends. *The Book of Addiscombe*
    (2000)
Carpenter, Edward. *My Days and Dreams:
    Being Autobiographical Notes* (1916)
Carpenter, Edward. 'Love's Coming of Age:
    A Series of Papers on the Relations of the
    Sexes' (1902)
Chesterton, G. K. *What's Wrong with the World*
    (1910)
Congregational Union of England and Wales.
    Congregational Yearbooks (1901, 1904)
Corrin, Jay P. *Catholic Intellectuals and the
    Challenge of Democracy* (2002)
Davies, W. H. *The Autobiography of a Super-
    Tramp* (1908)
Dawson, Jill, ed. *The Virago Book of Love
    Letters* (1994)
De Bellaigue, Christina, ed. *Home Education
    in Historical Perspective: Domestic
    pedagogies in England and Wales, 1750-
    1900* (2016)
Ellis, Havelock. *Studies in the Psychology of
    Sex, Volume 2: Sexual Inversion* (1900)
Emerson, Ralph Waldo. 'Self-Reliance' (1841)
Ehret, Ulrike. *Church, Nation and Race –
    Catholics and antisemitism in Germany and
    England, 1918-1945* (2012)
Eliot, T. S. *Selected Essays, 1917-1932* (1932)
Evans, Clifford. *The Story of Walter Road
    Congregational Church, Swansea 1869-
    1969* (1969)
Fleetwood, Mick and Bozza, Anthony. *Play
    On: Now, Then, and Fleetwood Mac: The
    Autobiography* (2014)
Gerhardie, William. *God's Fifth Column: A
    Biography of the Age, 1890-1940* (1981)
Harney, George Julian. *The Chartists Were
    Right: Selections from the Newcastle Weekly
    Chronicle, 1890-97* / ed. David Goodway
    (2015)
Harrison, Shirley. *Sylvia Pankhurst: A
    Crusading Life 1882-1960* (2003)
James, Reverend Daniel Bloomfield. 'A Manual
    for the Use of the Church and Congregation
    Assembling in Castle Green' (1869)

James, Norman. *The Autobiography of a Nobody* (1948)

Kaye, Elaine. *The History of the King's Weigh House Church: a Chapter in the History of London* (1968)

Keohane, Leo. *Captain Jack White: Imperialism, Anarchism and the Irish Citizen Army* (2014)

Koven, Seth. *The Match Girl and the Heiress* (2014)

Langland, William. *The Vision of Piers Plowman* (fourteenth century)

Light, Alison. *Common People: The History of an English Family* (2014)

MacEwan, Grant. *Eye Opener Bob: The Story of Bob Edwards* (1957)

Macmurray, John. *The Clue to History* (1938)

Merton, Thomas. *Elected Silence* (1949)

Merton, Thomas. *The Waters of Silence* (1950)

Mitchell, W. O. *Who Has Seen the Wind* (1947)

Pulsford, John. *Infoldings and Unfoldings of the Divine Genius in Nature and Man* (1887)

Pulsford, John. 'Fear Not – A Sermon Preached in Offord Road Chapel, London' (1874)

Roberts, T. R. *Eminent Welshmen – A Short Biographical Dictionary of Welshmen Who Have Attained Distinction from the Earliest Times to the Present* (1908)

Rutherford, Mark. *The Revolution in Tanner's Lane* (1887)

Southern Alberta Pioneers. *Our Foothills* (1975)

Thompson, Francis. 'The Hound of Heaven' (1893)

Thompson, Tierl, ed. *Dear Girl: The Diaries and Letters of Two Working Women, 1897-1917* (1987)

Tiley, W. E. C. 'Castle Green Congregational Church, Greenbank'

Trinity Congregational Church, Walthamstow. *Trinity Record* (1906)

Underhill, Evelyn. *Mysticism: A Study of the Nature and Development of Spiritual Consciousness* (1911)

Underhill, Evelyn, *The Mystic Way: A Psychological Study in Christian Origins* (1913)

Vellacott, Jo. *Bertrand Russell and the Pacifists in the First World War* (1980)

Wallis, Jill. *Valiant for Peace: A History of the Fellowship of Reconciliation, 1914-89* (1991)

Weller, Ken. *Don't Be a Soldier! The Radical Anti-war movement in North London 1914-18* (1985)

Whitman, Walt. *Complete Poems* (1995)

Wister, Owen. *The Virginian: A Horseman of the Plains* (1902)

Zuehlke, Mark. *Scoundrels, Dreamers and Second Sons: British Remittance Men in the Canadian West* (2001)

Newspapers, Periodicals

Secular

British Medical Journal
Calgary Herald
County Observer and Monmouthshire Central Advertiser
Croydon and County Pictorial and Surrey Magazine
Crusader
Daily Herald
Daily Mail
Daily News
Edinburgh Evening News
Evening Standard
Falkirk Herald
GK's Weekly
Labour Leader
Leighton Buzzard Observer
Lethbridge News
Lincolnshire Chronicle
Manchester Guardian
Monmouthshire Merlin
New Crusader
Nottingham Journal
Pontypool Free Press and Herald of the Hills
South Wales Daily News
Star
Surrey Comet
The Bailie
The Clarion
The Times
Times Literary Supplement
Tribune
Voices for Women
Walthamstow and Leyton Guardian
Western Mail
Woodbrooke Chronicle

Religious

Assisi
Baptist Times
Blackfriars
Catholic Advance
Catholic Fireside
Catholic Herald

Catholic Standard
Catholic Times
Christian Commonwealth
Christian World
Clergy Review
Columba
Hibbert Journal
Irish Monthly
Methodist Times
St Francis' Home Journal
The Cross
The Month
The Tablet
The Universe
Venturer

Websites
Ancestry.com
Spiers, Dale. 'Journal of Alberta Postal History'

Broadcasts
'Friend to Friend', Radio 4 (25 July 1984)

Plays
Dear Girl by Tierl Thompson and Libby
    Mason, Women's Theatre Group 1983-84

INDEX

Printed in Great Britain
by Amazon

59647212R00185